GARVEY, Terence. **Bones of contention: an enquiry into East-West relations.** St. Martin's, 1980 (c1978). 203p map bibl index 79-21623. 12.95 ISBN 0-312-08772-1. CIP

A short, balanced, sensible introduction to East-West relations is rare. Thus this unpretentious, literate book by the recently retired British ambassador to the USSR is especially welcome. Given the heightened public anxiety that the new Middle East crises have prompted, and the predictable excesses of political rhetoric that will accompany the 1980 US elections, the intelligent layperson would find Garvey's informed, moderate exploration of the issues a most useful set of benchmarks. The rise and decline of détente sets the stage for brief but accurate accounts of the Russian and Marxist-Leninist roots of Soviet behavior. The complexity of SALT is lucidly summarized; the human rights issue and the impacts of economic trends are assessed and integrated. One only regrets that the story, completed in late 1977, could not include the significant changes of the past two years. Still, it offers a sound perspective in which to evaluate those more recent events. For college and public libraries.

Bones of Contention

The Author

A professional diplomat for thirty-seven years, Sir Terence Garvey was successively Head of the British Mission in China, Assistant Under Secretary of State at the Foreign Office, Ambassador to Yugoslavia, High Commissioner in India and Ambassador to the USSR. He retired in December 1975.

Bones
of Contention

An Enquiry into East –West Relations

Terence Garvey

Routledge & Kegan Paul
London and Henley

First published in 1978
by Routledge & Kegan Paul Ltd
39 Store Street, ·
London WC1E 7DD and
Broadway House,
Newtown Road,
Henley-on-Thames,
Oxon RG9 1EN
Set in Plantin by
Computacomp (UK) Ltd, Fort William, Scotland
and printed in Great Britain by
Lowe & Brydone Printers Ltd,
Thetford, Norfolk

British Library Cataloguing in Publication Data

Garvey, Terence

    Bones of contention.
    1. Communist countries – Foreign relations
    2. World politics – 1965 –
    I. Title
    327'.0917'3   D850   78–40527

    ISBN 0 7100 0010 3

Contents

Preface

This is an enquiry into the present state and future prospects of East–West relations, and in particular into the obstacles to their improvement which result from the specific characteristics of Soviet society.

Aspects of the subject have, in recent years, been dealt with authoritatively and in detail, both in academic works and in articles in the press, by scholars of various disciplines and specializations, old and new – Russian historians, students of Marxism-Leninism, Sovietologists, Soviet economists, Kremlinologists, strategic analysts, arms controllers and chroniclers of Soviet dissent – who, collectively, have covered virtually the whole extent of the front. If little that is both new and true remains to be said, the general reader may, if the author's own experience is any guide, welcome assistance in picking his way through the multitude of information and interpretations which confront him, and it is to him that this book is addressed. Having been written at a period of considerable fluidity in East–West exchanges, it runs more than the normal risks of being overtaken by events before it sees the light of day.

Since it has no pretensions to being a work of scholarship, the customary apparatus of footnotes and source attributions has been dispensed with. The short bibliography at the end, intended to provide suggestions for further reading, may also be taken as indicating some of the sources consulted.

London, 1977

Snakes
and Ladders

This book is about East–West relations in the 1970s and the prospects of so regulating them that both sides may live to tell the tale. 'East–West' today (it had quite different connotations in the recent past) is shorthand for the Soviet Union and the East European countries on the one hand, and North America and Western Europe on the other.

The two groups are fundamentally at odds about the goals of human society and the functions of the state. An accommodation between them is hard to achieve because accommodations involve give and take and, all else apart, the Soviet Union's position is too integral to allow of much give. It follows that ambitious patterns of East–West co-operation are likely to prove utopian, realizable only over a very long period, and then only on the assumption that quite radical changes meanwhile occur in the premises of both sides, but most of all the Soviet side. In the perspective of ten years, which is as far as most people can usefully attempt to look ahead, relaxation of tension will be less than total and brought about, if it can be achieved at all, by the readiness of both sides to show restraint and to be guided by a sober view of their real interests. The thesis of this book is that a *détente* of this modest character is, obstacles of ideology notwithstanding, a feasible objective.

By the autumn of 1947 the wartime marriage between the Soviet Union and its Western allies had irretrievably broken down. The decree absolute came in the following summer when Stalin blockaded the

Western garrisons in Berlin and tried to starve them out. The two ensuing decades were years of persistent hostility and tension, punctuated only, once Stalin had died in 1953, by three ephemeral attempts at accommodation. The cold war froze and consolidated the division of Europe along a line from the Elbe in north Germany to the Black Sea, preventing the conclusion of a peace treaty and leaving uncleared the mess that the war had made of national frontiers. With both sides armed with nuclear weapons and collisions liable to occur whenever paths crossed, the tensions were patently dangerous in the highest degree. A miscalculation by Stalin set off a large-scale conventional war in Korea in 1951. Another by Khrushchev in 1961, when Soviet missiles were furtively installed in Cuba, came within hours of provoking a nuclear exchange. In the eastern Mediterranean, where the interests of East and West faced one another, the smouldering conflict between Israel and the Arab states broke into flames in 1956 and again in 1967, with continuing risks that the super-power protectors of the two parties might be drawn in. Deepening American involvement in Indo-China from 1963 onwards, though not touching vital Soviet interests, severely tested the Soviet Union's patience and restraint. These acute surface tensions were the outward marks of a deep underlying hostility characterized by ideological aggression, commercial discrimination, espionage, counter-espionage and propaganda.

The years 1970–77 saw the latest and by a long way the most systematic, longest-lived and most intensive effort so far made to moderate and regulate the hostility and reduce the tensions between East and West. These have been the years of what the West calls *détente* and what the Russians call the 'relaxation of international tension'. Public reactions to this phenomenon have varied, at different times and in different places, from high euphoria to deep suspicion, and there have been wide divergences of view as to what the word means and how much can reasonably be expected of it. It is well, in analysing *détente*, to keep as close as possible to the basic connotation, common to both cultures, which is the elimination of undue strain. The implication is palliative rather than curative. General de Gaulle, who for specific reasons of his own was the first to enter the *détente* field, defined the path forward as *'détente, entente, coopération'*. Views may differ on the correct order of the second and third members of this trinity: it will suffice here to side with the General in identifying the first as a preliminary phase, designed to remove obstructions to possible subsequent improvement and enjoining on both parties a measure of restraint. It is not a valid criticism of *détente*, as the world uses the term, to say that it has not produced peaceful and fruitful co-operation between East and West. Co-operation involves a measure – hopefully a widening measure – of agreement as to objectives. That is still some distance off. Even in the narrow definition here adopted the experience of the 1970s has shown *détente* to be an exercise of considerable difficulty and the odds against its successful prosecution have undoubtedly lengthened.

Nevertheless, the achievements – and the term is here used to mean the contribution which the quest for *détente* has made to the end in view, rather than the gains or losses made by either side – are striking, and the more striking by contrast with the immobility of the preceding twenty years. They could hardly have come about but for the concurrent appearance on the scene of three men – Willy Brandt, Henry Kissinger and Leonid Ilyich Brezhnev: Brandt, first as foreign minister and then as chancellor of the Federal Republic of Germany, prepared to accept the consequences of Germany's defeat and division, and to rely on his country's regained economic strength in rationalizing its relations with its eastern neighbours; Kissinger, the emissary of a new Republican president whom none could suspect of 'softness' on communism, himself a man of sharp perception and resource, impressed by the acute dangers and waste of the cold war, and believing that they could be reduced and made manageable by creating a 'web' of shared interests between the United States and the Soviet Union; Brezhnev, heading a Soviet collective leadership of sexagenarians who, having survived Stalin's purges and lived through Khrushchev's unpredictable adventures, needed time and tranquillity to solve domestic problems, saw in the early 1970s opportunities for shortening the USSR's long road to development and plenty.

In the aftermath of war the Soviet Union had taken drastic steps to ensure that Germany, which had twice invaded Russia in this century, should not be able to do so again. A slice of East Prussia on the Baltic was directly annexed to the USSR. German territory west of the Oder and Neisse rivers was handed over to Polish administration and colonization, in compensation for the Polish eastern provinces annexed by Stalin in 1939 by agreement with Hitler. By common consent of the victors, Austria, seized by Hitler in 1938, was separated from Germany, and the Sudetenland, acquired by him under the Munich agreement in the same year, was restored to Czechoslovakia. Thus cut down to size, destroyed and impoverished, Germany could hardly, for a long time to come, prove a serious threat. But the Russians were taking no chances. Having established that a communist government under Soviet control could not successfully be imposed on a united Germany, they opted to instal one in their own zone of occupation, which became the German Democratic Republic (GDR) and in due course joined the Warsaw Pact. The resultant division of Germany into the Federal Republic (FRG) and the GDR, with the former capital Berlin marooned deep in GDR territory, sustained by Western garrisons and FRG money, became the source of multiple tensions, complications and crises during the years of the cold war. Underlying all else was the provisional character of the post-war arrangements establishing national frontiers in central Europe. On top of this, the absence of diplomatic relations between most of Eastern Europe and the FRG, and the refusal of the West to recognize the GDR, ruled out the possibility of official contact or negotiation, and the vulnerability of west Berlin was a recurrent target of Soviet pressure.

Brandt's 'eastern policy' (*Ostpolitik*), once launched in 1969, made short work of these problems. The Federal Republic negotiated bilateral treaties with the USSR (Moscow, August 1970) and Poland (Warsaw, November 1970), providing for mutual renunciation of the use of force and of territorial claims, and recognizing the inviolability of all European frontiers, including the GDR's frontiers with Poland and the FRG. Treaties between the FRG and the other Warsaw Pact states followed, the last to be signed, in December 1973, being that with Czechoslovakia which liquidated the consequences of the Munich agreement. A quadripartite agreement between the USA, Britain, France and the USSR, regulating the anomaly of Berlin, was signed in June 1972 following the ratification of the Moscow and Warsaw treaties by the Bonn legislature; and a 'basic treaty' – regulating the relations between the two Germanies, and permitting the recognition of each of them by the members of the other alliance, and the admission of both to the UN – was concluded in November 1972. In a short space of time much of the old lumber that had for so long cluttered the European stage was thrown on the bonfire. Though it had not been a push-over for them, the Russians could be well pleased with the results.

When the *Ostpolitik* had got well under way, they reckoned that the road was clear for tackling the still more difficult task of improving relations between the Soviet Union and the United States. The American nuclear monopoly had long disappeared and the Russians, by the late 1960s, had reached approximate parity in nuclear armaments. The cost of competing had been punitive for both sides and already in President Johnson's time a tentative beginning had been made with 'strategic armaments limitation talks' (SALT). The Nixon administration, after an interval, took up the talks where their predecessors had left off. Mutual suspicion and the extreme technical difficulty of the matters at issue made sure that progress, when achieved, came slowly. Brezhnev visited Washington in September 1971 and an agreement on 'measures to reduce the risk of the outbreak of nuclear war' was signed. When Nixon paid a return visit to Moscow in the following May it was plain that matters had moved forward far and fast. Two important agreements were concluded – a treaty on anti-ballistic missile systems (ABMs) and an interim agreement on the limitation of strategic offensive arms (commonly known as SALT I), the first attempt to set an agreed common ceiling on the number of nuclear missiles at the disposal of the two sides. The groundwork was laid for a trade agreement, concluded some months later, which was to give most-favoured nation (mfn) treatment to Soviet goods entering the United States and to make available US government-guaranteed credit for financing American exports to the Soviet Union. A settlement of the Soviet debt for wartime lend-lease supplies, a long-standing obstacle to normal commercial relations, would be negotiated at the same time. Further agreements provided for US–Soviet co-operation in science and technology, joint space activity (the Apollo–Soyuz project), education and culture, environmental protection, health and other fields. Dr Kissinger's 'web' of shared interests was beginning to take shape. In particular, a bilateral statement of 'basic principles of relations' expressed the 'common determination that in the nuclear age there is no alternative to conducting their mutual relations on the basis of peaceful coexistence'. They undertook that they would 'always exercise restraint in their mutual relations' and would 'negotiate and settle differences by peaceful means ... in a spirit of reciprocity, mutual accommodation and mutual benefit'. They declared that the pre-conditions of peaceful relations between them were the 'renunciation of the use or threat of force' and the recognition of one another's security interests 'based on the principle of equality'. Ten years earlier equality would have been a pious formal expression. In 1972 it corresponded closely enough to reality: the military balance between the two had, by sustained effort on the Soviet side, moved into rough equilibrium. For the Russians, parity of strength was something to be proud of, but parity of esteem, achieved after fifty years of inferiority, was of capital psychological importance. For the first time the Soviet Union could feel that it confronted the United States, the principal 'imperialist' power, on equal terms.

Having seen the colour of Brandt's money in 1970, the Soviet leadership lost no time in organizing its response to the changed climate in Europe and the opportunities opening up in the wider world. The quinquennial jamboree of the Soviet Communist Party (CPSU) – the twenty-fourth party congress – was to be held in February 1971. In the course of his keynote speech to the congress Brezhnev proclaimed a 'programme of peace', calling for new efforts to achieve 'peaceful coexistence' with the capitalist world, a relaxation of tension in international relations, an end to the 'arms race' and technological and economic co-operation with the West. To achieve these ends he proposed, among other things, the convocation of an all-European conference on security and co-operation.

Several of these ideas were already familiar. Brezhnev himself had given them an airing, more tentatively and less concretely, at the twenty-third congress five years earlier, and the project for a European conference had been advanced, with increasing insistence and definition, at a succession of inter-party and Warsaw Pact meetings since July 1966. The concept of a 'collective security system' for Europe had been a recurring theme of Soviet propaganda and diplomacy since the early 1950s. (Soviet historians go one better, asserting its direct descent from Lenin's 'Decree on Peace' of 1917 and the Soviet government's manoeuvrings in central Europe during the inter-war years.) In the modern context it aimed at the settlement of the 'German problem' and the recognition of the post-war frontiers as definitive and inviolable. To it had been joined the notion of the development of co-operation between European states, particularly in trade, technology and science. The Western response was for a long time notably unenthusiastic: the 'German problem' was a matter for serious diplomatic negotiation, which a conference of upwards of thirty states was most unlikely to promote and for which neither the FRG nor its allies in NATO appeared to be ready; and 'co-operation' seemed likely to amount to furnishing the Soviet Union, free or on favourable terms, with finance and technology which the Soviet economic system had failed, through its own shortcomings, to generate, and which would no doubt be used to the West's disadvantage. Moreover, a strictly European conference, from which the USA was excluded, would be heavily loaded against the Western participants.

Now, however, Brandt's *Ostpolitik* was well on the way to taking the 'German problem', as so far understood, off the European agenda. The initial Soviet resistance to the participation of the United States (and Canada) vanished and the Nixon–Kissinger team were prepared to invest serious efforts in co-operation as a means of reducing tension. When Brezhnev and Nixon met in Moscow in May 1972, they agreed that 'multilateral consultations looking towards a conference on security and co-operation in Europe' could shortly begin. The meeting would admittedly require 'careful preparation' but should be convened without undue delay.

In agreeing to collaborate in the consummation of this long-cherished Soviet aim, Western statesmen were conscious that, for a square deal, balancing concessions were required from the Soviet side. The 'conference on security and co-operation in Europe' (CSCE as it became known) would serve to legitimize the post-war territorial order in Europe, adding multilateral recognition to the gains which the eastern countries had already secured by direct negotiation with the FRG. If the Soviet blueprint for the conference were to be followed, the CSCE could be relied upon to stick to generalities and would do nothing to reduce the size and armament of the Warsaw Pact and NATO forces confronting one another in central Europe. Mutual and balanced force reductions (MBFR) had been proposed by the NATO council meeting at Reykjavik in June 1968, but it was not until three years later, in a speech at Tbilisi, that Brezhnev, already pursuing the indications that *détente* was negotiable, gave a cautiously favourable response. At the Moscow summit a year later he agreed with President Nixon that negotiations on reciprocal force reductions should be prepared, but separately from the CSCE.

Even so, many in the West still felt that the balance of advantage tipped in the Soviet direction. The outcome of the MBFR negotiations was unpredictable and the Russians had shown no real keenness on starting them. The CSCE, as projected, could hardly fail to result in net gain to the Soviet Union. The Western governments accordingly insisted that the conference, if held, must deal, in addition to 'security' and 'co-operation', with 'humanitarian questions', leading to the freer movement of people and ideas across the European divide. A real relaxation of tension, the argument ran, presupposed not merely a changed attitude on the part of the governments concerned, but increasing contact between ordinary people, cultural and educational exchanges, improved access to the written and spoken word and the reunion of divided families. This would entail a relaxation of the tight control imposed by the Soviet government on many aspects of the life of its citizens. Not least, the Soviet government would be required to endorse, among the principles guiding the relations between the signatory states, the obligation of governments to respect 'human rights and fundamental freedoms'.

'Co-operation in humanitarian and other fields' – the 'third basket' as it became known – was the subject of prolonged and acrimonious argument in the protracted process of negotiation that followed. The CSCE began at Helsinki in July 1973 and its 'final act' was signed there by thirty-five heads of state or government on 1 August 1975. The main negotiation, lasting twenty-two months, took place in Geneva, providing an unrivalled opportunity for all participants, from Eastern, Western and neutral countries, to gain an insight into one another's minds. The final act never purported to be a legally binding document creating obligations binding under international law. The obligations it contained were 'adopted' by the participants. A number of them were less concrete and more optional in character than many of the Western signatories would have wished. No machinery of enforcement was established (the Russians had dropped their earlier idea of a continuing 'organ' to monitor compliance), but a 'follow-up' meeting was to take place in Belgrade in two years' time. However, the ten principles adopted to 'guide' relations between signatories represented a sound and satisfactory basis for the conduct of sovereign nations seeking to coexist in goodwill. The Russians fought stubbornly against the inclusion of passages in the 'principles' and in 'basket three', securing the excision of some and the dilution of others; but, faced in the early summer of 1975 with the choice of resting content with these gains or forgoing the long-heralded summit-level third stage of the conference, they opted for acquiescence. So the president of the United States, the secretary-general of the Soviet Communist Party and the prime ministers or presidents of thirty-three other states came together in Helsinki to sign the 'final act'. Brezhnev, in a speech afterwards, declared that there had been no losers: all had been the gainers, and the foundations of *détente* had been securely laid. All must work together to make it 'irreversible' and to 'complete' the political measures just taken with measures of 'military *détente*'.

Already, however, the euphoria of the Moscow summit three years earlier had begun to subside. Whatever Brezhnev might say about military *détente*, his negotiators in Vienna, where the MBFR talks had begun in January 1974, were displaying a stone-bottomed immobility which made even their colleagues in Geneva look flexible, refusing even to disclose the current size of the Warsaw Pact forces and, if appearances were any guide, seeking only to perpetuate the Warsaw Pact's margin of military superiority in central Europe. The pace of advance on the arms control front had also slackened. Continuing work by both sides had earlier made possible the conclusion of an understanding, reached between Brezhnev and President Ford at Vladivostok in November 1974, on the outline of a second strategic armaments limitation agreement (SALT II), replacing, reinforcing and extending the scope of the 'interim agreement' of May 1972. But technological developments since 1972 had deepened the inherent difficulties of arms control negotiations; and arms limitation had always had its opponents in the Pentagon and in the US Congress, as also in the Soviet military establishment. Critics in Washington soon discovered loose ends in the Vladivostok understanding which Dr Kissinger, with much energy and resource, but with indifferent success, sought to tie up. Meanwhile the momentum of *détente* slackened. Earlier still, while the CSCE negotiations were in full swing, congressional critics had got their teeth into the draft legislation − clauses in the trade bill of 1974 − introduced to give effect to the US–Soviet trade agreement. The Jackson and Vanik amendments made the extension of most-favoured-nation treatment, and of Exim Bank credits, to the Soviet Union, conditional on the Soviet government's performance in permitting the emigration of Soviet citizens of Jewish blood. Prodigious efforts by Dr Kissinger to soften the sharp outlines of the blackmail were unavailing and the Soviet government, with some dignity, announced that it was suspending the operation of the trade agreement. The experience was an unnerving one for the Soviet leaders. They had done their bit by settling the lend-lease debt. Exim Bank credits and mfn status had been part of the same package agreed between Brezhnev and Nixon at the 1972 Moscow summit. The good faith of the United States of America had been engaged. But it was now clear that even a presidential commitment was not gilt-edged. With less dignity, the Soviet press and radio unleashed a campaign of polemics against the 'enemies of *détente*' – the Pentagon, the US defense secretary, the Zionist lobby and Senator Henry Jackson – who were depicted as set on wrecking the wise and peaceful policies of the president and his secretary of state.

The Soviet leaders had regarded Watergate as no more than a little local difficulty and President Nixon's resignation in 1974 took them by surprise. But Dr Kissinger was still there and it seemed reasonable to expect that, with time, a no less satisfactory relationship could be established with President Ford. They were slower to apprehend the breadth and depth of the congressional reaction to the trespasses of the Nixon administration upon the preserves of Congress. The resultant reassertion of congressional authority in foreign affairs was essentially a response to the involvement of the United States in foreign wars by arbitrary acts of the president done in secret. But this response merged with suspicions that, in his *détente* policy, President Nixon (and Dr Kissinger) had been taken for a ride by the Russians, and with a resurgence of old, unreconstructed anti-Soviet sentiments and prejudices. The approach of the 1976 presidential elections intensified the recoil from euphoria, and, with President Ford fighting to retain the Republican nomination against a right-wing challenger who personified all that was hostile to *détente*, the momentum of US–Soviet exchanges slowed to walking pace. In March 1976 Mr Ford, finding himself in the position of St Peter when the cock crew, declared that he would no longer use the word *détente* to describe US policy towards the Soviet Union, but would speak instead of 'peace through strength'. With the trade agreement unstuck and SALT II impaled on the snags of the Vladivostok understanding, the Russians could but wait and see what the election would bring forth.

Prejudice and animosity apart, what did the case against *détente* amount to? Its critics argued that the fine words of the Helsinki final act added nothing to the engagements which its signatories had already assumed, and in binding form, in the charter of the United Nations. The final act had not reduced by a single soldier or a single rifle the burden of armed forces and armaments. The Soviet armed forces, launched in the mid-1960s on a massive arms development programme, continued to pile up strategic weapons of high sophistication and versatility. Soviet naval expansion was being pressed forward at an alarming rate. The force reduction negotiations were getting nowhere in Vienna. Meanwhile the Russians had harvested the fruits of the *Ostpolitik*, securing the legitimation of their ill-gotten gains from the Second World War, perpetuating the division of Germany and tightening their grip on their vassal states – the 'captive nations' of Eastern Europe. The Helsinki 'third basket' was another scrap of paper. The obligation to respect 'human rights', to which the Russians had subscribed, was being flagrantly violated. The spectacle at Helsinki of American statesmen hobnobbing with the Soviet leaders must, the critics continued, have been deeply discouraging to all in the Soviet Union and Eastern Europe who were rightly struggling against the injustices of communist society. What was more, 'peaceful coexistence' as propounded by the Russians was a snare and a delusion. On the morrow of Helsinki, Soviet spokesmen from Brezhnev downwards had hastened to reassure their party constituents that *détente*'s effects were limited to the Soviet Union's official relations with foreign states; the 'ideological struggle' between socialism and capitalism, long regarded in the West as a euphemism for Soviet subversion, espionage and dirty tricks, would proceed inexorably forward. Viewed in this light, *détente*'s critics concluded, Brezhnev's 'peace programme' should be recognized for what it was – a bare-faced attempt to disarm the free states of Europe physically and morally and to encourage the American forces in Europe to go home, so that in due course, the Europeans, left alone to face Soviet military power, would capitulate without resistance and submit to Soviet control. Finland, retaining democratic forms, but submissive to the Russians in the conduct of its foreign affairs, was seen as the prototype of this relationship. 'Findlandization' was Europe's appointed destiny if *détente* were allowed to proceed according to Soviet plans.

Exaggerated as some of these expressions might appear, they gained credibility from the indications, provided by the Portuguese revolution and its aftermath, that whatever the documents might say about restraint and reciprocal respect for interests, the nature of the Soviet animal had undergone no real change. The Caetano dictatorship in Portugal had fallen in April 1974 to a *coup* by a group of officers weary of fighting interminable colonial wars. Coming hot-foot from exile in Moscow, the Portuguese Communist Party leader Alvaro Cunhal made a sustained and very nearly successful attempt to take over the Portuguese democratic revolution for communism by methods strongly reminiscent of Lenin's when the Bolsheviks seized power in 1917. What was more, Cuban troops, ferried by Soviet transport aircraft, in the autumn of 1975 intervened decisively in the civil war in the former Portuguese dependency of Angola, securing the defeat of the factions opposing the Popular Movement for the Liberation of Angola and installing in Luanda a government amenable to Moscow. Dr Kissinger vainly besought Congress to provide money and arms for resisting this intrusion: but memories of Vietnam and the recoil from foreign adventures were too strong for him, and a new bond between Marxism-Leninism and national liberation movements in southern Africa was forged without American opposition.

For reasons such as these, *détente* was already a widely derided notion by the time the Carter administration took over in January 1977. The new president's utterances during the campaign had been of an opacity which left the world, the Russians included, guessing at what lay in store; though it looked likely that what Mr George Kennan, writing in 1951, identified as the 'legalistic-moralistic' strain in American foreign policy would once more come to the surface. It did. Shrewdly apprehending the revulsion of public opinion from the Nixon years and the prevailing disenchantment with Dr Kissinger's style of diplomacy, Mr Carter selected human rights as the centre-piece of his presentation of the problems of US–Soviet relations. In the first days of his presidency he put the Russians on notice that a real *détente* would require them to comply to the full with the engagements entered into at Helsinki to respect and promote human rights and fundamental freedoms. Lest there be any doubt about his meaning, he addressed, and published, a personal letter to Academician Andrei Sakharov, the standard-bearer of Soviet dissent, and ostentatiously received at the White House the dissident Vladimir Bukovsky; and American concern for human rights campaigns in Czechoslovakia and elsewhere in Eastern Europe was made abundantly clear. In terms of American domestic politics Mr Carter had picked a winner; after years of whispering and furtive compromise, the authentic voice of America had sounded loud and clear and the electorate liked what it heard and felt much better. Not so the Russians. For, in choosing to join battle on human rights, the president had selected the front on which Soviet freedom of manoeuvre was most circumscribed. As seen from Moscow, Mr Carter's gambit strongly suggested that, under cover of the elections, the 'enemies of *détente*' had captured the White House; but it was plainly premature to jump to this conclusion before the new administration had shown its hand on the central element and anchor of *détente*, strategic arms limitation.

Here too shocks were in store. As befitted matters of great technical complexity and political inflammability, previous SALT negotiations had been conducted discreetly and in conditions of secrecy. Now the new secretary of state, bound for Moscow to resume talks, called in the journalists and gave them, for publication, a preview of what he was going to tell the Russians. The new administration's assessment of the limitations negotiated by their predecessors was that they had never touched the heart of the problem; they had brought no actual reduction in the burden of armaments, merely limiting expansion in certain directions which were not of real importance, and had imposed no real constraints on either side. If the Russians were serious about disarmament, the message ran, they would now be required to join in a reciprocal programme of 'deep cuts', the outlines of which Mr Vance proceeded to sketch. If deep cuts were not to their taste, they could have the Vladivostok package in the form that Brezhnev and President Ford had left it, loose ends and all, without gloss or addition. The Russians were indignant. Since Vladivostok, exchanges had continued with the Americans in a joint effort to reconstitute the package in a form that both sides could accept; and some progress, albeit not enough, had been made. These matters had been allowed to rest by tacit consent until the election was over. Now, Mr Vance was telling them, all that had happened since November 1974 was a false trail and must be deleted from the record. Instead, the Soviet government was being offered, on what sounded like a take-it-or-leave-it basis, an entirely new set of proposals, broadcast to the world before Moscow had had a chance to consider them. They might suit the Pentagon but, for that if for no other reason, were most likely to work to the serious disadvantage of the Soviet Union. The Soviet government would not do business on these terms. Mr Vance, after three unhappy days in Moscow, was sent home with a flat refusal to both his proposals.

Some more hopeful initiatives were taken during those three days and, after the initial shock of the Soviet rebuff had worn off, contacts on SALT were resumed at working level. But the search for *détente* had taken another knock. The Soviet press, a sure barometer of the state of mind of the leadership, moved in to attack the United States, and for the first time the attack turned on President Carter personally. Across the Atlantic American commentators wrote of renascent confidence and a welcome return of realism after the years spent in the never-never land of *détente*. It was hard to see how these attitudes differed from those of the cold war which had been officially lain to rest, with such high hopes, five years before. Hostility, suspicion and polemics seemed to be the natural condition of the East–West relationship.

When the logic of arms limitation drove the Secretary of State and the Soviet Foreign Minister back to the negotiating table at Geneva in May the atmosphere was still frosty and the going slow. The suspension a month later of an important US weapons programme and the deferment of another were at first greeted in Moscow with suspicious incredulity. Then, in a pondered speech delivered at Charleston on 23 July 1977, the President emitted an unmistakable signal to Moscow that, human rights, deep cuts and brash rhetoric notwithstanding, the quest for *détente* remained the central preoccupation of the US government. After a very bumpy start, the new administration was evidently back on course. Three weeks later Brezhnev, welcoming a visitor to Moscow, went out of his way publicly to record the view that the Charleston speech contained elements which sounded 'positive'. And when Gromyko came to the United States in September for the annual session of the United Nations assembly, discussions between him and the president and Mr Vance evidently broke the deadlock over arms limitation that had continued since Vladivostok nearly three years earlier. Hopes rose for the conclusion of a SALT II treaty and perhaps also of a comprehensive ban on nuclear tests, to be signed at a new summit meeting in 1978.

Meanwhile, however, representatives of the thirty-five CSCE

participants had kept their appointment to meet in Belgrade to review progress towards the implementation of the Final Act. It was a foregone conclusion that the discussions would fasten on the only live issue outstanding, namely the shortcomings of Soviet performance in compliance with the human rights provisions of the Final Act and with its obligations under Basket Three. The closing months of 1977 were spent in the exchange of charges and counter-charges between West and East. The process may have modified or delayed the Soviet government's plans for dealing with outstanding cases of dissent, and it certainly provided a demonstration, if one were needed, of the deep and widespread obloquy which the Soviet Union's treatment of its own citizens inspired. But the problem of how to bring this undertaking to a useful conclusion remained over for resolution when the Belgrade meeting reconvened in the new year.

As this much foreshortened narrative draws to its close, we can hardly fail to be struck by the ups and downs, the snakes and ladders, that have characterized the recent course of East–West relations. The imperative of survival is strong and insistent, but the underlying distrust and hostility between the parties periodically reassert themselves, breaking out in crises which threaten to wreck all prospect of accommodation. Underlying the whole relationship are the three prime bones of contention – the reservations which the Russians attach to their version of 'peaceful coexistence' and their readiness for opportunist adventures; the unremitting competition in armaments between them and the United States; and the contempt which the Soviet Union shows for human rights as understood in the West.

The bones of contention will be examined in later chapters of this book, which will go on to consider the factors – the Soviet economy's failure to go it alone, the expectations which past promises have engendered in the Soviet consumer, and the fading of the dream of world revolution – which today reinforce the imperative of survival and permit us to retain a wary optimism about the outcome. But first, since Soviet reality can hardly be understood without reference to what went before, it will be necessary to turn back for a while to the past.

Old Ways

2

In a world divided into over one hundred and fifty nation-states the Soviet Union, occupying about one-fifth of the earth's surface, rich in natural resources and with a population of upward of 250 million souls, has an incontestable claim to have its voice heard in international affairs. The fact that that voice so often sounds discordant and menacing to others is in part explained by factors of geography and historical experience.

The Western view of the world's shape is heavily influenced by youthful acquaintance with Mercator's projection, centred on Western Europe and the Atlantic seaboard of the United States. The view from Moscow is strikingly different, as the map opposite shows. The Soviet Union is a huge continental country stretching from the Baltic to the Pacific Ocean. But it is enclosed between the polar seas to the north and, to the southward, the chain of mountains and deserts running from the Caucasus to the Chinese frontier, which substantially inhibit exit in either direction. At the westward end the Soviet Union has gateways on to the Baltic and the Black Sea, but passage in and out of each of these seas is through straits controlled by foreign countries. Murmansk, in the far north-west, alone provides a way out independent of foreign goodwill, but in winter requires continuous effort to keep the approaches free of ice. At the eastern end Soviet territory abuts directly on the Pacific, but until the trans-Siberian railway has been several times replicated, and Siberia itself opened up by industrial development,

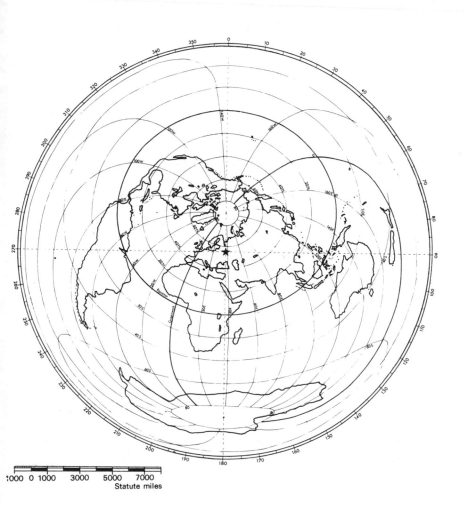

1000 0 1000   3000   5000   7000
Statute miles

The world centred on Moscow

This map is constructed on an Azimuthal Equidistant Projection centred on Moscow (Lat. 55°45' N., Long. 37°42' E.)

Distances from Moscow to any point in the world may be found by connecting it to the point by a straight line and measuring this on the linear scale provided. Bearings from Moscow may be read off by carrying the line through the point until it intersects the protractor at the border. Note: All distances and bearings other than those radiating from Moscow are NOT true. (Crown copyright. Reproduced by kind permission of The Controller of Her Majesty's Stationery Office.)

the Soviet Far East will remain a rather thinly held bridgehead. Seaborne communications from one end to the other are long and circuitous. The sea route from Leningrad to Nahodka on the Pacific runs by way of the North Sea, the Bay of Biscay, the Mediterranean (when the Suez Canal is open; otherwise by the Cape of Good Hope), the Indian Ocean and the China Sea. Aviation has considerably mitigated these handicaps, at least with regard to the transport of people and light freight. But for heavy cargoes, whether industrial equipment, raw materials or munitions, the limitations of geography remain a serious continuing disadvantage. The cardinal problems are those of lateral (east–west and west–east) mobility within the Soviet Union, and unimpeded exit into ice-free waters. The former can be mitigated by a massive and sustained effort of construction and development, but will require decades to surmount. The latter, exemplified by the constant elbowing and nudging of Russian nineteenth-century diplomacy towards the Mediterranean and the Adriatic, can only find solution by sacrifices, enforced or voluntary, on the part of others. Meanwhile, the 'world ocean', as the Russians call it, linking the Soviet Far East with European Russia, to the west via Suez and to the east by Panama, strikes them as an environment in which the presence of Soviet naval power is eminently natural and necessary.

An observer placed in geostationary orbit over Moscow, and scanning the southern horizon, would see a panorama of great peninsulas – Indo-China, Malaysia, the Indian subcontinent, Arabia and Africa – protruding into the 'world ocean'; and, on the far right, curling round behind him, the minuscule spit of Western Europe and its off-shore islands. Beyond the Soviet border to the west no natural feature inhibits either Soviet expansion or foreign intrusion. Historically, Western Europeans, and Germans in particular, have brought much trouble, though also much benefit, to Russia. For most of the nineteenth century the Russian frontier ran west of Warsaw. Today it still envelops much historically Polish territory, but essential Soviet security interests are reckoned to be met by political arrangements giving Moscow effective control over formally independent neighbouring states, which form a *glacis* against any attacker and a forward base for counter-attack or aggression.

Soil and climate add to the country's handicaps. High-quality agricultural land is found in the 'black earth' regions – the Ukraine and the steppe extending across Russia's southern fringe and into Kazakhstan. Elsewhere, land improvement demands decades, perhaps a century, of unremitting investment and hard work. In most of the USSR the growing season is short. Winter ends late and begins early and one crop a year is as much as can be won. Drought and excessive rainfall recur and, when they strike in a country as large as the USSR, the resultant disaster is proportionately large-scale. Almost all natural resources – petroleum, iron, coal, metals and minerals of all sorts – are to be found somewhere in the USSR, but climate and difficulty of access often make them hard to extract.

It is possible to conceive that Russia, so placed and so handicapped, might have remained wholly isolated from the world around her, eking out a meagre living from the soil, her entire energies being taken up with the problem of subsistence. In the event, her response to the challenge of her environment was different. When resources and effort could be spared, she looked outward for solutions to the problems of her remoteness, unwieldly geography and inclement weather. Her very size ensured that foreigners viewed her with a certain awe. She was a difficult one to get on with. But the obverse of her many disadvantages was that she was also hard to beat on her own ground, as Napoleon discovered to his cost. Once conscious of the world around her, Russia was a power to be reckoned with. And once she had advanced some distance along the road to economic development she could not fail to become a world power. By the nineteenth century her frontiers marched with those of half the world, in the Far East, in Persia and the subcontinent, in Arabia and Turkey and the Mediterranean and central Europe. In each of these areas she confronted the schemes and designs of great powers set on keeping what they held or gaining what they coveted.

Russia's historical experience differed considerably from that of other European states. All that can be attempted within the compass of this book is to abstract, at some sacrifice of chronological sequence, a few of the aspects of this experience which left an abiding mark. But the attempt is worth making, if only because many features of present-day Soviet behaviour, commonly ascribed to communist inspiration, will be seen to have much older antecedents. The rest of this chapter examines successively old Russia's social development, and her external relations, in this light.

The feudal states and principalities of medieval Christendom differed widely in habits, attainments and language, but they shared what was recognizably the same culture, in which the legacies of Rome – Rome as law-giver and administrator as well as Rome the fountainhead of the Christian faith – were interwoven with indigenous influences. Russia followed a path of separate development. Geographical remoteness had a lot to do with this. So too had religion. The first Russian state, with its capital in Kiev, was, Hungary alone excepted, the last European country to embrace Christianity. Legend records that in AD 987 the grand prince of Kiev held what we would today call an audition, at which divines from Islam, Judaism and Christianity were invited to compete for the privilege of providing Russia with an established church. The choice fell on the eastern Orthodox church with its headquarters in Byzantium (Constantinople). More was involved in this choice than those who made it could foresee. Thereby Russia unwittingly cut herself off from the mainstream of Christian civilization flowing from Rome; and when, in due course, Byzantium fell to the Turks and the remains of the Eastern Roman Empire disintegrated, she became the principal state professing Orthodox Christianity, and its defender against the inroads of Moslem and Roman Catholic states. Kievan Russia's belated conversion, though it led initially to some dynastic marriages with European royal houses, did not generate any enduring links with Western Europe, but served in the longer run to compound her isolation from other Christian and civilized countries.

Primitive monarchies, as a general rule, have claimed total authority for the sovereign, who was literally the owner of his realm, to which, as opportunity offered, he added land, things and people by process of conquest. In Western Europe the sovereign's arbitrary authority over his subjects was gradually worn away by the emergence of a system of law and institutions which, in time, conferred on the ruled rights no less definitive in the areas to which they applied than the sovereign's right to rule them. Not least important among these was the right to own property not subject to distraint at the caprice of the ruler. The evolution was not a linear process. It had its ups and downs, as witness the life and death of Charles I of England. Nor did it unfold evenly, with all countries moving in step. It marked time for a long period in France in the seventeenth and eighteenth centuries, requiring a bloody revolution to regain its momentum. In Germany and Italy it largely preceded national unification, achieved only in the nineteenth century. In Russia things turned out quite differently. The disaggregation of the powers of the crown took place hesitantly and late and was still a very long way from completion when the monarchy was finally swept away in 1917. The rights of the subject were never a matter which caused Russia's rulers much loss of sleep.

Until the reign of Peter the Great (1689–1725) old Russia retained the essential features of what historians have called the 'patrimonial' state, the land, its produce and the people who lived on it being reckoned to be the inherited property – the 'patrimony' – of the tsar, its ruler. It was a highly differentiated society but not, strictly speaking, a hierarchical one; its various orders existed by virtue not of their subordination to one another but of their relationship to the tsar, the source of all status and privilege. The tsar and his household administered directly a substantial part of the realm. The rest was in the hands of landlords who, however, held their lands not absolutely, but at the sovereign's pleasure, and conditionally, in consideration of the performance of military and other service. Alongside the landholding interest there grew up a bureaucratic class, originally the managers of that part of the realm under the sovereign's direct administration, but gaining in numbers and influence as the importance of the territorial class declined. But landholders and bureaucrats, though numerous, accounted for only a fraction of the tsar's subjects. The great majority of Russians were peasants – serfs – living in one form or another of bondage, increasingly tied to the soil and becoming with time, for practical purposes, indistinguishable from the personal property of those who held the land on which they lived. They were the source of manpower on which their masters drew in discharging their military service obligations to the crown. Unlike the other orders of society, they paid taxes. Finally, there was the Orthodox church.

The alliance between the monarchy and the church was rooted in mutual interest, for the crown safeguarded the extensive real estate accumulated by the monasteries from the benefactions of the faithful, and the church took on the role of ideologist and rationalizer *ex post facto* of the absolutist, patrimonial, state. The church taught that the tsar was invested with divine authority. He was not merely the autocrat of Russia; he was a universal Christian sovereign with the right and duty to rule and protect all the Orthodox faithful in the world. Moscow, the seat of the Russian empire and church, had become the metropolis of the Christian faith, the 'Third Rome'. Rome, and Byzantium after it, had been swept away, both suffering divine punishment for corruption and heresy. Moscow had inherited the mantle, becoming the third, and eternal, centre of the Orthodox Christian faith. In a further flight of fancy, Muscovite divines concocted a bogus pedigree, purporting to demonstrate the direct genealogical descent of the Russian royal house from the emperor Augustus Caesar. In propounding this egregious piece of humbug the leaders of the Orthodox church no doubt reckoned that unstinting support for absolutism offered at the same time the best guarantee of its material interests, and the best prospect of mobilizing the tsar's imperial power against the Catholic 'heretics' and Moslem 'infidels' in neighbouring lands. For the tsars, the doctrine of divine authority legitimized a system which otherwise rested on naked force alone. Resistance to state power invited sanctions not only in this world but in the world to come. Tranquillity on the home front was heavily reinforced, and, in the outer world, the martial operations of 'holy Russia' were invested with a mantle of obedience to God's will. In due course, the church became corrupt, worldly, ignorant and torn by schism; and the tsar, reckoning that the benefits of the alliance were by that time securely and irreversibly his, expropriated most of its lands and wealth, converting it into a mere adjunct of the bureaucracy.

At first sight there is no obvious reason why a state so organized should not have continued indefinitely. The tsar, as autocrat — a title which he retained right up to the revolution of 1917 — and defender of the faith, was effectively the owner and operator of the entire realm. The various groups that made up his people were separated from one another and bound by interest, as well as by loyalty, to him. Geographical remoteness and the absence of communications kept disturbing foreign influences at a distance and, for full measure, news of events at home and abroad was regarded as a state secret reserved to the tsar and those close to him.

Nevertheless, from about 1700 onwards radical changes began to occur: radical but, as will appear, not radical enough. One of their propellants was the technology of war. Russian armies had hitherto managed, more often that not, to win. Now the part-time soldiers, officered by landholders owing service to the crown, and returning home each winter, were no longer a match for the professionals put in the field by some of Russia's neighbours. Foreign advisers were brought in to reorganize the armed forces and the foundations of a modern munitions industry were laid. But modernization was needed on a much broader front if Russia were to compete. Peter the Great took the unprecedented step, shortly after his accession, of spending several months abroad in the West, returning convinced that Russia must change. But his reforms were made in the spirit of borrowing from, not assimilation to, Europe. 'We need Europe for a few decades', he is reported as saying, 'and then we must turn our back on it.' In fact, though the process of modernization ebbed and flowed during the two centuries that followed, Western influences and Western ideas proved much harder to turn the back on than to introduce, and many of the institutions of the old patrimonial system in time fell victim to them. With a professional army the *raison d'être* of the upper classes' obligatory service to the crown disappeared, and in the 1760s they were finally relieved of it. Landlords received unconditional title to their estates and the institutional link that bound the landed interest to the crown was dissolved. Slower to go was serfdom which was finally abolished a century later in 1861. One thing that did not change was the tsar's monopoly of political power. A limited measure of local government was introduced in 1864, but representative institutions at the national level were avoided like the plague until they were forced on the tsar by the revolution of 1905.

Russia had stumbled belatedly into the modern age equipped with a rather large leisured class, often talented and increasingly well educated, for which society as constituted offered no outlet by way of political activity or participation. The Russian intelligentsia read and discussed most of what was written in the West, but the narrow choices open to them — regimental soldiering in youth, a bucolic existence punctuated by social seasons in the capital, a routine job in the civil service – left them feeling futile and unfulfilled. The nineteenth century was the era of the 'superfluous man' who realized that his environment did not suit him and that he had nothing useful to do. Some took to literature and established a brilliant tradition of creative writing. Others went abroad. But other bright spirits, recognizing the autocracy as the prime source of their frustrations, turned their thoughts to political change. Against such an adversary, gradualism and partial reforms were, they felt, pointless. A clean sweep was necessary. Among the earliest were the

'Decembrists', a group of idealistic and wellborn young officers, whose soldiering in the West had familiarized them with the idea of constitutional government. When Alexander I died in 1825 they moved to displace his legitimate successor and instal another brother on the throne as a constitutional monarch. The revolt was quickly suppressed and its participants executed or exiled. As the nineteenth century wore on, there developed what became recognizable as a Russian revolutionary tradition, violent in its methods, for violence seemed to offer the only prospect of change; conspiratorial in its organization, for secrecy was necessary for survival; and total in its aims, since nothing short of the liquidation of absolutism, bag and baggage, looked like doing the trick. The proponents of this tradition came, almost without exception, from the propertied and official classes. Many of them were less sure what should be put in tsardom's place once the old order had been swept away. Like others a century later, they were content to destroy what was and see what happened. Assassination was their prime weapon and the murder in 1881 of Tsar Alexander II the unavailing summit of their achievement. Their terrorist methods were too undiscriminating to achieve much, but their legacy of revolutionary violence, disciplined and refined by Lenin, was to become an important weapon in the armoury of revolutionary professionalism which carried the Bolsheviks to power, and kept them there.

Just as absolutism radicalized part of the intelligentsia, so educated radicalism mobilized the defensive machinery of repression. Revolutionaries representing any serious threat to the autocracy could be counted in hundreds at most in a population numbering in the 1890s about 125 million, but they had succeeded in badly frightening their masters, who now forged a sledge hammer to crack the nut. A political police force charged with scotching seditious activities was a long-established feature of the Russian state. It had been reorganized and modernized following the revolt of the Decembrist officers in 1825, its functions including undercover operations, surveillance of foreigners, and censorship. It was the custodian of sections of the criminal code which made punishable by death any attempt to alter the system of government, and by hard labour any expression of disrespect for the authority of the sovereign. After Alexander II's murder, the tsar's minister of the interior was empowered to declare a state of emergency in any part of the country and, over the ensuing twenty-five years, contrived to apply this provision progressively until it covered the entire territory of the Russian empire. The state of emergency enabled the police to dispense with judicial procedures, to imprison, or exile to Siberia, on suspicion alone, and to hand over trouble-makers to courts martial for disposal. Officials could be dismissed on suspicion of untrustworthiness, and a police certificate of 'reliability' – or what the modern idiom calls 'positive vetting' – was required from entrants to universities and candidates for responsible posts. The system operated on the presumption that most acts of the subject were illegal unless specifically sanctioned by law or administrative permission. It was the prototype in modern times of the police state; not yet a wholly efficient one, since communications were poor and criminological techniques still in their infancy, but it executed, imprisoned and exiled enough people who were not themselves revolutionaries to establish the presumption that absolutism must go.

It was not, in the event, the professional revolutionaries that won the first two rounds of the long-drawn struggle that ensued. The first Russian revolution, coming in 1905 in the wake of Russia's defeat by Japan, was made by peasants, industrial workers, mutinous troops and liberal intellectuals who sought, and on paper obtained, a form of constitutional government. But Tsar Nicholas II paid little more attention and respect to his Duma than Charles I had paid to his parliament. Absolutism was not dead yet. By February 1917 the strains of the First World War and the losses suffered by the Russian armies became too much for the system to withstand. After disorders in Petrograd, in which mutinous troops joined, the tsar was forced to abdicate and a provisional government of liberal complexion was appointed by the Duma. The entire tsarist apparatus of repression, terror and censorship was dismantled and for almost eight months Russia was free as she had never been before. But the chaos was extreme, as conflicting elements struggled with one another to fill the vacuum left by the disintegration of the autocracy. The moment of the professional revolutionaries had come.

But how to smash the provisional government? The Bolsheviks had no power base of their own, nor would their aims, if disclosed, have had much popular appeal. Among the many contending forces the most militant and most cohesive was the Petrograd Council ('Soviet') of Workers' and Soldiers' Deputies, which had sprung up spontaneously in 1905 and surfaced again in March 1917. 'Soviets' modelled on it had appeared in other Russian cities. The Bolsheviks proceeded to gain political control of the Petrograd Soviet and to enlist the support of disaffected troops stationed in Petrograd and at the nearby naval base. On 26 October, under the slogan 'all power to the Soviets', Lenin moved in his forces and arrested the provisional government. On the following day an all-Russian congress of Soviets invested him with authority, and the Bolshevik Party formed a 'council of people's commissars' to govern the country. Parallel action followed through the Party's network in other cities. It was as neat a job as human ingenuity had ever contrived, speaking volumes for the dedication, meticulous preparation and 'scientific' attainments of the professional revolutionaries. It had had very little to do with the spontaneous, elemental groundswell of discontent and indignation that had swept the old system aside, though the Bolsheviks had known how to exploit these to bring themselves to power. Its success, then and later, was not a foregone conclusion. Though the plan was masterly, there had been a good deal of bungling and hesitation. The result was a close-run thing, but it was definitive. The eight months' interlude of freedom, licence and debate was over. The victory of the Bolsheviks marked the confluence of the Russian revolutionary tradition – violent, conspiratorial and total – with the Russian state tradition of absolutism briefly interrupted in the spring of 1917. The combination is formidable both for the Russians themselves and for their neighbours.

So far this account has assumed the existence of 'Russia' as an entity – remote, huge and governed in a fashion all of its own. To complete the picture, some account must now be given of how Russia became what she was, and is, and how her relationship with the outside world developed.

A point of departure is the disintegration, towards the end of the twelfth century, of the Russian state centred on Kiev and controlling part of what is now the Soviet Ukraine and Belorussia. The princes of Kiev, under attack from Turkic tribes from the neighbouring steppe, withdrew from their rich black-earth lands northward into the forests and established a series of small principalities of which Moscow was but one, and far from being the greatest. In 1237 the Mongol successors of Genghis Khan invaded Russia, and for 150 years the Russian principalities formed part of the dominions of the 'Golden Horde', a province of the Mongol empire with its capital on the lower Volga. The Mongol khans were generally content to run the outlying and unpromising lands of northern Russia by indirect rule, and found the princes of Moscow notably serviceable in keeping order and collecting tribute. As agents for the occupying power, the Muscovites showed considerable diplomatic skill in maintaining the favour of their masters, and turned this to good account in annexing, as opportunity offered, the lands of their immediate neighbours. But it was not until after another conqueror, Tamerlane, emerged from central Asia and smashed the Golden Horde at the end of the fourteenth century that Moscow and its neighbours were liberated from foreign overlordship and tributary obligations.

Mongol rule had been a disagreeable experience, but Moscow had learnt much from it, not least about methods of running a state. With the burden of foreign occupation removed, the Muscovites set about absorbing the remaining independent principalities surrounding them. In 1547 Ivan IV, grand prince of Moscow, had himself crowned 'Tsar of all Russia' and within ten years he had attacked and captured the khanates of Kazan and Astrakhan, two of the units into which the state of the Golden Horde had disintegrated. These conquests took the Russians out of the woods and back into the black-earth lands from which the princes of Kiev had been driven. Success bred confidence and the romanticists began to take a hand, proclaiming Moscow to be the heir of the Kievan state, and the tsar's rightful inheritance to consist of all lands formerly Russian. It was the era in which the ideology of absolutism and the 'third Rome' took shape. Imperceptibly the reintegration of historically Russian domains shaded off into the acquisition of territory for its intrinsic utility. From the accession of Ivan IV until the end of the sixteenth century Russia approximately doubled in size, from less than three million to five-and-a-half million square kilometres, and in the first half of the seventeenth century another ten million square kilometres were added. Once launched on an easterly course, Russian fur-trappers and traders moved practically unopposed across the great land mass of Siberia, reaching the Chinese border and the Pacific by the middle of the seventeenth century. The flag followed trade as new territories were claimed for Russia. It was an achievement comparable in significance to the extension of the American frontier from the Alleghenies to the Pacific two centuries later, and greater than it in more geographical scope.

If anything, however, the conquest of Siberia served to accentuate Russia's sense of remoteness and isolation. In terms of real estate, the traditional store of value of the patrimonial system, the acquisition was colossal: but Siberia was a poor, cold and underpopulated place and, without manpower and investment, little could be done to make it profitable. The Russian empire might be quantitatively immense, but qualitatively it was poor stuff, and all the best seats elsewhere seemed to be occupied. Southward expansion into Asia was blocked by geographical features. Russia's south-western flank was contained by the Ottoman empire which controlled the exit from the Black Sea into the Mediterranean and occupied the Balkans as far west as the Adriatic. To the north-west Sweden, commanding the Baltic exit from Russia, was a martial and efficient neighbour who not merely resisted subjection but was capable of carrying the war deep into Russian territory. To the westward Catholic Poland, united by a dynastic marriage with Lithuania and still holding the Russian lands that Lithuania had picked up when the Kiev state dissolved, for a long time blocked all possibilities of expansion. Indeed in the 'time of troubles' ending with the accession in 1613 of the Romanov dynasty, the king of Poland came within measurable distance of adding the crown of Muscovy to that of his other realms, with consequences that could not have failed fundamentally to alter the course of East European history.

The later history of tsarist external policy is largely taken up with Russia's efforts to break out of the constraints. In 1709 Peter the Great, having reorganized Russia's armed forces, decisively beat the Swedes, and in the same year began to build his new capital at St Petersburg on the Gulf of Finland. It was Russia's window on the West, marking a shift of emphasis away from the 'oriental', Asia-oriented, past. Polish power was liquidated in a series of partitions, beginning sixty years later, in which Polish territory was carved up between the Empress Catherine II, the emperor of Austria and the king of Prussia, with Russia getting the lion's share. Warsaw and its surrounding territory, which had gone to the Prussians under the partitions, and been taken from them by Napoleon, was picked up by the tsar in the aftermath of the Napoleonic wars. Finland was detached from Sweden in 1809 and incorporated in the Russian empire with untypical guarantees of autonomy and constitutional government.

In dealing with Turkey, however, the tsars ran up against the material interests of the great powers of the day, who had no desire to see a Russian presence in the Mediterranean. At the beginning of the nineteenth century the Ottoman empire extended from the Persian Gulf to the Adriatic. At its height it had controlled the whole south shore of the Mediterranean as well. Now its further disintegration was plainly only a matter of time, promising glittering prizes to whoever was on hand to pick up the bits. For Russia, at last, possession of Constantinople and the Black Sea straits seemed an attainable goal. Besides, the European provinces of Turkey — present-day Greece, Bulgaria, Romania and southern Yugoslavia — were largely inhabited by Orthodox Christians, many of them of Slav blood, chronically misgoverned by their Moslem masters. The key to getting control of the straits was to promote the independence of the Christian provinces in the Balkans, after which the Turkish foothold in Europe would have lost its justification. Western practitioners of the balance of power, Britain more than most, found themselves frequently, as the years wore on, in incongruous support of Turkish absolutism and in opposition to 'liberal', freedom-fighting causes, in order to contain Russian westward expansion. In 1878 it looked for a short while as though the Russians had finally done the trick. Having beaten the Turks in the field, they obliged them to sign the peace of San Stefano which, among many other benefits to Russia, created an autonomous, jumbo-sized Bulgaria extending far westward into the Balkans and including a substantial slice of the Mediterranean coast west of the Black Sea straits. The prospect of Russian power rampaging in the eastern Mediterranean by courtesy of this newly created Slav satellite state was too much for the European powers to stomach. Summoning Russia to meet them in Berlin, they undid the three-month-old San Stefano treaty, cutting Bulgaria down to size, restoring Turkish sovereignty in the coastal strip and substituting a settlement tolerable to themselves. Today, a hundred years later, Istanbul is still Turkish. Meanwhile the aeroplane has removed many of the constraints which Turkish possession of the straits imposed on Russia. British and French interests in the eastern Mediterranean have diminished as decolonization progressed and the Soviet Black Sea fleet moves with growing freedom in and out.

A conspicuous feature of Russian history is the recurrence of ideological themes, and their exploitation to legitimize the pursuit of

Russia's material interests. In the sixteenth century, it was the myth of Moscow as the 'third Rome'. In the years following Napoleon's defeat it was the Holy Alliance. This was the personal contribution of Tsar Alexander I, now sitting at the top table as one of the principal victors, to the contemporary struggle of ideas. Signed in the first instance by the tsar and his fellow-autocrats of Austria and Prussia, and later acceded to by other European sovereigns, it was a multilateral pact binding the signatories to be guided in all things by the precepts of the Christian religion, practising justice, Christian charity and peace. It was in itself too airy and abstract to have any practical significance. What gave it a bad name was the zeal with which the tsar sought in the years that followed to mobilize his fellow-signatories in opposition to liberal and constitutional movements in Europe. The royal houses of Spain, Portugal and other states, deposed by Napoleon and restored to power by the victors, were soon faced with demands for representative institutions and, when these were refused, by revolutionary uprisings. The tsar, persuaded that peace and order everywhere were threatened by a revolutionary conspiracy, urged in vain, at successive congresses of the great powers, the need for military intervention in support of the established order of things, offering to supply Russian troops for the purpose. Such intervention was quite unacceptable to Britain and the prospect of Russian armies at large in Western Europe was too much even for the tsar's fellow-autocrats in Vienna, Berlin and Paris, who duly arranged for the dirty work to be done by other means.

Russia remained, however, the obvious point of recourse for absolute monarchs in trouble and when in 1848 − the 'year of revolutions' − Hungary demanded parliamentary government and attempted to secede from the Austro-Hungarian empire, Tsar Nicholas I provided an army to put the insurrection down. Likewise, the nineteenth century saw a recrudescence and development of the 'holy Russia' theme. What could be more right and proper than that holy Russia should take on the protection of her co-religionists languishing under the Turkish yoke, or that Byzantium, the seat and origin of Orthodox Christianity, should be redeemed from Moslem rule? In the second half of the century Russian publicists went one better, propounding the notion that it was Russia's historic mission to liberate from foreign rule not merely orthodox Christians but also all peoples of Slav blood. Panslavism, as this ploy was known, implied a simultaneous challenge to two major powers at once, since it encompassed not merely the Serbs, Macedonians and Bulgars in European Turkey, but the Czech, Slovak, Croat, Slovene and Polish subjects of Austria-Hungary as well. As such, it never received full official endorsement, but the appeal to Slav solidarity was freely used, where applicable, to reinforce that of common religion in Russia's campaign for the liberation of Turkey's European provinces.

What inferences can be drawn from this perforce abbreviated and selective account of Russia's past? Some Western historians have displayed prodigious industry in identifying and excavating the precise prototypes of the many features that most displease them in the current Soviet scene, and establishing thereby to their own satisfaction that Russia, tsarist or Soviet, is set in a mould of incorrigible malice and mischief. Without following them along this melancholy path, we may reasonably accept that Russian history is a continuum, and that the pre-revolutionary past offers valuable clues about why much that is done in the Soviet Union today is done in the way that it is: and we may note some conditioning experiences which seem to have left an abiding mark on Russian behaviour and habits of thought.

With the exception of those seven months in 1917, Russians have been accustomed to have a government claiming, and exercising, a monopoly of political power. It was the ruler's job to rule and the subject's to obey. The conception of law, binding on the ruled and ruler alike, was largely omitted from Russian experience: the ruler did, by and large, what his interests, as he saw them, or his caprice, might dictate. Where Western societies, shaped by Roman law or by English common law, have shown a recurrent preoccupation with the rights of the subject, and achieved thereby a progressive erosion by irregular stages of the power of the state to dispose freely of his person and property, Russia has continually failed to extract from its rulers liberties which were not revocable at pleasure or liable to be overridden in practice. Much has flowed from this tradition of absolute government. Bureaucrats, the doers of the ruler's will, are unloved the world over. In the West they have been widely regarded as the new despotism, begotten of the enlarged scope of the state's intervention in human affairs. In Russia they have been pushing their clients around since time immemorial, a phenomenon as natural as death, taxes or foul weather. Political policemen as an institution have been accepted as the protectors and guardians of the state's absolute authority − guarding first against sedition, then against conspiracy to promote change and finally against the very discussion of it; acting first on evidence and then on suspicion, in a legal vacuum. None of these phenomena should be interpreted as meaning that Russians like things to be done in this way. All that is suggested is that historical experience has taught Russians to regard them as normal, as something causing neither shock nor surprise.

Attitudes to the outside world have been contradictory. Deep down, Russia has often seemed to adopt Uncle Matthew's position: 'abroad is unutterably bloody, and all foreigners are fiends'. Strangers in Russia could be assumed to be up to no good and needed a sharp watch kept on them. Russians travelling abroad could be expected to pick up ideas disturbing to the tranquillity of the empire. The passport and the exit visa, scarcely known in the West before 1914, were essential Russian institutions. Yet 'abroad' was reluctantly recognized as the source of so much that Russia had to have. We have seen that Peter believed that she could have it and not get hooked, turning back to her roots once the foreigners' tricks and techniques had been mastered and assimilated. The disengagement was never completely achieved: at times it seemed that the objective had been almost abandoned. But the logic of westernization was never allowed to proceed to the point of political participation by the governed. Despite oscillations, the trend has been to recurring suspicion and fear of Western foreigners.

The methods by which the tsar's dominions were expanded were in substance neither better nor worse than those by which the Americans subjugated their continent in the nineteenth century or the British, then and before, built up their overseas empire, but the style was different and, from the point of view of this enquiry, instructive. Military power was a constant preoccupation, excessive in relation to the rather remote threat of foreign aggression, and demanding a larger slice of the national resources than needs could reasonably be thought to warrant. So also were grand ideological ploys − the 'third Rome', the 'holy alliance' and panslavism − all of them ideas of high explosive capability, purporting to legitimize Russia's power and to enlist external support. So again was the habit of secrecy and clandestinity under which tsarist diplomacy uninhibitedly pursued its ends.

The ends themselves emerge, in the perspective of two centuries, as having a certain permanency – to break out from the cage into which Russia was locked by geography, above all to find exits into warm, ice-free waters and into the seas and oceans beyond; to own, or at least command, the belt of territory on the Western frontier separating Russia from the martial powers of West and central Europe; to exclude these powers from areas contiguous to Russia's land frontier across Asia. Collectively these ends added up to a major undertaking, for the principality of Moscow, partly by accident of history, partly by design, had grown into a European and a world power. In taking on where the tsars left off, the Bolsheviks were not inheriting a *tabula rasa,* a clean slate. Both at home and in their foreign relations they were to build on what had gone before. To this task they brought a new propelling element, the ideology of Marxism-Leninism, which must now be briefly examined.

New Myths

3

In the last years of the nineteenth century, two generations after Karl
Marx and Friedrich Engels had published the Communist Manifesto,
European socialists were assailed by insistent doubts about the validity
of Marx's predictions, too long unfulfilled, and had begun to 'revise'
Marx's teaching, shifting the emphasis from revolution to reform.
These doubts were indignantly repudiated by Vladimir Ilyich Lenin,
leader of a radical faction of the diminutive Russian Social Democratic
Workers' Party, founded in 1898, a latecomer to the Marxist labour
movement and an otherwise indistinguished member of the second
Workers' International. Since Lenin was to imprint his revolutionary
Marxist views on his party – the nucleus from which the Soviet
Communist Party sprang – and on Soviet society as a whole, some
familiarity with what Marx taught is indispensable to an understanding
of what makes the Soviet Union tick. To acquire this familiarity is a
forbidding task, for Marx covered reams of paper and buried his
meaning in language which defies translation into plain English. What is
more, he was at once philosopher, social scientist, political scientist,
ideologue and prophet, claiming to encapsulate in a single
comprehensive system ultimate truths about the nature of man and
matter, about man's social organization and the course of human
history. All that can be attempted here is to extract a few of Marx's
main political and social themes, and to state them so far as possible –
more than that would be too much to hope – in layman's language. The

first few paragraphs that follow are the worst. Thereafter the going gets easier.

It should be said, by way of preface, that Marx claimed that his analysis of human society and human history was 'scientific', that is to say that it followed the strict methods and processes of verification applied by natural scientists, and enabled him to propound 'laws' of history comparable in nature and validity to, for example, Newton's laws of physics. He asserted that the development of history was conditioned by material, primarily economic, factors. This is not to say that he denied the importance of human acts, aims and aspirations: indeed he saw man as the prime mover in all change. But man's ideas, strivings and achievements were a response to the material environment that conditioned them and determined events. And events unfolded by a 'dialectical' process which postulated that all change came from the struggle of opposite forces. We cannot here follow Marx into the maze of argument by which he sought to substantiate these claims. It will suffice to note his assertion of historical determinism, and to observe that this and the laws that he purported to deduce from scientific observation impart to his teachings a quality of certitude and inevitability which, if it leaves the logicians unimpressed, has added greatly to his political appeal. Thus armed, Marx felt able not merely to say why what had happened in the past had happened, and indeed had to happen in that way, but also to predict what inevitably, inexorably, would happen in the future.

Marx's theory of the development of human society asserted that in his original state primitive man, a creature of inherently good nature and infinite potentialities, lived in freedom, equality and brotherhood with his fellows, battling against, and eventually taming, his natural environment and consuming what he himself produced. Organized society 'alienated' him both from his environment and his own good nature. This occurred because the 'forces of production' altered and corrupted the relations between man and man, sorting mankind out into antagonistic classes. By the 'forces of production' Marx meant, in the first place, the skills and tools which man progressively acquired in his struggle with nature – that is, roughly, what would today be called technology; but also the ways in which he applied them and the social and organizational consequences of their acquisition – the transition from subsistence activity to the economy of specialization and exchange, the social division of labour, the development of the market and the growth of the use of money as a means of exchange. Marx argued that, at any given moment, the level of development of the 'forces of production' determined the prevailing modes of production, commerce and consumption; these modes in turn determined the structure of civil society; and the structure of civil society determined the political conditions obtaining in it.

The class structure of society came into being as a by-product of the social division of labour, which assigned different functions to different individuals or groups, giving rise to inequalities of opportunity and inequalities of distribution. The source of these inequalities is identified as control over the means of production. For the class that controls the means of production is in a position to 'exploit' those that do not. The argument is that human labour alone creates value: but, as soon as the social division of labour comes into the picture, man finds himself selling his labour to an employer: and what he receives in return is less than the labour-value he produces. The difference – 'surplus value' – accrues to the employer by virtue of his control over the means of production. This is exploitation. In sum, the exploiting class uses its control over the means of production to appropriate to itself part of the value created by the labour of others, thus accumulating capital and enjoying leisure, while those who bear the main burden of labour receive less than their proper share of the social product. The resistance of the labourer to this exploitation ensures that the constant condition of society is one of 'class struggle' or 'class war'.

To moderate the acute tensions thus generated, and to stop their tearing society apart, society, as Marx saw it, creates a whole apparatus of institutions – a legal system, a political framework, a way of life, a religion or ideology – which collectively make up the 'state'. The state is the embodiment of the interests of the ruling class, that is to say the class that controls the means of production. It exists to conserve and promote those interests, coercing the exploited classes into submission to them and seeking to invest the existing order of things with a halo of righteous inevitability, obscuring the injustices of society's class structure. But the state is essentially a superstructure. Its character and institutions are not immutable. Society will change from time to time in response to technological and other developments in the underlying 'forces of production '; one class will displace another in control of the means of production, and the state superstructure will be adjusted accordingly to the interests of the new masters of society. The political power achieved successively by tyrannical autocrats, feudal lords, landowning aristocracies, merchants and manufacturers exemplified, in Marx's view, the truth of this analysis.

Industrial capitalism was, for Marx, the most complex and developed, and at the same time the most inhuman and depraving, form of social organization yet devised. The transition from primitive subsistence to an economy of commodity exchange had propelled man from self-employment to craft workshop separating production from use, and from workshop to factory, deepening his 'alienation' at each stage. It had spawned a new class, the heirs of the industrial revolution, which, equipped with the new mechanical technologies, had gained control of the means of production and, in the nineteenth century, were busy adapting the state to their own image and interests. Their driving force was greed and their means of satisfying it the accumulation of capital derived from the exploitation of human labour. Their advent brought the class struggle to a new pitch of intensity, for the industries they created achieved a new low point in the corruption and degradation of man. His labour had become a commodity, to be bought and sold for what it would fetch on the market, like potatoes or pig-iron. He faced the bitter choice between starvation and accepting employment for a pittance, working long hours in degrading conditions. Factory production had turned human labour from an exercise of skill into repetitive drudgery. It took the labourer out of his natural environment and crowded him into squalid urban slums. The emergence of a capitalist class had been matched by that of an industrial proletariat. The common man had been turned into a proletarian, a member of a dehumanized propertyless class, leading a wretched existence, the chattel of a state controlled by and run in the interests of the capitalist bourgeoisie. His condition was the apogee of alienation. But the moment would come when the constraining superstructure of the state would no longer suffice to contain the tensions within. The capitalist system bore in itself the seeds of its own destruction. It would inevitably perish by its own 'contradictions'. Its mainspring was competition – dog eating capitalist dog. The stresses set up by competition – falling yields, oligopolistic concentration, depressed wages and mounting unemployment – would generate recurring crises, each more disastrous than its predecessor. At that point the class struggle would reach its climax. The proletariat would rise in revolution, seize control of the means of production, and smash the capitalist exploiter and the state he had created.

Initially the proletarian society born of the revolution would be a class society, just as much as its predecessor had been. All that the revolution would have done would be to substitute control of the means of production by the proletariat for control of the same by the bourgeoisie, thereby enabling the proletariat to reconstitute the state and its institutions so that they reflected its own interests. The task of reconstruction would be enormous in scope. Since the capitalist bourgeoisie would fight the revolution every inch of the way it would have to be eliminated by force. So the proletarian state, so long as other classes existed, would have to sustain itself by dictatorial methods to ensure against a capitalist come-back. The post-revolutionary 'dictatorship of the proletariat' would perform the necessary surgery, expropriating the bourgeois owners of the means of production, dispossessing them of their ill-gotten gains and replacing the entire exploitation-oriented legal system by new laws giving expression to the rights of the workers. But proletarian dictatorship would not last forever. As the 'class enemy' was progressively liquidated, and control of the means of production vested in public hands, a 'classless' socialist society would emerge and the curse of exploitation of man by man would be finally exorcized. But even this was not yet the end of the road. Just as the material determinants of man's condition had, by successive transformations, produced industrial capitalism, and capitalism, because of its inherent nature, would necessarily give place to socialism, so socialism, applying the entire product of human labour for the common good, would in due course be transformed into communism, the final and perfect form of human organization, in which there would be abundance for all, with each man contributing according to his capabilities and receiving from society everything that he needed. With the advent of communism the state would 'wither away'. Class, its *raison d'être,* would have disappeared and it would be left with nothing to do. So too would alienation. Man would have regained the freedom he had lost when primitive society took its initial wrong turning. The inherent goodness of his nature would reassert itself and he would devote his increasing leisure to the further development of his potentialities for the common good. If anyone objected that human nature would need to change rather radically before 'full' or 'true' communism could be expected to work these miracles, the answer was that there was no problem. The elimination of class, the absence of exploitation and the progressive refinement of proletarian man by education and culture could be counted on to bring about such a transformation. Communist man would be a new man.

Before leaving Marx behind a further dimension needs to be added. In what has been said so far, Marx's ideas have been presented as relating to a single, if unidentified, society. His analysis, however, applied with equal force to all societies of the world, or more exactly to all societies in that part of the world that fell within Marx's field of vision, namely the industrially developed states of Western and central Europe and North America. The historical process had unfolded by precisely the same path in each of these countries, though it was further advanced in some than in others. The real interests of the bourgeoisie and the proletariat were respectively the same in each of them, and the class struggle common to them all. Proletarian solidarity transcended national sentiment and cut across frontiers. The revolution, when it came, would be no mere national upheaval. Proletarians of all lands were in the same boat. English, French and German workers would find themselves fighting shoulder to shoulder on one side of the barricades against their combined capitalist exploiters on the other.

This is not the place to develop the numerous lines of criticism to which the Marxian system is vulnerable. Several of them had already made themselves felt by the turn of the century. Having waited two generations for Marx's predictions to be fulfilled, the 'revisionist' stream of European socialist thought pointed out in the 1890s that a number of the premises underpinning Marx's argument had disappeared. The life of the factory worker in the 1840s had indeed been very much as Marx had described it. But now, so far from collapsing, the capitalist system was booming. Trade unionism had developed and demonstrated the ability of the working class to combine and fight for, and to win, its rights within the existing industrial framework, without having to make a revolution. And humanitarians and utilitarians had pushed legislation through parliaments − factory acts, public health and education − which took much of the edge off Marx's critique of bourgeois selfishness and proletarian misery. By

1900 the greater part of the labour movement, while paying lip-service to proletarian revolution as an ultimate goal, had become far more interested in promoting democratic reforms of the capitalist system, in getting better wages and shorter hours, in strengthening the legal position of trade unions, in consumers' co-operatives and in maximizing labour's share of the social product.

Not so Lenin. For reasons partly personal and partly intellectual, he was a revolutionary. He reckoned, with many others of his own generation and its immediate predecessors, that Russia could only be set to rights by violent revolutionary action, and Marx's analysis of the ills of capitalist society seemed to him both persuasive in itself and a first rate rallying-point for the mobilization of the oppressed of Russia. True, Russia did not fit precisely into Marx's frame of reference. It was then what would today be called an undeveloped country. Industrialization had come slowly and late. The poor of Russia were, first and foremost, not proletarians but peasants, the descendants of the serfs emancipated forty years before. Marx himself had certainly never thought of Russia as anywhere near ripe for his sort of revolution: he saw it as an odious oriental despotism just emerging from the twilight of feudalism. But Lenin reckoned that the beginnings of an urban proletariat had been brought into existence by the reforms and industrial development of the late nineteenth century and that, with a few necessary adjustments, Marx's reach-me-down ideas could be made to fit its needs.

But Marxism was not the only spring from which Lenin had drunk. The indigenous Russian revolutionary tradition, which was mentioned in the preceding chapter, was part of the environment in which he grew up. His formative years were passed in the atmosphere of deepening repression following the murder of Alexander II and were overshadowed by the death on the gallows of his elder brother for conspiring to murder Alexander III. Like other revolutionaries of his time, he believed that the existing order was so unjust that only a clean sweep would change it, and so heavily armed that force alone could make any impression on it. Those who had gone before him along the revolutionary path were persuaded that in dealing with such an adversary, with a system so steeped in iniquity, all means were permissible. Conventional morality had no relevance to their struggle. Revolutionism was a profession with infinitely lofty objectives, but the professional revolutionary could not afford the luxury of boxing in accordance with the Marquess of Queensberry rules. Likewise, in the conditions of the time, revolutionary activity was necessarily underground activity, requiring absolute dedication, steadfastness of purpose and, above all, secrecy. In establishing the separate identity, within the wider framework of the Russian Social Democratic Party, of the Bolsheviks (the title, meaning 'majority group', stems from a crucial debate in 1903, which they won by the casting vote of the chairman − Lenin), Lenin took all this for granted but added specific contributions of his own. They related to organization and to revolutionary ethics.

Divided councils were, he recognized, the curse of democracy. To make a successful revolution, the first requisite was the unity of his party in action. His doctrine of 'democratic centralism' laid down that a decision of the party, once taken by majority vote, was binding on the minority with the force of law. It became part of the party's 'line'. And decisions of higher organs of the party were binding on lower organs. This principle was justified on a pragmatic plane by the practical necessity for centrally directed, co-ordinated action, but also, on the theoretical level, by the notion that the party, equipped with the scientific truths of the Marxian analysis, conscious as the generality of mankind was not of the full meaning of the situation confronting it, and knowing clearly where it was going, was in a position to render 'correct' decisions. Its decisions took on a mantle of infallibility. The party could not be wrong. It could, of course, take a new decision which might change the line, thus giving the impression that it followed a zigzag course, but that would be because the conjuncture, the situation confronting it, had changed. This device, as will be apparent, was more conspicuously centralist than it was democratic. Its claim to democratic character rested first on the fact that the membership of decision-making bodies was constituted by election from below, and second that, until the chairman's gavel came down, debate, at least within the limits set by ideological rectitude, was unconstrained and the majority view prevailed. Both these saving graces withered away with the passage of time, as leaders came to be selected by co-option not election, and debate at all levels but the very top increasingly conformed to the known predilections of the leadership. Along with centralized decision-making went the growth of bureaucratic procedures for execution.

Administration was a subject close to Lenin's heart. The party's job was to establish the line; thereafter it was the task of the official apparatus below, whether in party or state, to carry it out. If anything went awry it could only be through bungling, neglect or sabotage on their part.

The amorality preached by the nineteenth-century Russian revolutionists was erected by Lenin into a principle of statecraft. Marxist teaching reinforced his personal disgust with the society in which he lived, whose destruction became for him a necessary, and sufficient, moral goal. Once that goal was established, expediency – the aptness of the means to the end in view – became the sole criterion for action. The selection of the proper means to that end became for Lenin a pragmatic, not an ethical problem. He had no use for misdirected terrorism, but his was not the half-regretful attitude, common to politicians elsewhere, that 'you can't make an omelette without breaking eggs'. That one course of action might be morally acceptable, or morally less unacceptable than another, left him cold. What was important was a realistic appraisal of a situation and of what was needed to change it in the desired direction. All means must be used, and all forces manipulated, to achieve the end. The end justified the means. He was a man in a hurry. The means to be adopted were those that led fastest and most surely to the end. This amorality was most conspicuous in the in-fighting within the Social Democratic Party, and between it and other parties in the pre-revolutionary and revolutionary period. As a tiny minority the Bolsheviks could come to power only through alliances with others, notably the Socialist Revolutionaries and the Mensheviks, whose objectives were quite different but whose momentary interests might be, or could be made to seem, temporarily or partially compatible with its own. For Lenin these alliances were to be made, used and discarded ruthlessly. Profit from them should be taken rapidly before the other party himself treacherously broke them. By these means the Bolsheviks climbed to power. The success of their revolutionary coup was sufficient justification for Lenin and is certainly reckoned as such by the Soviet society that grew from his revolution. But, sixty years on, the world has good grounds for regretting the systematic debasement of the currency of politics which his teaching inculcated, with results extending far beyond the confines of Russia, and with devastating effects upon the credibility of his own country in international affairs.

It is now time to consider some of the adaptations and additions which Lenin made to the theory and practice of socialism, inherited from Marx and crossed with the Russian revolutionary tradition. First, and perhaps most striking and long-lived in its effects, is his shaping of the role of the party. Marx had postulated the inevitability of a socialist revolution, to be brought about by the uprising of the proletariat, the propertyless working class, against its bourgeois exploiters. As a practical politician and professional revolutionary, Lenin recognized the indispensability of the proletariat as an instrument for destroying the old regime; but he was sceptical of their ability, having once taken power, to run society and to keep it on a revolutionary course. The proletariat lacked what he called 'consciousness', by which he meant an understanding of its own role in the class struggle. Left in charge, it would be prone to lower its sights and settle for some mere charter of trade union rights and the gradual transformation of the old society, as a large section of the nominally Marxist labour movement in more advanced societies had already unashamedly done. The Russian revolutionary tradition had been carried forward in the nineteenth century not by working men but by the middle-class intellectuals. Lenin, as one such, saw that the revolution must be led by men who had acquired 'consciousness', who were guided by ideas and convictions and whose vocation it was to conspire against and destroy – not amend – the existing order.

He organized his Bolshevik Party with this end precisely in view. Its claim to leadership was founded upon the unquestionable superiority, as Lenin saw it, of socialist theory over the elemental, irrational force of the proletariat, which, left to itself, would lose its way and end up with some form of gradualist social democracy. The making of revolution and the running of a post-revolutionary state was far too serious a business to be left to amateurs. Clear thinking, ideological inspiration, strong control from the top and tight discipline below, and rational and methodical administration, were the prerequisites of success. So, though the revolution would be made with, and in the name of, the proletariat – how, indeed, could it be otherwise? – the directing role, both on the day and after, must be reserved to the party as the proletariat's conscious 'vanguard'. The big battalions of the proletarian rearguard might catch up in time, indeed the party would constantly train them for greater participation. But it would be a long business. The history of the Russian revolution testifies with devastating clarity to the practical success of Lenin's conception of the party: a minuscule group of professional Marxist revolutionaries was enabled to outmanoeuvre other socialist and reformist parties, to take control of a popular movement of massive discontent and to establish itself as the ruler of Russia. By substituting the party for the victorious proletariat and ruling in its name, Lenin fundamentally altered the character of the post-revolutionary society and state. The dictatorship of the proletariat was henceforth to mean the dictatorship of the party. This is the first of Lenin's great legacies.

The second concerned the behaviour of the new state in relation to the outside world. Marx, we have noted, deduced his 'laws of history' from a study of the advanced societies and economies of Western Europe, giving little or no thought to the prospects of social revolution in tsarist Russia. It was in England, Germany and France and the United States that capitalism had matured to a point where, once the conjuncture was right – once a 'revolutionary situation' had been generated by the mounting injustices of the system – the proletariat would rise and take power. And it was assumed that the flame of revolution, once lit in one or more of the developed societies, would spread – much as the revolutionary upheavals of 1848, different as they were in nature and fruitless in their outcome, had spread – and would engulf all or most of the developed states of the world. The coming revolution was a world revolution. Proletarians of all lands were united in their common condition of subjection and exploitation, a unifying factor far more potent than the divisive factor of national allegiance, already sapped by the manifestly unjust nature of bourgeois rule, and would rise in unison when the moment came.

Lenin certainly recognized that Russia was far from being a natural, still further from being the ideal, spot from which to set this process in train. Yet, having, by methods of which Marx never dreamed, captured control of the Russian revolution and installed the dictatorship of the Bolshevik Party, Lenin and his associates steadfastly believed that, in a matter of days or weeks, the spark struck in Petrograd would kindle the proletariat everywhere, and that the sovereign states of Europe would collapse. It was not a wholly implausible thought. For the preceding three-and-a-half years the great powers of Europe, Russia included, had been locked in the bloodiest war yet known. Governments were close to bankruptcy. Privation, war-weariness and casualties must surely move the conscripted workers of Germany, France and Britain to recognize the folly of further slaughter and to dethrone their rulers who had willed it. The Bolsheviks accordingly called on Russia's enemies and allies to make peace without annexations or indemnities, reckoning that this appeal would touch off the expected explosion. But nothing of the sort happened. Instead, the German high command, summoning Russian plenipotentiaries to Brest-Litovsk, proceeded to impose on Russia a peace more punitive than even the most pessimistic had thought conceivable. And in due course Russia's former allies moved in troops to intervene in the civil war waged by tsarist remnants against the Bolsheviks. Evidently Marx had been wrong. The Bolsheviks were on their own. World revolution had failed to march. Alone and exposed, socialist Russia was confronted by a ring of hostile capitalist states. The question was not how far and how fast the revolutionary movement would sweep across the continent of Europe. It was rather how Russia, backward, isolated and impoverished by the war, could keep the spark of socialism alive.

Successive disappointments did not quench Lenin's belief that world revolution would eventually come, and triumph; but they did induce a basic revision of his thinking. The Soviet state, he now saw, would have to be kept in being throughout what might turn out to be quite a long transitional period until, in the fullness of time, the capitalist order beyond Russia's frontiers was swept away and replaced by socialism. This consummation would be brought about by an era of world wars and revolutions, but its timing remained highly uncertain. Meanwhile, if the Soviet state were to survive, Soviet attitudes and policies would have to change. Hitherto patriotism had been a sentiment much derided by the Bolsheviks. They were, above all, internationalists and had been defeatists, in the proper sense of the term, reckoning that the defeat of their country in the squalid and acquisitive war then ending was a necessary condition of revolution at home and of the coming together of the proletariat in the world at large. In the changed circumstances the preservation of the gains of the revolution obviously demanded the preservation of the Soviet state. So, Lenin found, there was nothing wrong with patriotism, provided that it was patriotism of the right sort. Nor, for that matter, with wars: it was indeed contemptible to fight for a government representing an exploiting class, but, once one had rid one's country of bourgeois rule, what could be more just, righteous and

necessary than to fight to strengthen and spread socialism in the world?
Imperciptibly at first, a new doctrine was emerging, greatly to be
elaborated by Lenin's successors. It was the doctrine that, while the
transitional period lasted, while the historical process marked time, the
interests of socialism and of world revolution were, for practical
purposes, synonymous with those of the Soviet Union, the homeland
and first country of socialism. These interests were to be sustained at
home by the inculcation of Soviet patriotism and pursued, as necessity
dictated and opportunity offered, by waging 'just wars'. In the wider
world the Soviet Union took the lead in bringing together in the
Communist (third) International the communist parties of all lands. The
manifesto of the second congress of the International in 1921 records
that 'the Communist International has declared the cause of Soviet
Russia to be its own cause'.

A third legacy of Lenin's that is relevant to our enquiry is his 'theory
of imperialism', a word which he employs in a specific sense only
distantly related to its meaning in common English usage. Lenin's main
work on this subject was written in exile in Zurich in 1916, but his
optimism in the following year about the spread of the Russian
revolution to the other capitalist countries suggests that he had not fully
appreciated the practical implications of his theory. The failure of the
spark to ignite gave a new relevance to the conclusions of what had
initially been a piece of painstaking theoretical research. Something had
obviously gone wrong with Marx's prognosis. The walls of Jericho had
not fallen. The historical process had not come up with the promised
dénouement. The proletariat in the countries where capitalism was ripe
for revolution had not risen and overthrown its oppressors. Why?
Because, Lenin concluded, the 'contradictions' by which capitalism was
supposed to perish – the anarchy of the market, planlessness, cut-throat
competition, dwindling returns on capital – had been relieved by
processes which Marx had failed to foresee. The contradictions had not,
for the time being, intensified to the point of revolution because
developed capitalist societies had managed to shift the stress on to the
undeveloped regions of the world. Unbridled competition, as Marx's
'law of capitalist concentration' taught, led to the progressive
elimination of the weakest and the gradual emergence of monopolies.
Lenin's researches showed that monopolies appeared at first within
developed capitalist states but later internationally and multinationally.

The process of monopolization and concentration into large units generated immense accumulations of 'finance capital', seeking opportunities for further profit and, at the same time, brought about a divorce between the producer of goods and the financier who juggled with the funds thereby accumulated. Ruthless though it was in its monopolistic stage, capitalism was no longer chaotic and planless. It worked by rational criteria and knew what it was doing. It could even transform itself into 'state capitalism' by getting the state to take a hand. But, whether ownership was private, nationalized or mixed, monopoly capitalism, the 'highest stage of capitalism', lived by the export of its accumulated surplus funds which were put to work in backward countries, exploiting their natural resources and underpaying their plentiful work-forces for the benefit of the metropolis. Colonialism was one mode of this exploitation but not the only one. Weaker and less developed capitalist countries were victims of it too, the difference being only in degree. The material point was that the super-profits gained by this process enabled the monopolists to avoid revolution at home by buying off their metropolitan proletariats with better wages and conditions of labour, introducing the paraphernalia of 'democracy' and extending the suffrage to the working class.

By these means, proletarians in the advanced countries became accessories after the fact of monopolist exploitation, growing fat on their share of the inflated profits of injustice, and losing their revolutionary consciousness and their desire for change. They had placed themselves on the side of the exploiters, acquiring in the process a status similar to that of the capitalist *rentier* whose income is derived from the sweated labour of others. It was not surprising that their enthusiasm for the barricades had waned. But this, Lenin insisted, did not mean that Marx's analysis was fundamentally mistaken, merely that there was one more twist in the path of history which Marx had not foreseen. For capitalism in its monopolist, or 'imperialist', stage had the same vices, the same contradictions, as Marx's more primitive model, and they would assuredly bring it down by the same process as he had foretold. All that had changed was the theatre, and some of the actors, in the drama of world revolution. Also the time-scale. With the benefit of hindsight it was clear that the Bolsheviks had been wrong to look to the proletariat of Western Europe for early support for their revolution. They must now turn their attention to the 'oppressed peoples' in distant lands, where the seeds of revolution had been planted by the imperialists. After that harvest had been gathered, the time would come when the scythe of revolution, sharpened by use in the backward countries, could be turned back on to the lusher fields of Europe and north America.

The 'theory of imperialism' was a creditable, even an imaginative, shot at updating Marxist doctrine, introducing and digesting many developments which had taken place since Marx wrote, failure to deal with which impaired the credibility of his entire system. But it left many loose ends, many questions unanswered and Lenin himself died before it could be put very far to the test of experience. Though he was in general remarkably uninhibited in his readiness to manipulate and adapt Marxian theory in the light of his own revolutionary experience, insisting that Marx's writings were a guide not a set of rules, Lenin, whether from cynicism or faith, was careful to keep the Marxist revelation, the declaratory framework of certitude, intact. This was important for the Russian people, shorn as they now were of their traditional Orthodox Christian faith, and called upon, as they were, to man the long vigil until the age of world revolution should dawn. Forearmed with the revelation, they could be sure that they were betting on a certainty. As sure as eggs were eggs, socialism would triumph. Capitalism, though Marx had been a bit hasty in issuing its death certificate, was doomed and, with its disappearance, freedom, plenty and the brotherhood of man would supervene. It might prove to be a long haul, and it would be necessary for all to fight, and many to die, before the victory of socialism was achieved; but others would live on to enjoy the sweets of victory. For it was written. History was on the side of socialism, and socialism for the time being at least, and until further notice, was Soviet Russia.

In this spirit Lenin's successors set out on the long haul. They too saw the inestimable value of Marxism as a revealed religion. Under them, Lenin's legacies – the dictatorship of the party, the consolidation of socialism in one country and the theory of imperialism – acquired the same sanctity as the original prophecies. But, underdeveloped as she was, weakened by the ravages of war, and surrounded with enemies, Russia must first industrialize and arm herself before her role in the historical process would be much more than passive. She must set about building 'socialism in one country'.

Trial and Error

4

Seventeen years after Lenin's death in 1924 the Soviet Union was attacked by Hitler. In September 1939 the imperialists had come to blows, as Lenin had said they would. As war approached, Soviet diplomacy sat on the fence seeking to gain time. A week before Hitler invaded Poland, Stalin signed a non-aggression pact with him, purchasing thereby almost two years' respite and regaining in the ensuing carve-up the borderlands lost to Poland in the aftermath of the First World War. He also obtained a free hand to deal with Finland, from whom he grabbed, in the squalid and bungled winter war of 1939–40, a strategic slice of contiguous Karelia; and then with the Baltic states – Estonia, Latvia and Lithuania – formerly tsarist provinces, which were reincorporated six months later. But these strategic dispositions availed nothing. Having battered Western Europe, Britain alone excepted, into submission, Hitler turned on the Soviet Union and by Christmas 1941 was at the gates of Moscow and Leningrad. The 'second imperialist war' had become the 'great patriotic war' and for the ensuing three years the Soviet people responded with outstanding endurance and heroism.

Two decades of socialism had not, if the truth be told, brought very much in terms of human welfare to justify this heroic defence, which must be explained in large measure by visceral national sentiment; but the Soviet system had been formidably consolidated and ramified on the foundations that Lenin had laid. Consolidation had not been achieved without some false starts. From 1918 to 1921 the economy had been brought to a standstill by a doctrinaire attempt (subsequently known as 'war communism') to establish, by recourse to requisitioning and direction of labour, a non-monetary, non-market economy. By early 1921 mounting disorder, including mutiny at the Kronstadt naval base, hitherto a stronghold of revolutionary power, convinced Lenin that war communism had to be abandoned. Its successor, the 'New Economic Policy' or NEP for short, was a mixed economy. The 'commanding heights' of industry were nationalized, but most of the rest and small businesses, crafts and services remained in private hands. Goods, whether produced by state or private entities, changed hands on the market at the price they could fetch. The NEP worked, in a manner of speaking, and the country settled down. But it was not socialism as the Bolsheviks saw it, for it left a substantial part of production in the hands of an exploiting class and it retained the spontaneous, unplanned characteristics of the capitalist market economy. With the introduction of Stalin's first five-year plan in 1928 all that was to change.

Since it was to prove so durable – in its main outlines it persists to the present day – Stalin's economic model merits closer examination. With the exception of collective farms (a form of agricultural co-operation nominally preserving the fiction of individual peasant tenure, symbolized by the retention of a half-hectare 'private' plot per family), the entire means of production were brought under the ownership of the Soviet state. Henceforth the functions which under capitalism are performed, and under the NEP had still been performed in part, by spontaneous forces were transferred to a central planning organization. Though money was retained as an accounting medium and means of exchange, production was henceforth to be determined not by demand and profitability but by social requirements. Applying social criteria, the plan established priorities for production and investment and decided what should be produced, where and by whom and in what quantities, what additional capacity was needed and whence the resources for creating it should come. Stalin's economic strategy was to give top priority to the industrialization of the country. Electric power, coal, steel and heavy engineering were to come first. Satisfaction for the consumer would have to wait, and agriculture, once collectivized, would have to muddle along as best it could until the main task of building the industrial base had been completed.

The first two five-year plans (1928-37) and the first half of the third (which was interrupted by the war) changed the shape of the economy almost beyond recognition. Planning made possible the mobilization of resources on a gigantic scale. The industrial labour-force increased hugely as more and more peasants were brought into the factories and phenomenally high rates of investment were achieved. But the detailed performance of the planned economy was a good deal less satisfactory. In banishing the traditional motivations of management, the planners had taken on themselves the responsibility for prescribing product, price and utilization. But, since one man's output is another man's input, they found themselves obliged also to organize the supply interrelationships between raw-material producer and manufacturer, and between enterprise and enterprise in the manufacturing industry. Lacking the technical capability and the information – indeed, the omniscience – that these tasks demanded, they frequently got their calculations wrong and muddles and nonsenses were endemic at the micro-economic level. The five-year plan was subdivided into annual plans and each annual plan into monthly plans, with targets for each period which had to be fulfilled on time on pain of sanctions. The resultant emphasis on haste and on the achievement of gross output targets, at the expense of reliability and quality, did not matter so much in the early days of the system but was to prove a serious drawback later on. The social, and in the longer run the economic, costs of Stalin's planning priorities were high. The capital accumulation required to build the great hydro-electric schemes, steelworks, oil refineries and defence factories was wrung out of agriculture, which was systematically starved of investment. The prices paid by the state to collective farms for compulsory deliveries of foodstuffs were niggardly and the personal income of the peasant barely enabled him to sustain life. Those who from time to time starved were casualties of the strategy of putting industrialization first. The longer-term consequences of Stalin's neglect of Soviet agriculture have survived to plague his successors who in recent years have had to spend hugely to make good his omissions.

The other principal casualty was the standard of living of the urban proletariat, in whose name the revolution had been made. The preemption by heavy industrial development of most of the disposable resources of the economy meant that there was nothing over for housing, and only the barest minimum for the light industries that might have catered for the needs of the common man. Hopes of eventual improvement were held out, but not until the country had developed and mobilized its extensive natural resources. Autarky was the long-term aim. If imports were indispensable for accelerating the development of heavy industry, products were set aside to pay for them, but the Soviet Union intended in the long run to be self-sufficient.

Stalin's years of power brought back in new guise familiar features of old Russia. The tsarist bureaucracy had been swept away by the revolution, but the planned economy gave birth to another even more extensive. Planning meant that what formerly happened spontaneously must now happen by command. Hence there evolved, as of necessity, a bureaucratic structure charged with formulating the commands, monitoring compliance with them and accounting for the resources expended in the process. There was thus interposed between the central planners and the factory or farm manager, a hierarchy of state agencies. Ministries at the centre proliferated, one each and sometimes more than one, for each branch of the economy; below the ministries a second tier of central administrations, and below them ministries of the republic in which an enterprise was situated. The party too had its own bureaucracy, both at the centre, where the party Secretariat replicated within itself most of the main branches of government, but also at republic level, and in every *oblast'* (province) and *rayon* (district). The elite of 'conscious' proletarians had expanded in response to the demands that faced it. It was now present everywhere, the repository of Marxist-Leninist lore and myth, more skilled, more active, better educated and more privileged than the common man, and keeping closely to itself the monopoly both of decision and of the information on which decisions were based. In the proletariat's name the party exercised dictatorship. But dictatorship bespoke vigilance, for the 'class enemy', the classes dispossessed by the revolution, must not be allowed to come back, and the waywardness of human nature needed constant restraint if the Russian people, not the least susceptible of God's creatures to temptation, were to be kept on the rails. This called for more than the blue pencil of the tsarist censor. Control of ideas required the inculcation of socially acceptable views through the written word, in education and in the arts, which in turn meant more men in offices, more committees and more directives.

It also meant policemen. Lenin's Cheka, reckoned in its day to be the indispensable arm of the Bolsheviks in suppressing counter-revolution, took on with a minimum of dislocation and interruption the methods of the old Okhrana, the tsar's secret police, and Lenin himself had not scrupled to use terror when his power was challenged in the early days. Under Stalin, the secret police under various labels (GPU, NKVD, MVD, MGB – later KGB) shook off the party's control and became the personal fief of the dictator himself, as its predecessor had been of the tsar. With its 'archipelago' of prisons and forced labour camps it became a state within the state and Stalin used it for the summary liquidation of all whom he suspected of conspiring against him, unleashing it successively on the state bureaucracy, the officer corps and the upper echelons of the party. Stalin's rule was every bit as arbitrary and ruthless, and infinitely more efficient than the tsar's had been. Under the pressures of war the rigours of the system were somewhat relaxed, but when peace came Stalin was still there and the screws were once more tightened.

But the war had made possible a forward movement on socialism's long static international front. The Communist International (Comintern) had pursued its conspiratorial way under Soviet tutelage through the inter-war years, but the great depression of the 1930s, for all its apparent similarities to the final crisis of capitalism that Marx had predicted, evoked no successful proletarian uprisings. Instead, overtly anti-communist dictatorial governments were installed in Germany, Italy and Spain, and elsewhere the writings of John Maynard Keynes seemed to point to the solubility of many of capitalism's 'contradictions'. In 1943, in deference to the susceptibilities of his capitalist co-belligerents, Stalin formally dissolved the Comintern, though the Soviet Communist Party (CPSU), always the International's mainspring, carried on as though nothing had happened. In 1945 Hitler's retreat after the great battles on his eastern front brought the Red Army into Poland, into the Balkan countries that had been Hitler's satellites and eventually into Germany itself.

'Liberation' provided the opportunity for giving proletarian revolution a much needed push forward. Bulgaria, Romania, Hungary and Poland were, by various devices, equipped with communist governments. A *coup* in Prague, not then under Red Army control, in February 1948, added Czechoslovakia to the list; and in September 1949 the Soviet zone of occupation in Germany, with the Soviet sector of Berlin, was established as the German Democratic Republic (GDR), thus consummating the division of Germany. Communist governments also emerged from the war in Yugoslavia and Albania. The outcome, in sum, was a belt of territory under communist control on the Soviet Union's western frontier, running from the Baltic to the Black Sea and, if Yugoslavia and Albania were included, to the Adriatic. After almost thirty years, it was no longer a case of 'socialism in one country'; the victory over Hitler had made it possible to speak of a 'socialist camp' or 'commonwealth'. The new regimes were in full subjection to Stalin and the CPSU, which had set up a new institution, the Communist Information Bureau (Cominform or Informburo) to co-ordinate them. Unlike the Comintern it embraced only those parties that had gained power in their countries, plus a few others, notably the French and Italian, which were reckoned to be in sight of power. In 1949 the Chinese Communist Party (CPC) took Peking and established the Chinese People's Republic. The Chinese party's victory had been won by reliance not on the relatively sparse industrial proletariat but on the peasantry. Though observers in the West, with some encouragement from Soviet publicists, hastened to brigade China together with the other communist states in a single 'Sino-Soviet camp', the Chinese was a revolution of a different sort. The institutions and much of the machinery of the CPC were the same but its base in popular support was different, and conditions in the two countries – the one primitive and agrarian, the other with thirty years of industrialization behind it – could scarcely have been more disparate.

The camp, from the outset, was an unhappy undertaking. The disparity, on the one hand, in power and, on the other, in culture between the Soviet union and its vassals was too great. Yugoslavia was the first to go, in 1948, sent to Coventry for insubordination, blockaded, provoked and reviled, but not attacked. Before long Stalin was firing, imprisoning and murdering the leaders of the other 'fraternal' countries as though they were his own people. The Council for Mutual Economic Assistance (Comecon or CMEA) established in 1948 in response to the Marshall Plan in Western Europe, looked, and initially was, too much like an instrument for the economic exploitation of the vassal states by the Soviet metropolis. The Warsaw Pact, set up in 1955 to defend the socialist camp against NATO's 'aggressive' designs, placed the national armies of Eastern Europe under Soviet command

and control and afforded a basis for the stationing of Soviet troops in those countries. Violence broke out in east Berlin in 1953, as it was to do elsewhere in the Soviet orbit before the decade was out.

In the spring of 1953 Stalin died. It was the end of an epoch, and the new epoch was slow in getting off the mark; but when the CPSU's twentieth congress was convened in 1956 it was already clear that great changes were in gestation. They are associated with the name of Nikita Sergeyevich Khrushchev, the most important figure in the collective leadership that initially succeeded Stalin, and his eventual sole successor. The Soviet Union was declared to have become a state of the whole people. Forty years after the revolution the class struggle inside the Soviet Union was reckoned to be over. The dictatorship of the proletariat in whose name so many inhumanities had been committed was pensioned off. Stalin's excesses were condemned and disowned, attributed to the 'cult of personality' which had grown up in the dictator's latter years. Many of his dead victims were posthumously rehabilitated and most of the millions still alive in prisons and camps were discharged. The new leadership pledged itself to work in future within the framework of 'socialist legality', a concept a good deal narrower and less satisfactory to the governed than the rule of law as understood in non-socialist countries, but offering some protection against the arbitrary use of state power. But the party was to remain the monopolist of power and of political action. Its essential dictatorial role was untouched, though it was now, with the demise of proletarian dictatorship, dubbed a party of the whole people.

Of more direct significance to the outside world were Khrushchev's revisions of doctrine about the means by which the cause of revolution, and the material interests of the Soviet Union as the standard-bearer of that cause, were to be carried forward in the world at large. The necessity to promote both of them was axiomatic, for the struggle for 'world revolution' was nothing less than the projection on the international plane of that 'class struggle' that had been already resolved within Russia. Lenin, as we have seen, took an entirely uninhibited view as to methods. Capitalism being limitlessly evil, all methods, legal and illegal, overt and covert, were permissible in encompassing its overthrow. His theory of imperialism taught that competition between monopolist, imperialist states would inevitably lead to wars between them; and how right this prediction seemed, when one considered that two world wars had broken out within twenty years of one another. The quarrels between bourgeois states were socialism's opportunity. Besides, the inherent irreconcilability between the two systems – socialism and capitalism – pointed unmistakably towards resolution by war. The allied intervention in Russia in 1918–19 had been an attempt to strangle the proletarian revolution in its cradle. Its failure did not exhaust the set purpose of the bourgeois states to make an end of socialism. True, Lenin and Stalin after him proclaimed their dedication to peace, indeed the pursuit of peace, in their time and this subsequently became an essential feature in the stock-in-trade and image of socialism. But it was to be a peace after socialism's objectives had been achieved. Till then, the watchword was struggle, and, unless – which would be quite foreign to their nature – the imperialists threw in the towel, struggle meant war. The assumption, sometimes explicit, sometimes tacit, of Soviet thought in the first thirty years of the Soviet Union's existence was that, sooner or later, there would have to be a showdown, by force of arms, with the imperialists. There was felt to be nothing discreditable or immoral about this assumption. It was a matter of having the means ready to hand, and of 'correctly' assessing the moment for their use.

Now, however, an entirely new situation had arisen. Nuclear weapons, first used by the Americans in the closing stages of the war with Japan, had brought about a 'qualitative change' in the nature of warfare. The USSR lost no time in developing her own nuclear armoury, but it was obvious that – even given parity, which the Soviet Union was still a long way from achieving – war between combatants so armed would most likely lead to the extinction of both imperialists and socialists alike. In Khrushchev's words, 'the atomic bomb does not recognize the class principle'. Plainly an ideology which relied on the arbitrement of war for the final settling of accounts with imperialism was insolvent and self-destructive. The direct route to the victory of socialism was closed. War had become too dangerous.

If, as had hitherto been assumed, war between the two systems was inevitable, then there could now be no future for socialism. So inevitability had to go overboard. What, then, was the correct course for the CPSU to adopt? When world revolution had missed its cue in 1918, and the prospect of 'socialism in one country' had begun to materialize, Lenin had written of the tactical necessity of 'peaceful cohabitation' or 'peaceful coexistence' with the capitalists. 'Peaceful coexistence' was now taken out of the attic and dusted off and, under Khrushchev and his successors, was to become the pivot of Soviet external policy. In its modern formulation, of which more will be said later on, it represented the minimum and unavoidable adjustment of Soviet doctrine to the nuclear age. It applied only to the official relations between states – the 'ideological struggle' between the two systems continued unabated – and only between states having different social systems. Important consequential changes of doctrine followed from it. Shorn of its assumed *dénouement* by military confrontation, the struggle with imperialism would be carried on by 'peaceful competition', in which the inescapable superiority of socialism would make good its claims by rapidly outstripping the capitalists in the production of material wealth and in creating a more humane society. And, since the advancement of world revolution now involved risks of opposition or intervention by nuclear-armed capitalists, the possibility was now entertained of 'peaceful transition' from capitalism to socialism, including even the possibility of communist parties taking power by the parliamentary, constitutional, route. These were the 'three peacefuls' which, together with the 'two alls' (the all-people's state and the all-people's party, already referred to), became the target of the bitter ideological polemic that broke out in public between Peking and Moscow in the early 1960s.

Mao Tse-tung was, of course, wildly wrong (as his subsequent conduct implicitly admitted) in earlier dismissing the atom bomb as a 'paper tiger'. But he was perfectly correct in stigmatizing these revisions of doctrine as heretical. They did not, however, exhaust Krushchev's errors in Chinese eyes, for in his initial zeal to abjure the inevitability of major war he had recoiled also from advocacy of local wars and wars of liberation, on the ground that they might escalate and involve the nuclear powers. It was by such wars that the Chinese party, its eyes fixed on the undeveloped third world, believed that socialism must for some time develop and expand. What was more, having, as the Chinese saw it, made a proper mess of socialist theory, Khrushchev went on, in a futile endeavour to prove his manhood, to commit disastrous errors in practice. His furtive attempt in October 1961 to checkmate the American imperialists in one move by installing Soviet medium-range missiles in Cuba seemed to the Chinese the act of a

hare-brained adventurist. Anyone having a vestige of scientific insight
into the historical process could have seen that it was an enterprise
bound to end in tears. And when the imperialists called his bluff,
Khrushchev, with his tail between his legs, had meekly dismantled his
missiles and taken them back to Russia, thus capitulating to the class
enemy. His disastrous combination of 'adventurism' and
'capitulationism' made him patently unfit to lead the CPSU, let alone a
world-wide socialist camp.

But, loudly as the Chinese might rage, the revisions of doctrine made
by the twentieth congress had for the most part come to stay and were
duly absorbed into the body of Soviet socialism. However hedged – and
the incompatibility of some of them with what had gone before called
for a good deal of hedging – they recognized aspects of reality which the
Soviet leadership could not afford to ignore. The Soviet Union, now a
relatively developed industrial and urban society, had changed. Stalin's
(and Lenin's) way of doing things might still make sense when applied
to the barefoot millions of China, but the Soviet Union as it now was
could not grow and prosper by such methods. Abroad, the interests of
socialism, and of the Soviet Union, its first country, could not be
advanced by going bald-headed for the imperialists. And if revolution in
the developed countries of the West were not to be indefinitely
postponed socialists there must be prepared to work, at least initially,
within the framework of the societies they sought to destroy. In due
course, the CPSU's twenty-second congress in 1962 adopted a new
party statute incorporating the new ideas propounded at the twentieth
and, as the quarrel with the Chinese party spread and deepened, the
attempt to preserve a united 'socialist camp' was abandoned, leaving
the CPSU more free to go its own way. On one point Khrushchev's
revision of doctrine proved ephemeral. The risk of great-power
involvement in small wars was recognized as a valid limitation, but to
erect it into a prohibition of principle was reckoned to be too much,
imposing an altogether excessive curb on revolutionary initiative.
Already dead before Khrushchev fell in 1964, the interdict on small
wars was effectively erased from the record by his successors.

Those successors, initially the team of Brezhnev and Kosygin, but
with Brezhnev in time increasingly achieving pre-eminence, came to
power conscious that the country had had its fill of innovations and
surprises, and that the twentieth congress, in making its, doubtless

necessary, modernizations of Leninist mythology, had come close at several points to upsetting the applecart. The campaign to discredit Stalin had gone too far. 'Socialist legality' was necessary and (within proper limits) commendable, but the dictatorship of the party must not be undermined, for it underpinned everything from the maintenance of public order to the management and control of the economy. Peaceful coexistence, properly understood, was impeccable, but it needed to be founded on Soviet strength, and there was still much leeway to be made up before the military balance with the United States was satisfactory. Not least, care must be taken, as Khrushchev had failed to take it, to ensure that any unnecessary changes in the tone and temper of Soviet society should not have disturbing repercussions in the socialist countries of the Warsaw Pact, whose fidelity to the Soviet line was essential to national security.

Though views might differ about their formulation, Khrushchev's revisions of doctrine about relations with the capitalist world were well-founded and his successors could not neglect the objective changes that had made them necessary. Since war was no longer an option and competition with the imperialists must perforce be peaceful, the old attitudes of abuse and defiance no longer served a useful purpose. This was not to say that anything like a truce was in order. Even if that were not ruled out on ideological gounds, the capitalist bogey was far too valuable an instrument of home-front propaganda to be lightly discarded. But the logic of the changed situation called for a measure of contact with the 'class enemy' and for a cautious look at the possibilities of reducing the area in which clashes of interest might lead to conflict.

In fact Khrushchev had already made inconclusive moves in that direction. While Stalin had been content, except on a very few occasions during the war and immediately after it, to sit at home and leave diplomacy to professionals, Khrushchev had been to the capitalist countries to see for himself. He had addressed the United Nations General Assembly and had on at least two occasions – at Geneva in 1955 and at Camp David in 1959 – seemed briefly to be working for an understanding with the West, only to give up when difficulties later arose. He had even begun in 1962, at a moment when American military superiority was at its height, to toy with unilateral reductions in Soviet defence expenditure, but had been obliged to come off it. The new leadership had no intention of making that sort of mistake, but the possibility of other moves – the tidying up of European frontier problems and the final emasculation of the German threat – had obvious attractions for them.

Their first years in office were, as it turned out, preoccupied by other problems, both at home and in the socialist camp. At home it was the steadying of the boat after Khrushchev had rocked it, and the attempt made in 1965–6 to get the economy working by new reforms. Abroad it was the headlong rush by the new Czechoslovak leadership in 1968 towards democratization which, as seen from Moscow, put at risk the achievements of socialism in Czechoslovakia and imperilled by its example the dictatorship of ruling communist parties throughout the camp. The military action taken against Dubček put the Soviet Union into the international doghouse for a year or more; Western contacts with Moscow at all levels were reduced to a minimum and the move to explore the chances of less dangerous relations with the West was stalled. But in the FRG the first signs of the coming *Ostpolitik* were already visible and, as the blight cast by the Czechoslovak 'events' spent itself, Brezhnev and his companions realized that the moment for launching a new 'programme of peace' was approaching.

What they had in prospect was an undertaking of considerable difficulty. A relaxation of tensions with the West had, for reasons which will appear later on, very considerable attractions for them if it could be got on terms which would not unacceptably cramp their style. But such terms were demanding in the highest degree and the chances of bringing Western governments to accept them in full were highly problematical. The main Soviet requirements were three. First, and axiomatically, that *détente* must not get in the way of the continuing struggle of the two systems. Second, that the hard-won shift of the military balance in the Soviet Union's direction should not be redressed. Third, that the relaxation in tension should be confined to international relations: *détente* abroad must not be allowed to spill over on to the home front and undermine the party's dictatorship. In these requirements we catch a first glimpse of the three great bones of contention. Foreseeably, the Western negotiators found inconsistency between the Soviet Union's professions of peace and the free hand it concurrently claims in carrying on the battle by all means short of war, its insistence on arming itself to the teeth, and its disregard for human rights. It is now time to unearth the bones and examine them more closely.

Double Talk

5

International negotiation, if it is to be fruitful, demands an irreducible minimum of confidence by each side in the good faith of the other. In the context of *détente*, the recurrent doubts which normally assail the parties in any negotiation are multiplied a hundredfold by reason of the ideological preconceptions with which the Soviet Union approaches the business of negotiation. We need recall only that their ideology has taught the Russians to see international relations as a struggle to the death between socialism and imperialism the outcome of which – the victory of socialism – is historically determined. Because the Russians hold this view of history (and they make no effort to conceal the fact) the question is posed whether negotiation with them, in the normal sense of the word, is possible at all. Negotiation is a process of give and take, directed to securing an accommodation tolerable to both parties but certainly falling short of the maximum aims of both. But the Soviet side, if it follows its preconceptions, will not be content with such an accommodation. It wants, indeed it is required, to win all along the line. It would be untrue to itself if it acted otherwise. And Lenin, as we recall, taught that, where the great issues of history were at stake, conventional morality must be discarded, that the end justified the means. For him it was 'Them, or us' (*Kto, kogo*?). For these reasons those who negotiate with the Russians are troubled by suspicions that any agreement reached with them will be found later to contain concealed escape-clauses; or that, even if the agreement is itself watertight, the Russians may not feel bound by its terms.

These suspicions have been much magnified by the persistence with which Soviet negotiators have attempted to write into agreements with non-socialist countries a formula which defines the relationship between the parties as being one of 'peaceful coexistence between states having different social systems'. 'Peaceful coexistence' (as we shall usually call it for short) has come to be regarded in the West as implying a number of reservations, qualifications and unspoken conditions which, like the fine print on the back of an insurance policy, limit the liability of the Soviet negotiator and leave him free to do things which, on a reasonable construction of the agreement, he has promised to refrain from doing. The 'peaceful coexistence' formula, with its overtones of duplicity, has become the first main bone of contention in *détente*. Are the difficulties to which it gives rise real or imaginary?

We noted in Chapter 3 how Lenin coined the expression 'peaceful coexistence' as an answer to the problems raised by the failure of the revolution to spread beyond Russia, and how it was resurrected by Khrushchev as a rationalization of the fact that nuclear weapons had closed the direct route to the victory of socialism by force of arms. Since Khrushchev's time the theory of 'peaceful coexistence' has been much elaborated and articulated and it now occupies a central position in the picture the Russians paint of the Soviet Union's relationship with the outside world. To understand the meaning of this picture we must revert for a moment to the full text of the formula. The first two words, 'peaceful' and 'coexistence', are in themselves unexceptionable. Countries exist side by side, and it is common ground that in the nuclear age they should coexist peacefully, since war would risk destroying all of them. But we note that they are described not as countries, nations or societies, but as 'states', and not merely as states in general, but as states 'having different social systems'. Here the choice of language is not random. For where 'social systems' differ, that is where one party is socialist and the other capitalist, it is axiomatic to the Marxist-Leninist that the relationship between them should be one of struggle, and the inevitable outcome of the struggle should be the defeat and destruction of capitalism. So we have at one and the same time, existing side by side, an imperative to coexist peacefully and an imperative to continue an implacable struggle whose outcome is a foregone conclusion.

How to reconcile these opposites? The key to the synthesis lies in the use of the term 'states'. We became familiar in Chapter 2 with the Marxist-Leninist theory of the state. Here it will suffice to recall that, for Marxist-Leninists, the state is a superstructure of laws and institutions, a creature not of principle but of practical expediency, set up by every society and reflecting the interests of the class which for the time being dominates that society. It has specific functions, domestic and external. It makes laws which entrench the interests of the ruling class and coerce the citizen into complying with them. It defends society, its parent, against foreign enemies. But it remains a superstructure, and a transitory one at that, for the capitalist state will be destroyed by the proletarian revolution, giving place to the proletarian socialist state, and the socialist state itself will in the fullness of time wither away with the onset of true, or full, communism. Society endures, developing and changing in accordance with the immutable laws of history. Thus the dichotomy between the evolving society and the transitory state is, for the Marxist-Leninist, a familiar and well-worn concept. When confronted with the contradictory imperatives to coexist in peace with the 'imperialists' and, at the same time, to pursue against them a struggle to the death, he encounters no difficulty, intellectual or moral, in concluding that the regime of peaceful coexistence, a matter *par excellence* of expediency and practical convenience, applies to the area of relations between states; elsewhere the abiding struggle between the two systems continues, as it is bound to do, unabated.

When it comes to giving practical effect to this theoretical conclusion, policy falls naturally into two complementary parts. As between states having different social systems, peaceful coexistence involves acceptance by the socialist state of the rules that make up the regime of bourgeois international law – the sovereignty, equality, independence and territorial integrity of other states and non-interference in their internal affairs. But this regime is accepted as applying only on the 'state' level, that is to the formal and official dealings of the socialist state with capitalist states and the conduct of normal diplomatic intercourse between them. Elsewhere the axiom of struggle applies. It could not be otherwise. (We should take note in passing, for future reference, of an important corollary. Peaceful coexistence, being relevant only to 'states having different social systems', has no application in the relations between one socialist state and another; for in states that have had their socialist revolutions the struggle has already been won. Between them the relationship is one of fraternity and 'proletarian internationalism'. Any problems that arise here relate to the preservation of the gains and achievements of the revolution. This requires mutual vigilance lest these gains should be squandered or frittered away, as would have happened, for example, in Czechoslovakia if Dubček had been given his head.)

A substantial majority of Western Sovietologists are content, having thus established to their satisfaction the sophistical and contrived process of Soviet reasoning, to let the case for the prosecution rest. It is as plain as a pikestaff, they say, that Brezhnev's 'programme of peace' is a humbug. The Russians have not changed by one iota. They are not a bit interested in genuine accommodation with the West. They are concerned only to bring the struggle between the two systems to its appointed conclusion, the victory of socialism. *Détente* for them is no more than a tactical gambit, undertaken because the hazards of direct confrontation have proved to be too dangerous. To pursue negotiation with an opponent who is patently bent on doing you down is folly. *Détente* is best left alone. 'Peaceful coexistence' as offered by the Russians is a snare and a delusion.

This position strikes many intelligent men of goodwill as unduly pessimistic and prejudiced. They are bored and irritated by the zeal which Western scholars bring to the exposition of Soviet ideology. Being practical people themselves, they question whether ideology any longer has any serious importance. And they are sceptical that, at the end of the day, the Russians can really mean all the claptrap that they continue to repeat. One does not have to accept, they argue, everything that the Russians do or say, much of which is in our eyes reprehensible and wrong. But no one, surely, is asking us to accept the Soviet view of the world, merely to live with it, as the Russians are asked to live with ours, without coming to blows over our differences. We may be forced in the end to conclude that the game of negotiation with the Russians is not worth the candle. But we refuse to be diverted by the ineradicable prejudices of cold warriors, reactionary ideologues and bureaucrats from making the attempt. When we hear such people pontificating about peaceful coexistence, we reach for our gun.

There are elements of truth in each of these conflicting assessments.

To discover what they are, and hopefully to reach a conclusion, let us consider successively what it is that the Russians say, whether they actually mean what they say, and how to rate the chances of their being able to carry out what they say in practice.

We must concede from the outset the impressive character of the evidence supporting the pessimistic view of Soviet *détente* policy. The Russians, assuming that they wish to impress us with their good faith, are their own worst enemies. Because they are ideologues, and their society a society built to give effect to an ideology, they are not content to let actions speak for themselves. Every step must be explained, co-ordinated and brought into line with the ideology. It must be clearly shown to conform with the Marxist-Leninist view of the world, indeed to have been undertaken in order to advance the achievement of the goals which the ideology has set. So *détente* is held out not merely as a package of measures designed to prevent a world war, an aim which would enlist general support, but also as advancing the goals of Soviet society. And, since these goals are advertised as including the revolutionary destruction of the capitalist world, Soviet proposals for relaxation of international tension are naturally received with extreme caution in the West. The testimony given by Soviet spokesmen against the credibility of their own case merits examination.

Détente, they tell us, has become a practicable possibility only because of the shift that has taken place in the 'correlation of forces' in the world. The forces in question, they explain, are 'political, economic and military'. The apparent implication of this is that so long as the USSR was in a position of inferiority *vis-à-vis* the West, negotiation with the West was bad business and better left alone. Now that the West is obliged to negotiate not from a position of strength but from one of approximate parity, the USSR is able to contemplate the relaxation of international tension without the fear of being forced to agree to arrangements disadvantageous to herself. There is, so far, nothing particularly heinous in this view, the less so if account is taken of the series of shocks and unpleasant surprises which the Soviet Union experienced in the first fifteen years of the arms race. But, the Russians continue, the correlation of forces, including military, is continuing to move in the Soviet Union's favour, and the relaxation of international tension (that is, *détente*) will serve to intensify the shift in the international power balance. Indeed *détente* is good business for the

USSR and the socialist countries. It provides an environment favourable to the realization of their goals. It will leave the socialist countries relatively stronger and the imperialists relatively weaker. Look, Soviet publicists were saying in 1974–5, at what is happening in NATO countries. Greece (which withdrew from the NATO military organization) and Portugal (whose revolution had brought the Communist Party into the government) are forsaking the imperialist alliance and tying NATO's plans in knots. *Détente* pays! These are sentiments of an entirely different order and they have an ominous ring when the continuing build-up of Soviet armaments, which the next chapter examines, is called to mind. The shift in the 'correlation of forces' emerges not as a decent adjustment permitting negotiation on terms of equality, but rather as a stage on the road leading to the same old goal, the defeat and destruction of capitalism. The effect on the credibility of Brezhnev's 'programme of peace' has been disastrous, enabling Western students of Marxism-Leninism to portray *détente* (Moscow style) as designed to disarm the West physically and morally, as a preliminary to dictating the future of Europe and the world on Soviet terms. Hence the popularity of the theory of 'Finlandization'.

Besides, it was not just what the Russians said that undermined confidence in their good faith; it was what they did. Intervention in third-world countries with money, arms, military advice and, on occasion, troops was a regrettably standard adjunct of super-power diplomacy during the years of the cold war. But the Moscow summit of 1972 had to all appearance drawn a line under that chapter. 'The USA and the USSR', Brezhnev and Nixon had declared, 'attach major importance to preventing the development of situations capable of causing a dangerous exacerbation of relations between them. ... Both sides recognize that efforts to obtain unilateral advantage at the expense of the other, directly or indirectly, are inconsistent with these objectives. ... The prerequisites are the recognition of the security interests of the parties based on the principle of equality and the renunciation of ... force.' The final extrication of the United States from Vietnam seemed a happy augury for a new epoch. But, as soon became clear, the Russians had learnt nothing and forgotten nothing. The destructive effect on Soviet credibility of the Angolan adventure, embarked on in the autumn of 1975 at a moment of rising doubts in the West about the future of *détente,* can hardly be overstated. The revolution in Lisbon and the ensuing collapse of Portuguese resistance to the wind of change in Africa threw up opportunities that were too good to miss for stealing a march on Western governments and consolidating Soviet influence. In Mozambique and elsewhere past Soviet investments in arming the anti-colonial movements paid off smoothly enough. In Angola the Soviet-sponsored faction was one of three locked in civil war with one another and the stakes were too high – Angola being contiguous with both Zaïre and South African-held Namibia – to leave the outcome to chance. So Cuban troops were flown in and in due course established the Popular Movement in control of the new government, if not of the entire territory. The psychological legacy of Vietnam sufficed to prevent American counter-action, but it spent itself in the process. Soviet arms had prevailed, by proxy, on the field of battle, but the new dispensation which the fine words of May 1972 had ushered in was the main casualty, and the months that followed came close to marking the abandonment of the quest for *détente.*

As though bent on dispelling the benefit of any lingering doubts, the Soviet leadership and the whole Soviet publicity machine set out, on the morrow of the signature of the Final Act, to reassure their constituents that nothing had been done at Helsinki that in any way blunted the sharp edge of the ideological struggle. All that had been agreed fell in the area of peaceful coexistence between states. There was not, indeed there could not be, any armistice in the war of ideas. These notions were not novel. They had been proclaimed incessantly, with prophylactic intent, ever since the prospect of *détente* with the West had appeared on the horizon. Their most articulate and readable exposition can be found in *The War of Ideas in Contemporary International Relations* published in 1970 by Georgi Arkadievich Arbatov, the leading Soviet pundit on Soviet–US relations. Now, with the ink scarcely dry on the Final Act, the message was put out once more to ensure against any risk of post-operative infection. The Soviet people were left in no doubt that, while important results had been achieved at Helsinki – the seal of permanence had been set on socialism's gains from the Second World War – these achievements, and any concessions made to get them, fell within the strictly insulated field of inter-state relations. In all other fields the war of ideas was uninhibited, and would be carried on until, as the Marxist scriptures prescribed, capitalism was defeated and destroyed.

Before adding this further count to the indictment we should, in fairness, reflect whether we actually disagree with the Soviet thesis that a 'war of ideas' continues between the socialist and capitalist systems. On the plane of ideas pure and simple, there can be no gainsaying the fact that socialism, as practised by the Soviet Union and those countries that have followed its path, is objectionable to us. We reject, too, the mythology in whose name Soviet socialism has been built. We regard as unacceptable the volume of human misery that has followed the Soviet attempt to transform the myth into social reality. We consider that, judged by its own canon of success in producing material wealth and well being, Soviet socialism has, over the years, done notably less well than capitalism. Offered a free choice between the two, we would not touch Soviet socialism with a barge-pole. The Russians take the diametrically opposite view, so our ideas and theirs are in frontal opposition to one another. If each side stopped there, both could safely leave the issue to be settled by results. But the Russians are not free to do so. The myth requires them constantly to encourage and assist the class struggle in the capitalist countries and to advance the coming of proletarian revolution in them. Soviet attempts to discharge this mission kept the Soviet Union in quarantine internationally throughout most of the inter-war period and, after the Second World War, led, as we have seen, to the breakdown of the wartime alliance and to twenty-five years of 'cold war'.

Although entering the cold war in a poor state of preparedness, the capitalist countries were not slow to learn how to strike back and within five years of its outbreak had developed a position of 'ideological' hostility yielding nothing to the Russians in the radicalism of its professed aims or its choice of methods employed. John Foster Dulles, the US Secretary of State, was its high priest. The proclaimed objective was to 'liberate' the captive nations of Europe from Soviet enslavement, to 'roll back' Soviet military power. The methods used were psychological warfare and propaganda designed to encourage resistance and subvert authority in communist countries, reinforced by espionage and special operations. Two large radio-transmitters (Radio Free Europe and Radio Liberty) were installed on the periphery of the Soviet empire (they are still there today) and became a mecca for *émigrés* old and new, defectors and any who had a grudge against the Russians. 'Liberation' and 'roll back' were discarded by American official policy in the late 1950s but remained part of the stock-in-trade of cold war publicists for some years longer. Thereafter official utterances of Western governments took the form of exposing Soviet initiatives in foreign affairs as propagandist (which they all too frequently were) and the media in the West adopted, with few exceptions, an attitude of set hostility in their reporting of events in the Soviet Union. More recently still, the emphasis placed by the Helsinki 'third basket' on freedom of information has been inspired as much by ideological considerations in the proper sense of the term as by considerations of real interest; and the same may be said of the current campaign for human rights in the Soviet Union. Western governments are therefore ill-placed to dismiss the 'ideological struggle', either in its proper sense or in its practical manifestations, as a one-way process or as something exclusively of Soviet manufacture. Nor should we here underrate the contribution made by Western cold war tactics to the reinforcement of existing Soviet preconceptions about the implacable hostility of capitalist countries towards the socialist system.

Is it then open to us to conclude that the Russians have been as much sinned against as sinning and that, with the end of the cold war, the war of ideas is reduced to a more or less amicable disagreement about how societies should be run? If so, Soviet insistence on the continuing ideological struggle need cause us no loss of sleep. Alas, no. The Russians are quick to claim that, with the cold war officially buried, the US and its allies must lose no time in dismantling and destroying the apparatus of psychological warfare and subversion with which they waged it. To retain these weapons, they say, is incompatible with peaceful coexistence and the relaxation of tension. But, conversely, they add, peaceful coexistence does not forbid, indeed it requires, the Soviet Union to go on assisting and encouraging the revolutionary transformation of capitalist societies. There is nothing new or strange about this; it merely represents a reversion to the *status quo ante* cold war. The laws of history are not rendered inoperative by a mere agreement between states. Nor can the ideological struggle be defined in terms which draw an abstract distinction between thought and action.

The reactions of Western governments to the doctrine of peaceful coexistence (and its corollary, the continuing ideological struggle) have varied quite widely. The document defining the 'basic principles of relations' between the United States and the Soviet Union states baldly that 'in the nuclear age there is no alternative to conducting their relations on the basis of peaceful coexistence'. Dr Kissinger, who negotiated this document in 1972, appears at the time to have taken the robust view that each side knew what the other meant, and the United States was big enough and powerful enough to deal with any backslidings. But the words have stuck in the gullet of most Western Europeans who have refused to endorse a formula which they reckoned to be bogus and which would, most likely, be used to their discredit. The French and Germans, in their respective 'principles' of bilateral relations, and in many long sessions before and since, have flatly refused to have it. So had the British, until Mr Wilson in February 1975, seizing on a phrase used by Brezhnev himself, scored a minor success by securing the insertion of a definition which, on paper at least, straightened out the record. The Anglo-Soviet 'statement of principles' speaks of 'peaceful coexistence, which means long term, fruitful and mutually beneficial cooperation of states with different social systems, on the basis of full equality and mutual respect'. The definition was impeccable and the proponents of the optimistic view were much encouraged. But the gain proved to be transitory. After a brief interval official Soviet spokesmen reverted to their old ways and Mr Wilson's gloss dropped out of sight.

The reader may well ask whether this quibbling over words is not a puerile exercise unworthy of grown men, let alone international statesmen. Maybe, and it certainly wastes an inordinate amount of time that could be better spent. But the Russians evidently do not see it that way. Those who have spent long hours negotiating with them will attest the single-minded persistence with which the Russians press for the inclusion of their formula in every public document, now wheedling, now threatening, now arguing that it is a mere form of words which their interlocutor can accept with a quiet mind, now asserting that there can be no agreement unless the phrase goes in. Quibble or not, the Soviet government patently attaches a high degree of importance to seeing that any transaction with non-socialist states shall be made expressly subject to the qualification of peaceful coexistence. All of which increases the natural tendency of their interlocutors to smell a rat.

So much for what the Russians say. Do they really mean it? To answer this question adequately we shall need to form a view on the importance attached to Marxist-Leninist mythology in the Soviet Union today. To those who fought on the barricades in 1917 it was a living faith. Many of Stalin's victims of the 1930s faced the executioner in the assurance that the vision of communism would come to pass, even though it was not given to them to see it. Today, sixty years after the October revolution, the flame of faith burns low. The years of terror, the war, the experience of destalinization, the modest growth of prosperity and the palpable stratification of Soviet society have all done their bit to blur the vision. In varying degrees, Russians have developed a healthy scepticism about the verbal inspiration of the Marxist-Leninist scriptures, just as many people elsewhere who were brought up as Christians entertain doubts about a wide range of biblical events and dogmas, from the creation and the flood to the immaculate conception and the nature of the holy trinity. But all Russians, with the exception of a handful of dissidents who have wrenched themselves free (and cut themselves off from their social environment), are intellectually the prisoners of the ideology in a way that Westerners have difficulty in comprehending. What locks them in is the fact that the prodigious effort in education, which has brought the Soviet people from mass illiteracy to post-doctoral research in the short span of three generations, has taught them to think in Marxist-Leninist terms. The tools, the software, with which their minds have been equipped – the categories, the modes of thought, the relations and associations that they make between ideas – are Marxist-Leninist. Marxism-Leninism is the only medium through which ideas, old or new, can find expression. This goes equally for the intelligentsia, the officials, the industrialists and policy-makers. But it is with the policy-makers and in particular with the leadership that we are here primarily concerned. If, for one reason or another, the leadership should wish to alter its course, the change would inevitably be ascribed and presented to those below in terms that not merely made it compatible with received doctrine, but were actually dictated by Marxist-Leninist premises.

The leadership, and the party behind it, have, however, an even more potent reason, whatever doubts they may individually or collectively entertain about questions of dogma, for maintaining the ideology through thick and thin. The party, as we have seen, exercises dictatorial power, and exercises it permanently, not because the Soviet people chose it and invested it with authority to do so, but because it claims to be made up of the 'conscious' minority of those who know what to do. This claim rests simply and solely on the party's exclusive custodianship of Marxist-Leninist social science. Marxism-Leninism is the legitimator of the party's title to rule. If its dogmas should be exploded, if the Soviet people should come round to the view that Marxism-Leninism, as Henry Ford is supposed to have said of history, is bunk, the party would be out of a job, for its entire stock-in-trade would have gone up in smoke. This would have profoundly disturbing effects on the country as a whole. But for the party and the leadership it would open the way to the loss of power, career, privilege and prospects for the future. The party bureaucracy and its leaders recognize that the ideology is their most important, indeed their only, marketable asset, and they must be expected in all circumstances to treasure, cherish and defend it, at all costs and against all comers.

What has just been said could provide an explanation why the Russians have gone to such lengths to present their 'programme of peace' (i.e. the relaxation of international tension or, as we would say, *détente*) as being in perfect consonance with Marxist-Leninist orthodoxy, even at the cost of seriously damaging its credibility in the eyes of those in the West whose co-operation is essential to its realization. But such an explanation in no way justifies leaping to the conclusion that ideological factors have no relevance to the goals of Soviet policy. Rather on the contrary, we have seen that Soviet thought (and Soviet policy as a specific form of it) has its roots deep in Marxism-Leninism; and we have noted that, however sceptical they may be about the literal truth of specific dogmas, the practitioners of Soviet policy have a vested interest in keeping the ideology intact and bright.

To carry the argument further we are obliged to have recourse to inference from observation of Soviet policy in action. Here again we must content ourselves with something less than a comprehensive answer. All we can assert with confidence is that, when it comes to policy, there is a good deal of room for motivations other than purely ideological ones, and that the party's position as sole interpreter of Marxist-Leninist science gives it considerable freedom to choose courses of action, provided only that they can plausibly be shown to be in consonance with the scriptures. This has been true for a long time. It has become more broadly true today, given the decline of faith that has meanwhile taken place and the increasing variety and complexity of the matters with which Soviet external policy now has to deal. Mixed motives began to creep in in the early post-revolutionary years when the Soviet Union, against its expectations, found itself building socialism in one country. In the conditions of those days, the internationalist notions of the revolutionists perforce gave way to the proposition that what was good for the Soviet Union, the first, and for the time being the only, socialist country, was good for the interests of socialism in the world at large. This proposition came to acquire a validity of its own which remains unchallenged, even though other socialist states have come into being. Today the interests of the Soviet state appear to weigh at least as heavily, in Soviet calculations, as do the interests of world revolution. In a majority of cases they can be made to look sufficiently alike as to avoid offence to the eye. Occasionally awkward problems of choice arise, as in the Middle East where the Soviet Union finds itself aligned with some notably reactionary Arab interests in pursuit of goals which have much more to do with the strategic and political needs of the Soviet state than with the class war. And communist parties in foreign countries — France, Egypt and India are recent examples — have repeatedly found their revolutionary struggles taking second place to the superior state interests of the socialist homeland. In the classic case, when ideology was propelling the Soviet Union towards a confrontation, which it could not hope to win, with nuclear-armed America, not merely did state interests come out on top, but the ideology itself was 'revised' to prevent recurrence.

We must hand it to the pessimists that the role of ideological factors is of high importance, and that those who neglect it in negotiating with the Russians do so at their peril. But this does not, in itself, justify their conclusion that *détente* as proposed by the Russians is a fraud, and negotiating with them about it a waste of time. On the one hand, there can be no doubt that the ideological packaging of the Soviet version of *détente* encourages the suspicion that the parcel contains a bomb. But, on the other, we have established that, if the Russians should perceive concrete reasons of national interest (other than simply an interest in winning the game by a trick) for seeking a relaxation with the West, they are unlikely to be inhibited by ideological considerations from pursuing such relaxation. It is therefore at least conceivable that we have in the 'programme of peace' a sheep, albeit a sturdy one and of uncertain temper, in wolf's clothing. The tenability of this hypothesis hangs on whether such concrete reasons of Soviet national interest are actually found to exist. Three possible candidates – the growth of economic interdependence with the capitalist world, the need to satisfy the expectations of the Soviet consumer and the fragmentation of the international communist movement – are examined in later chapters of this book.

6

How Much is Enough?

Keeping potential enemies guessing about the strength of one's own forces is of the essence of military rivalry and, until fifteen years ago, many ostensibly informed guesses about the size and armament of the Soviet armed forces were wildly wrong. Today the fog has, if not completely, at least very substantially cleared. The agent that dispersed it was space photography, a by-product of the space exploration programmes on which the United States and the Soviet Union embarked in the late 1950s. Each side can now launch reconnaissance ('spy') satellites which overfly the territory of the other and relay back to earth photographs, of increasing clarity and definition, of everything that is visible on the earth's surface. Much of what was formerly cloaked in mystery is now revealed, and this enables those who are interested – including military staffs on the one hand, and civilian 'analysts' on the other – to deal in many areas with ascertained fact, where they could earlier speak only in terms of conjecture.

The catalogue in Chapter 1 of *détente*'s shortcomings included statements that the Soviet armed forces, having launched in the mid-1960s a massive arms development programme, continued, *détente* notwithstanding, to pile up strategic weapons of high sophistication and versatility; that Soviet naval expansion was being pressed forward at an alarming rate; and that the force reduction negotiations in Vienna were getting nowhere. What, in concrete terms, is the basis of these assertions? Let us look first of all at figures, and then

Historical changes of strength 1963–76 (mid-years)

	USA			USSR		
	ICBMs	SLBMs	Long-range bombers	ICBMs	SLBMs	Long-range bombers
1963	424	224	630	90	107	190
1964	834	416	630	190	107	175
1965	854	496	630	224	107	160
1966	904	592	630	292	107	155
1967	1054	656	600	570	107	160
1968	1054	656	545	858	121	155
1969	1054	656	560	1028	196	145
1970	1054	656	550	1299	304	145
1971	1054	656	505	1513	448	145
1972	1054	656	455	1527	500	140
1973	1054	656	442	1527	628	140
1974	1054	656	437	1575	720	140
1975	1054	656	432	1618	784	135
1976	1054	656	387	1527	845	135

(Source: International Institute for Strategic Studies, *The Military Balance 1977–8.*)

at some of the strategic ideas underlying them.

The above table shows the relative strengths of the USA and the USSR in strategic nuclear delivery vehicles over the period from 1963 to 1976. The term 'strategic' in this context relates to weapons which enable one power, from sites in its own homeland or from vessels and aircraft based there, directly to attack targets in the homeland of the other. All strategic delivery vehicles are means of transporting a charge of nuclear explosive, or 'warhead', to its target. They fall into three main classes: the land-based 'intercontinental ballistic missile' (ICBM); the submarine-launched ballistic missile (SLBM); and the long-range manned bomber aircraft, capable of flying from its base to its target, unloading its bombs and returning. The figures for 1963 show the Soviet Union as outclassed by a factor of nearly 5 to 1 in ICBMs, of 2 to 1 in SLBMs and of over 3 to 1 in long-range bombers. The United States more than doubled its ICBM strength between 1963 and 1967, but stopped there and the figure has remained unchanged for the succeeding ten years. Soviet ICBM strength increased sixfold between 1963 and 1967, tenfold by 1969 when it approximately equalled that of the United States, and fifteenfold by 1971, achieving a 50 per cent margin of superiority, since when it has remained fairly steady. Relative strengths in SLBMs followed a very similar pattern of development, though it unfolded more slowly. The American figure doubled between 1963 and 1965, almost trebled by 1967, and has stayed at that level ever since. Soviet strength was unchanged between 1963 and 1967, quadrupled by 1971 and sextupled by 1973, when it nearly drew level with the United States, going on to establish a lead of approximately 40 per cent by 1977. The long-range bombers kept in service by the two sides decreased absolutely over the period, the ratio of approximately three to one in the United States' favour being maintained. Whatever qualifications and caveats may be introduced, and some will be introduced in due course, it is apparent that Russians, since the early 1960s, have deployed what can fairly be called prodigious efforts to redress their initial position of inferiority, and that they have not been content to achieve mere equilibrium but have pressed on to establish a substantial margin of quantitative superiority.

The 'alarming' rate of Soviet naval construction relates primarily to submarines. This is not to say that the Soviet navy has neglected other arms of the service. Indeed it has been very active in building new, and modernizing old, missile-equipped surface vessels in the 3,500–5,000 tons range, but so have the NATO countries. And it has recently caused a stir by commissioning the first of three aircraft-carriers, a type of vessel which it has not hitherto built, but of which the United States has 13 in service. The growth of the Soviet submarine fleet is a different matter. The greater part of it is linked to the rapid expansion, already noted, of the Soviet SLBM strength. Between 1967 and 1976 54 new Soviet nuclear-propelled ballistic-missile submarines have been commissioned, coming into service at the rate of 6 per year in the last five years. In the same ten-year period NATO countries built 9 in all. For the rest, the Soviet navy received in the same period a further 17 nuclear-propelled submarines armed with short-range (450 miles) cruise missiles, as well as 42 submarines equipped for firing conventional torpedoes, of which 22 were nuclear-propelled.

Next, the balance of strength in north and central Europe, the main area in which the forces of the Warsaw Pact and NATO confront one another. First, some figures about the main participants on each side. In 1962, American forces in Europe numbered 434,000. By 1967 they had dropped to about 300,000. In 1967 there were 26 Soviet divisions in Eastern Europe facing the NATO armies. There are now 31, and this despite the fact that Soviet strength on the border with China has increased in the same period by some 25 divisions – perhaps 250,000 men, or as much as the total manpower of the British Army and the Royal Air Force put together. Here again the effort made has been prodigious. Second, a comparison of the combined strengths of Warsaw Pact and of NATO forces in the 'reductions area' (GDR, Poland and Czechoslovakia; the Federal Republic, Belgium, Holland and Luxembourg) to which the force reduction negotiations relate. Here NATO estimates that the Warsaw Pact ground forces exceed its own by 150,000 men, but the differences in equipment are more striking still. Warsaw Pact tanks (16,200) outnumber NATO's (6,730) almost two-and-a-half times, and Warsaw Pact aircraft (3,075) outnumber their counterparts (1,344) by a similar margin. These are not the only variables in the equation, but it is noteworthy that the Warsaw Pact tank strength, five-eighths of which is provided by the Soviet Union itself, is considerably larger than a purely defensive posture could reasonably be held to warrant. In aircraft it is true that the Warsaw Pact's longest suit has been in the 'air defence' role. But the replacement of older types by new multi-role aircraft means that, in the air too, the Warsaw Pact has begun to acquire new capabilities running well beyond the needs of defence. Air force re-equipment is only a part of what appears to be a purposive attempt to reinforce quantitative superiority with improvements in quality and sophistication throughout the Warsaw Pact's armoury, so that the qualitative edge which the NATO forces have reckoned they possessed, and on which the balance in central Europe has been thought to rest, is showing signs of erosion. Almost four years of negotiation in Vienna have failed to reveal any Soviet willingness to strike a compromise. Indeed the Russians have seemed interested only in contractualizing their margin of superiority in central Europe.

The reasons why the military aspects of *détente* have proved so intractable will emerge more clearly if we examine the course of events which preceded, and gave rise to, the current Soviet military build-up.

At the end of the war both sides demobilized a substantial proportion of their wartime forces, as indeed they were bound to do in order to meet the demands of reconversion and reconstruction of their economies. Soviet demobilization went less far and, with the rundown and repatriation of American and British forces, the Western allies found themselves at a serious disadvantage in conventional forces in Europe. This might not have mattered had the prospect been one of fruitful and amicable co-operation between East and West. But events in the Balkans, in Eastern Europe and in Germany had effectively broken up the wartime alliance. The manifest weakness and disarray of the recently liberated countries of Western Europe offered the Russians the chance of seizing control there as they had already done in the East, and there was no conventional force that could effectively be interposed if they tried. A Soviet thrust to the westward could, it seemed, reach Bordeaux overland in a matter of days. All that stood in the way was the American monopoly of nuclear weapons. For four years after 1945 the monopoly was absolute; and after the first Soviet nuclear device was tested in 1949 the United States continued for several years to enjoy a strategically impregnable position. Possessing this advantage, the United States did not hesitate to threaten that any Soviet attack on America's vital interests would be met with 'massive retaliation', meaning that Soviet cities and Soviet industry would suffer the fate that befell Hiroshima and Nagasaki in 1945. The North Atlantic Treaty, concluded in 1949, established unmistakably that those interests included the security of the states of Western Europe. The latter substantially rearmed and reorganized their armed forces, and the American military presence in Europe was reinforced and consolidated. But considerations of manpower and geography ensured that continuing advantage, in terms of conventional capability, remained with the Soviet Union and its allies, whose forces in due course were integrated under Soviet command in the Warsaw Pact. Tension between the two blocs ran high and political relations could hardly have been worse, but the American nuclear threat sufficed to 'deter', as the phrase went, any Soviet attempt to change the situation in Europe by force.

In those days long-range bombers were still the sole means of delivering strategic nuclear weapons and the United States, with a long start over its rival, retained a significant lead. Obviously the Russians would spare no effort to catch up, but their aircraft industry had emerged from the war lagging far behind those of America and Britain and, so far as nuclear munitions were concerned, the Americans had been stockpiling warheads for four years before the Russians had reached the starting-post. But the fog of the cold war, and recognition of how great was the West's dependence on nuclear weapons, bred a mounting sense of insecurity in Washington. The evidence of Soviet devilry was unnerving. A power that could in three years mount the take-over of Czechoslovakia (1948), the Berlin blockade (1948–9) and the invasion by proxy of South Korea (1951) plainly recognized no limits. In the early 1950s intelligence of plans to expand the Soviet long-range bomber force became magnified in the American mind into the delusion that, somehow, the Russians had caught up and drawn ahead. A 'bomber gap' had opened up, which at all costs must be closed. There was in fact no 'gap' for the Americans to close. The only gap that existed was a Soviet problem. But the Americans, with characteristic thoroughness and speed, proceeded to build, and deploy in 1956, a fleet of B52 bombers exceeding by a factor of three-and-a-half the number of Soviet TU95s that eventually came into service the same year.

The same psychological pattern was to repeat itself before the decade was out. In 1957 the Soviet Union, without warning, put into earth orbit the first satellite, Sputnik. It was immediately clear that a new situation had arisen. The Russians could not have got Sputnik off the ground and into outer space unless they had succeeded in building a heavy-lift long-range rocket which could equally well be used to boost a Soviet nuclear missile on its path to targets in the United States. This, be it said, was unquestionably a correct inference. But the reaction in the United States and other Western countries far exceeded any rational limits. Sputnik left the world aghast. All of a sudden it seemed that the West must for years have been disastrously under-estimating the resources of Soviet science and technology. National priorities were revised over a broad front running from science policy and further education to investment and strategy. The Americans, whose scientists had been struggling for several years, with indifferent success, to solve the missile-launcher problem, jumped to the conclusion that their country was heading rapidly for the status of a second-class power under immediate Soviet threat. Once more the intelligence community took a hand, giving the administration hair-raising accounts of Soviet capability to deliver a nuclear attack. These accounts leaked, and the alleged evidence of a new 'gap', this time a 'missile gap', became an issue in the 1960 presidential campaign. Once more the Pentagon, the scientists and the aerospace industry rose to the occasion and by 1963 the United States had manufactured and deployed four times as many ICBMs and twice as many SLBMs as the Soviet Union had by that time been able to make. There had in fact been no 'missile gap'. The Russians had, as happens, experienced difficulty in the transition from development model to series production, and the deployment of Soviet ICBMs had slipped. But, regardless of the facts, the notion of Soviet pre-eminence in rocket technology had implanted itself. This impression was buttressed by the exploits of Yuri Gagarin, the Soviet cosmonaut, who was the first man to travel in outer space; and Khrushchev did all he could to inculcate and exploit it by uttering dire threats − notably during the Berlin crisis of 1961 − of nuclear retribution. The threats were bluff, designed to cover up the Soviet Union's real, but unrecognized, position of inferiority, and Khrushchev must bear his share of the responsibility for the impulse given to American nuclear expansion. The days of obfuscation were, however, numbered, for the new launcher technology had now placed the reconnaissance applications of earth satellites within the grasp of both sides. From the 1960's onwards it became possible, as already noted, for each to monitor, by photography from space, the state of readiness of the other and to identify and interpret new developments.

By thus reacting to supposed 'gaps' in her defences, the United States had established an impressive measure of nuclear superiority. But what had happened meantime to 'deterrence'? The days of American nuclear monopoly had long since gone forever. The problem of deterring a Soviet surge into Western Europe had yielded its place at the top of the list to another even more neuralgic. With nuclear warheads, long-range bombers and now ICBMs in their hands, the Russians now undoubtedly had the means of striking at the American homeland. Though quantitatively inferior, Soviet nuclear forces might be able, if they struck first, at best to weaken, and at worst possibly to knock out, American capacity to retaliate. Whether one liked it or not, the Russians had begun, if as yet only tentatively, to 'deter' the United States. If the military and political consequences of this shift were to be neutralized, it followed that what the United States needed was to develop and maintain a 'second-strike capability', that is to say the ability, having sustained a Soviet 'first strike' which might destroy not merely cities and industries but also a large part of its strategic nuclear forces, nevertheless to retaliate in kind, and to inflict unacceptable damage on the Soviet Union. Deterrence depended on the creation of second-strike, not first-strike forces. The shortest route to a reliable second-strike capability was by way of making American strategic forces invulnerable, or less vulnerable, to Soviet attack. The same, of course, was true of the Soviet Union. In the event, no Soviet first-strike on the United States materialized. The American position of superiority was unimpaired. The Soviet missile forces expanded at a measured pace, but well behind, and at no point came within sight of being able to knock out their American counterparts.

The lesson had, however, been learned and, by 1966 or 1967, both sides, unequally as they were armed, achieved second-strike capabilities. Either, after absorbing a surprise first strike, was in a position reliably and massively to retaliate on the other. Mutual deterrence had been established, based on the ability of the two sides to inflict 'mutually assured destruction' (MAD). It was a sombre position to have reached and one vulnerable to human error or rational failure on either side, but nevertheless embodying elements of stability and balance. It had been achieved mainly through the acquisition by both sides of submarine-launched missiles. Nuclear propulsion had made it possible for submarines to roam the world's oceans for months on end, submerged and unperceived, armed with strategic nuclear missiles dischargeable from under water at targets in the enemy's homeland, and wholly invulnerable to any first strike. Land-based missiles likewise became less vulnerable through the developing techniques of 'hardening' the emplacements ('silos') in which they were installed with deep excavation and prodigal use of reinforced concrete. It may be significant that the period following these developments saw the first tentative moves towards bilateral discussion of the possible limitation of strategic armaments.

But the balance of mutually assured destruction had, itself, to be maintained against the inroads of new technology, which at any time might re-establish the first-strike capability of one side or the other. One such destabilizing innovation, it was recognized, would be an anti-missile missile (ABM) which could shoot down approaching enemy missiles before they reached their target. Intelligence reports in 1966 began to suggest that arrays of missiles installed around two Soviet cities might have precisely this capability. Pressure developed in Congress for the United States to follow suit, while American technology was mobilized to devise an antidote. With the emergence of the antidote the race had entered on a new lap. The Multiple Independently-targeted Re-entry Vehicle, or MIRV for short, is a mechanism which enables one delivery vehicle to do the work of several, fitting into the nose of a single launcher a cluster of nuclear warheads which start their journey together but then peel off and home individually on separate, widely dispersed, targets. The MIRV had many obvious advantages, but its immediate appeal lay in its ability to confuse an ABM system by blanketing it with a clutch of warheads travelling on divergent courses. The more abiding result of its deployment was to impart a new impulse to the contest by enabling the United States to attack a far wider range of targets than the Russians could hope to do, and to attack them with much greater accuracy. So the Soviet Union had to equip itself with MIRVs too. By the middle of the 1970s it had begun to deploy them. The ABM itself had a curious, if instructive, fate. It had always been recognized as likely to prove inordinately costly and doubts spread about its reliability and effectiveness. In the event the United States half-heartedly installed one such system, and planned to install another. But at Moscow in 1972 Brezhnev and Nixon agreed, in the ABM treaty, not to build any more.

What had prompted the Americans to threaten nuclear retaliation in the first place was the need to deter a conventional attack by Warsaw Pact forces on Western Europe. Ironically, one result of the sequence of moves and counter-moves just related was to raise doubts about the effectiveness of deterrence in this contingency. The threat of nuclear retaliation remained an effective means of deterring an attack by the Soviet Union on the homeland of the United States and (in the absence of a technological breakthrough that enabled the Russians to knock the United States out with a first strike) would continue to be so. But it had begun to look increasingly improbable that an American president would respond, by what would be an American first nuclear strike on the Soviet homeland, to a Soviet threat with conventional forces in Western Europe, knowing full well that this must evoke a Soviet second strike, bringing devastation to American cities and involving the death of tens of millions of Americans. As a means of fulfilling the American guarantee to NATO, strategic nuclear deterrence was no longer fully credible. Not, of course, that the American strategic threat was the only weapon in NATO's armoury.

The United States had, over the years, established 'forward-based systems' (FBS) on the periphery of Europe, in Britain, Italy, Spain, Greece and Turkey. The FBS consisted in the main of medium-range nuclear armed aircraft deployed in a ring around the central European theatre and capable (though they were not 'strategic' in the proper definition of the term) of attacking targets in the Soviet Union. Furthermore, NATO's forces in Europe were equipped with 'tactical' nuclear weapons – battlefield weapons, artillery and short-range missiles equipped with miniaturized nuclear warheads. Even so, the outcome of a battle for Europe could not be predicted with any certainty. NATO's geographical handicap was increased when in 1966 General de Gaulle took France out of the organization (though not out of the treaty), thus narrowing to the territory of the FRG and the Low Countries the area in which NATO's forces in the central front could be deployed, and in which, since NATO would be on the defensive, the bulk of the attendant devastation would be concentrated. By contrast, the Warsaw Pact had all the room in the world to its rear; and, while the reinforcement of NATO's forces, in time of war or alert, would involve ferrying men and equipment from overseas, the Red Army had ample reserves of manpower and arms in western Russia, which needed only to cross the land frontier to join in the battle. Besides, the Warsaw Pact forces had been equipped with tactical nuclear weapons too, and in the 1970s the Russians began to deploy intermediate range missiles targeted on Western Europe. How, if it ever came to that, the battle would go on the day was anyone's guess; but if the tide began to run against NATO it was no longer axiomatic that the threat of strategic nuclear reaction would suffice to arrest it.

The great debate on nuclear strategy begun under Secretary McNamara in the 1960s, and continued in the Nixon years under Secretary Schlesinger, has lasted more than a decade, without, so far, yielding definitive conclusions about how deterrence can be re-established. Some things have, however, become clearer in the process. The mass destruction of populations may have been a good enough bogey in its day, but it is not, in itself, a rational object of policy. A far better way of crippling the enemy, if that is the objective, is to destroy his military capability, including his strategic nuclear capability. This is what the jargon calls a 'counterforce' (as opposed to 'counter-city') strategy. But, even so, even if one's entire armoury of nuclear warheads is targeted on strictly military objectives, it will not necessarily make sense to discharge the lot at once. The vice of 'massive retaliation' has always been that it poses an all-or-nothing choice, when 'all' may wildly exceed the needs of the situation, while 'nothing' is useless. Since, by hypothesis, the aim is to deter an enemy from taking some action or, if he has already begun to take it, to make him desist, the degree of force used should be roughly proportionate to the aim. If deterrence is to recover its credibility, nuclear response to an enemy's challenge needs to be organized flexibly, that is, in separable and controlled stages of mounting severity, permitting a halt to be called if the enemy desists, but keeping force in reserve for use in case he raises the ante. It is too much to say that these theoretical contributions add up to a comprehensive answer. They enabled Secretary Schlesinger to reorganize American nuclear strategy on the basis of 'limited nuclear options', which greatly increased its flexibility and sophistication. But it remains an open question whether these 'limited options' have actually succeeded in re-establishing deterrence. On the practical level, the debate certainly went some way to discrediting the axiom that a holocaust of Soviet cities was a desirable objective, which must be reckoned as a plus. But the resultant emphasis on counterforce strategy undeniably gave an impetus to the qualitative improvement of American ability to destroy hardened targets, thus reawakening Soviet fears that the United States was edging once more towards a first-strike capability.

The arms race need never have taken place had the Russians after 1945 not given grounds for believing that they were out to convert the victory over Hitler into the victory of socialism in Europe. But once the race was on, it was for the most part (an exception must be made for Khrushchev's bluffs and boasts) the United States that administered the successive upward boosts to the spiral of nuclear competition. Viewed from Moscow, American performance invited the conclusion that the United States aimed not to deter but to win by re-establishing the first-strike capability that it had lost in the early 1950s. Why else should America, already several laps ahead, repeatedly have doubled its bets? It would have been a sobering experience for any adversary, but for the Russians perhaps more so than for any other, given their pre-conceptions about the superiority and inevitable victory of their form of society. The evidence of the 1950s and 1960s was that in weapons technology (and it was not difficult at the time to draw the same conclusion in other fields as well) the Soviet system was not superior. It was trailing behind the 'imperialists' and its every effort to draw level was frustrated by a new demonstration of American technological prowess. These considerations may suffice to explain the single-minded resolve which the Russians have shown since 1963 to make an end of American nuclear superiority. They had had enough unpleasant surprises. They had learnt nuclear and rocket technology the hard way, and might have to learn more. But they would not be caught again if they could help it. Conveniently for them, the growth of American launcher strength flattened out after 1967, reflecting a tardy recognition that the Russians were not after all ten feet tall and that the mere piling up of further weapons added nothing to security. Enough was enough. But, as time went on, the world began to ask itself whether enough was also enough for the Russians. The Soviet programme of launcher expansion continued without let-up, overtaking the United States in land-based missiles in 1969-70 and in SLBMs in 1973-4. A second-strike capability had long since been acquired. Mutually assured destruction had been achieved. If the Russians were looking for parity, they had got it. Yet the build-up proceeded.

The two contestants are armed to the teeth, but the nature and composition of their respective armouries differs in ways which make precise comparison difficult. We have hitherto measured the strategic balance between them in terms of launcher strength. But there are other standards of measurement too. One is by counting 'deliverable warheads'. The United States, first in the field with nuclear weapons, and later with MIRVs, has long had nuclear warheads in series production and, in mid-1976, possessed more than double the Soviet stock. But, with the MIRV-ing of the Soviet ICBM and SLBM fleets, the American lead, measured by this yardstick, has been diminishing. The accumulation of deliverable warheads, of course, reaches its useful limit when the stock of warheads outruns the number of targets to be destroyed; and, in the American case at least, this limit may already have been reached.

Another scale of measurement is 'equivalent megatonnage', which seeks to compute the capability of either side to inflict damage on the other. Historically the Soviet Union has built its rockets big, and its warheads with yields counted in megatons (one megaton (MT) equals

one million tons of conventional explosive), the biggest yet being the
Soviet SS9 missile, deployed in the mid-1960s, with a maximum yield
of twenty-five megatons. Higher-yield warheads inflict more extensive
damage than those with lower yields, but the increase is not
proportionate and tails off as size increases. The concept of 'equivalent
megatonnage' provides an approximate basis of comparison between
the two sides by reducing the gross aggregate yield of their warheads to
take account of this factor. By this canon of measurement the Russians
are shown to be capable of inflicting more extensive, undiscriminating,
damage on the Americans than the Americans can inflict on them, for
what that may be worth. Another result of the Soviet Union's
predilection for size in launchers is that the Russians also lead by a large
margin if relative strength is measured in terms of 'missile throw-
weight'. 'Throw-weight' means the aggregate weight of everything –
warheads, guidance systems and ancillary apparatus – that proceeds on
its journey to the target once the booster stage of the rocket – the bit
that gets it off the ground and into space – has been discarded.
Conversely, the Americans retain a huge margin of superiority by the
analogous test of 'bomber payload' – the total weapons load that their
aircraft can deliver at intercontinental range. Neither throw-weight nor
bomber payload affords a measure of destructive capability, but both
give an indication of the versatility of the opposing forces, and in
particular of the range of choice open to each as between delivering
many smaller or fewer larger warheads. This choice is relevant because
of the different views taken at different times by the contestants of the
type of targets they wish to destroy and the vulnerability of those targets
respectively to high explosive-yield and to pin-point accuracy.

By whatever combination of these several tests the capability of the
two sides was judged, by the end of the 1960s a rough equipoise
between them was in sight, leading both sides to consider, on grounds
both of security and expense, the possibility of agreed limitation of
strategic armaments. 'Arms control' specialists in the West,
practitioners of a hybrid craft, part-military technology, part-politics,
born in the US in the 1950s and popularized through the successive
United Nations bodies dealing with disarmament, had for some time
been preaching such limitation. They had earlier scored successes on
the periphery of the armaments field – the US–Soviet–British treaty of
1963 prohibiting nuclear weapons tests except underground, the

nuclear non-proliferation treaty of 1968, and the multilateral treaties banning the use of outer space and of the sea-bed for military purposes. Their doctrines were now to be tested, in the Strategic Arms Limitation Talks (SALT), on the central problem of super-power strategic balance. The broad objective was, without disturbing the principle of mutually assured destruction, to halt the competitive accumulation of strategic nuclear armaments; and then, with the same proviso, to bring about their balanced reduction.

The Treaty on the Limitation of Anti-Ballistic Missile Systems (the 'ABM treaty'), concluded during President Nixon's visit to Moscow in May 1972, broke entirely new ground. The signatories undertook to limit the deployment of ABM systems to two per side, one defending the national capital and the other a single concentration of ICBM silo launchers. The treaty was of unlimited duration, with provision for review at five-year intervals and an escape clause permitting withdrawal by either party if it should reckon that 'extraordinary events' had 'jeopardized its supreme interests'. Compliance by the parties with their engagements under it was to be monitored by 'national technical means of verification' (meaning, primarily, by 'spy' satellites); and each side undertook not to interfere with the other's monitoring arrangements, and not to frustrate these by deliberate concealment.

The Interim Agreement on Limitation of Strategic Offensive Arms (the 'interim agreement' or SALT I) was made for five years and embodied the same six-month escape clause and monitoring arrangements. It and the accompanying protocol and minutes placed a numerical ceiling on ICBMs by prohibiting the construction after 1 July 1972 of additional 'fixed land-based inter-continental ballistic missile launchers'. This meant that the US was limited to a total of 1,054 ICBMs (consisting of 54 elderly Titan IIs (1962), 450 Minuteman IIs (1966), both unMIRVed; and 550 MIRVed Minuteman IIIs (1970)); and the Soviet Union to 1,618 (including 109 single-warhead SS-7s and SS-8s (1961–3) and 1,138 SS-9s, SS-11s and SS-13s (1965–8), partially MIRVed). It also limited SLBMs and ballistic missile submarines on both sides to numbers operational or under construction at the date of signature; but these numbers might be increased, on a one-for-one basis, as pre-1964 land-based missiles (the American Titans and the Soviet SS-7s and SS-8s) were retired. These limits gave the United States a ceiling of 710 SLBMs in 44 ballistic missile submarines, and the Soviet Union 950 in 62. No limit was placed by SALT I on long-range bombers. The quantitative inferiority accepted by the Americans in ICBMs, SLBMs and missile-launching submarines was reckoned to be offset by qualitative superiority in each category. However, the interim agreement failed to deal unambiguously with the problem of modernization and replacement of older missiles, which was highly material to the maintenance of the American margin of qualitative superiority. While prohibiting the conversion of land-based launchers for older and lighter ICBMs into launchers for modern, 'heavy' missiles, it failed, not through any lack of American effort, to define what was meant by 'heavy', and it expressly permitted the limited enlargement of the dimensions of existing missile silos.

While the parties had engaged themselves in the interim agreement to pursue negotiations for further limitation, the defects just noted were the source of much subsequent trouble, which was compounded both by political factors and by the blooming in the immediate wake of SALT I of a new crop of innovations in missile technology.

The new generation of Soviet MIRVed ICBMs (SS-17, SS-18 and SS-19), which began to be deployed in 1975, though they fitted into the numerical limits set by the interim agreement (which the Russians had tailored to accommodate them), were very much larger, more accurate and of greater throw-weight and megatonnage than those they replaced. And the intermediate-range SS-20 mobile launcher, to be deployed in 1977, against targets in Western Europe and eastern Asia, was evidently the precursor of a new intercontinental-range mobile launcher. These weapons, with their greatly enhanced ability to destroy hardened targets, were reckoned to threaten the survival of the American ICBM force of fixed-silo Minutemen, thereby eroding the US second-strike capability. Besides, the Soviet supersonic swing-wing TU-7 bomber, known in the West as Backfire, came into service from 1974 onwards. Though ostensibly of medium range, it was widely regarded as capable, with or without in-flight re-fuelling, of intercontinental strategic missions.

These Soviet innovations, destabilizing as they might prove to be, could all be related to the established categories in which arms controllers worked and in which the interim agreement had been expressed. But American scientists had since 1972 been developing a weapon which defied any traditional classification and eluded the limitations of the SALT I framework. It was a 'cruise' missile capable of strategic missions. The principle of the cruise missile was no novelty. In essence it was a sonic-speed pilotless turbofan aircraft, the lineal descendant of Hitler's 'flying bomb'. Both sides in the past had deployed cruise missiles in various ancillary and tactical roles. But now the Americans, by combining the results of technical advances on a number of fronts, were developing a cruise missile of a totally new sort which looked like being a match-winner. It could be launched with equal ease from the ground, from an aircraft in flight or from a submerged submarine. It could be armed equally well with a nuclear or a high-explosive warhead. It could be used on tactical or strategic missions and, in its strategic mode, it was reckoned to be capable of pin-point accuracy at ranges exceeding 2,000 miles. It was hard to shoot down because, though slow-moving, it operated well below the altitude at which radar detection was normally feasible. And it was cheap enough, and in engineering terms simple enough, for many medium-sized countries to make. The cruise missile bid fair to defeat attempts at negotiated limitation by blurring the accepted distinctions between strategic and tactical, nuclear and conventional, and to throw up insoluble problems of verification and proliferation.

Less bewildering, though potentially no less destabilizing of the military balance, were a series of further American innovations due to materialize towards the end of the decade. The B-1 intercontinental bomber, to replace the B-52 (whose service dates from 1956-9), would fly twice as fast as its predecessor, carry double the payload and be capable of operating at much lower altitudes. The Trident SLBM (to replace Polaris) would increase the sea-launched missile superiority already enjoyed by the Poseidon over its Soviet counterpart. The Mark 12-A warhead, to be deployed in 1978, would greatly improve the accuracy and penetration of the Minuteman against hardened Soviet silos. And the MX mobile missile, Minuteman's eventual successor in the 1980s, set on rails and firing from unpredictable positions in long, deep reinforced concrete trenches, would re-establish the invulnerability of the US ICBM screen and pose a threat to Soviet fixed-position ICBMs.

This, in rough outline, was the set of contingencies with which American and Soviet negotiators had to contend in pursuing further limitations.

For a while the momentum of apparent progress was sustained by concentration on two important, though peripheral, questions. In July 1974, with Nixon again visiting Moscow, a protocol was signed reducing the number of sites permitted under the ABM treaty from two to one a side; and on the same occasion a treaty was concluded (the 'threshold test-ban treaty') prohibiting the underground testing of nuclear weapons with yields exceeding 150 kilotons (one kiloton (KT) equals 1,000 tons of conventional explosive). It took almost two years more to agree on a complementary ban on so-called 'peaceful nuclear explosions' (PNEs) with yields exceeding the same figure. The significance of the threshold test-ban calls for a short digression.

The great developments in the sophistication and accuracy of nuclear weapons over the preceding twenty years had depended on the freedom of both sides to prove successive generations of weapons by test-firing. The 1963 treaty, while ending the hazard of atmospheric pollution, had done nothing to constrain this freedom, since the armourers on both sides had accommodated themselves with the minimum of inconvenience to the requirement for testing underground. Plainly, a comprehensive ban on all nuclear tests, including those conducted underground, would be the most direct and effective route to prevention of further innovation and development. A serious snag, however, was that neither China nor France, both late-comers to the field, had any intention of forgoing the knowledge that could only be acquired by nuclear testing; and the Russians fought shy of a ban which did not effectively tether all competitors. But, all else apart, a comprehensive test-ban had been, from the outset, blocked by problems of verification. For many years scientists were unable, for lack of the necessary equipment, to tell for sure whether a given disturbance, seismographically recorded from a distance, was due to an earthquake or a nuclear explosion, an uncertainty which, it was thought, the Russians could be counted on to exploit. So the United States (and Britain) insisted that a comprehensive nuclear test-ban must include arrangements for verification by inspection of the test site. This the Russians, evoking the spectre of 'foreign spies' on their territory, flatly refused to countenance. But, as time went on, improved seismological techniques progressively lowered the level of disturbance below which a nuclear explosion could hope to masquerade as an earthquake, and the way was thus opened, if not for a comprehensive, at least for a 'threshold' ban, prohibiting tests down to a level of yield that could be reciprocally policed, without on-site inspection, by using 'national technical means of verification'. The Russians, however, demanded that an exception should be made permitting underground nuclear explosions for 'peaceful' purposes, which they claimed – the Americans had discarded the hypothesis several years before – had a role to play (digging canals, reversing the course of rivers and excavating harbours) in accelerating the development of their vast Siberian wilderness. The Americans, reckoning that any exception would be all too easy to abuse for military purposes, insisted that, if the Russians wished to be free to conduct PNEs, on-site inspection of PNEs would be essential. And this the Russians, after a two-year haggle, untypically conceded.

But the threshold treaty in fact contributed very little to the original purpose of inhibiting innovation, since both sides, keener in 1974 on showing results than on solving problems, set the threshold at 150 KT, a level significantly – perhaps as much as ten times – higher than what could be policed by modern seismic monitoring, and too high to prevent the proving of the small, accurate and reliable MIRV warheads which had become the main preoccupation of nuclear innovators.

In the event, neither the threshold treaty nor the agreement on PNEs has yet been ratified by either party. So much, for now, for nuclear testing.

In November 1974, with the American election campaign and the CPSU's twenty-fifth congress both lying a year ahead, Brezhnev and the American President, meeting at Vladivostok, issued guidelines for a second SALT agreement, to run until 1985, which was to be concluded in the course of the following year. The guidelines restricted to 2,400 the aggregate number of strategic delivery vehicles (ICBMs, SLBMs and long-range bombers) which each side was entitled to possess and, within this overall limit, set a sub-limit of 1,320 on the MIRVed missiles of both sides. Dr Kissinger claimed that these limits 'set a cap' on the arms race for ten years; and the world at large seemed at first broadly to agree, though arms-control purists noted sourly that the limits spelt little contraction in the burden of armaments and scarcely incommoded the weapons development plans of either side.

In the ensuing two years, coinciding with the run-up to the presidential election of November 1976, the political decision taken at Vladivostok was rendered inoperative by obstinate technical factors, some of which have already been noted, assisted by the growing disenchantment of American opinion with the merits of *détente*. Troubles began when the ink on the Vladivostok guidelines was barely dry. Some of them proved soluble, at a price. The summit had made a commendable first shot at limiting the spread of MIRVed missiles; but had not settled what missiles should be counted against the MIRV ceiling, though the missile, MIRVed or unMIRVed, would look precisely the same to the eye of a satellite. This problem was eventually settled by Soviet acceptance of Dr Kissinger's proposal to count as MIRVed all missiles of any type that had been tested in a MIRVed mode. Nor, again, had there been any progress at Vladivostok on defining what was a 'heavy' missile. The giant SS-18, with its eight warheads, each with a yield of upwards of a megaton, was a clear case; but the smaller SS-19, with almost five times the throw-weight of its predecessor, was scarcely less so. Yet Dr Kissinger had to acquiesce in its exclusion from the 'heavy' category in order to gain Soviet assent to his proposal for counting the MIRVs.

The cases of the Soviet Backfire bomber and the American cruise missile proved much more intractable. President Ford appears at Vladivostok to have accepted the Soviet contention that Backfire was not a strategic bomber, and therefore should not count against Soviet entitlement of strategic delivery vehicles. But the US position was reversed following the President's return to Washington, facing the Russians with what amounted to a demand that other strategic delivery vehicles should be scrapped to make room for the Backfire, already coming off the production line; or alternatively that the Backfire itself should be discontinued. The Vladivostok summit had placed no constraints on the development of cruise missiles; and, indeed, as the Americans were able to point out, their new weapon, possessing the characteristics of a fixed-wing aircraft, fell quite outside the ambit of the Vladivostok limitations, which related to missiles that were ballistic (i.e. possessing the trajectory of a bullet) and to intercontinental manned bombers. Predictably, the Russians responded to the about-turn on Backfire by insisting that cruise missiles must either be counted against the American ceiling or banned altogether.

The Backfire and cruise missile problems were inconclusively discussed when Brezhnev and President Ford met at Helsinki to sign the Final Act; and Dr Kissinger had not abandoned hope of settling them when he visited Moscow for the last time in January 1976. The idea of separate and supplementary quotas began to take shape, but the positions of the two sides as to how, and to what, these quotas should apply were still far apart as the campaign for the US presidency gained momentum, calling a halt to negotiation. Meanwhile, public disappointment over the results so far achieved, allegations that the Russians had 'cheated' on their obligations under SALT I and growing disillusionment about *détente* in general combined to harden attitudes and inhibit the negotiating mobility of the outgoing administration.

Inheriting this situation when he took office in January 1977, President Carter was quick to respond to the new mood of the American electorate. The days of 'political' SALT agreements, made to America's disadvantage to keep the pot of *détente* boiling, were stated to be over. *Détente* was to be a two-way street. If the Russians wanted a real reduction in armaments, they could have it; but it would mean real sacrifices for them, as it would for the US. If not, America would show them what it could do.

All the same, behind this screen of brash rhetoric, the administration put together a package of proposals which sought to grasp the nettle of arms limitation in a way that its predecessor had not attempted. The 'deep cuts' which the Secretary of State proposed in Moscow in March 1977 were indeed, as Mr Brzezinski, the new President's national security adviser, later claimed, 'the first truly disarmament-orientated proposal introduced in SALT'. The chief elements of the package, as they emerge from a collation of published material, seem to have been these. The ceiling on strategic delivery vehicles of all sorts, set by the Vladivostok summit at 2,400, should be lowered to a figure between 1,800 and 2,000 and the ceiling on MIRVed missiles from 1,320 to between 1,100 and 1,200; the modification of existing and deployment of new ICBMs should be frozen; both sides should abandon their plans to deploy mobile missiles; the strategic version of the cruise missile and the strategic use of the Backfire bomber should be prohibited. These proposals involved the slaughter of many sacred cows venerated by hard-nosed men on both sides and it was not without difficulty that the President lined up the numerous American arms-control pundits and national security hawks in support of them. The alternative, 'fall-back', proposal which Mr Vance took to Moscow was that a SALT agreement embodying the Vladivostok ceilings should be concluded, covering ballistic missiles and strategic bombers only, and leaving Backfire (which the Russians claimed was not strategic) and cruise missiles (which were not ballistic) to be dealt with, along with the accumulating pile of other unsolved questions, in a subsequent negotiation.

In rejecting both proposals, the Russians were influenced alike by considerations of substance and style. The proposed lowering of the Vladivostok ceilings would have required a cut in the Soviet ICBM force while leaving American ICBM strength untouched (because of the lower ceiling accepted by the US in SALT I). The freeze on modification and deployment of ICBMs was unwelcome to them for many reasons, but first and foremost because it would have cut by 50 per cent their projected deployment of heavy SS-18s. The SS-20 mobile missile, which they were invited to abandon, was already on the point of being deployed. In its existing configuration it was, in any case, a medium-range, not a strategic weapon (though it could be made into one by adding a third 'stage'). As such, it was the centre-piece of the Soviet Union's warlike array both against China (which was none of America's business) and in central Europe, where it was the Soviet answer to the American forward-based systems (FBS). If it got dragged into the SALT negotiations, then the Soviet side would have to drag in the FBS too. All in all, while there were powerful attractions for the Russians in the American offer to kill the strategic version of the cruise missile and the (still unborn) MX mobile missile, and in conserving virtually unimpeded use of the Backfire in the European and Far Eastern theatres, these benefits were reckoned in Moscow to be too dearly bought by the sacrifices, in terms of military force in being, which President Carter was demanding in return.

The advance publicity given to the American two-pronged proposal, its ultimative overtones and, not least, its assumption that everything that had happened since Vladivostok, including negotiations at the highest level involving Brezhnev himself, could be struck from the record and consigned to oblivion, combined to harden Soviet objections of substance. Gromyko, when he spoke to the press after Vance's departure from Moscow, went so far as to say that the United States was seeking unilateral advantage and that the Soviet Union would 'never' agree. What Vance had proposed, he said, was that half the Soviet Union's rockets should be destroyed because 'someone in the United States' disliked them as being 'too heavy' or 'too effective'.

The *débâcle* in Moscow did not entail a complete severance of contact on arms limitation; indeed the two foreign ministers had established eight or more working groups to examine the chances of reaching agreement on several important, if less neuralgic, subjects – including a comprehensive test-ban, nuclear non-proliferation and Indian Ocean problems – and these groups started discussions; but it was not until 18 May that Vance and Gromyko met again, in Geneva, to pick up the bits of the main negotiation. They were reported to have agreed on a 'three-tier framework' which contemplated the conclusion of a SALT II treaty, to run until 1985, a protocol, to run for three years, intended to regulate for the time being the Backfire and cruise missile questions, and a 'statement of principles' which should point the way to a further balanced reduction in strategic armaments, but disputes continued for some time about what these documents should actually contain, evoking grumbles from Gromyko in Geneva and from Brezhnev in Moscow.

Two unilateral decisions by President Carter certainly helped to improve the atmosphere: the first, at the beginning of June, to postpone deployment of the Mark 12-A warhead, due to start that autumn; and the second not to proceed with the production of the B-1 super-bomber but to rely instead on air-launched cruise missiles mounted on his existing B-52s. Then, in a constructive and conciliatory speech at Charleston on 21 July, Mr Carter let fall that the US had put forward new proposals for dealing with Soviet worries over the cruise missile and American anxieties about the Soviet threat to the Minuteman force. By early September Gromyko was already saying that a new SALT treaty was 'completely possible'. Matters moved forward fast when he came to the United States in September. After a meeting with the president on 26 September Gromyko declared himself confident of reaching a satisfactory conclusion, and on 12 October Brezhnev himself conceded in a speech that the SALT negotiations had taken a turn for the better. Evidently a basis for compromise had been found. Meanwhile, in the interests of avoiding a legal hiatus, the two governments had agreed, in identical unilateral statements, informally to extend the life of the interim agreement of 1972 whose five-year term, lately squandered in inconclusive discussion, was due to expire on 2 October.

There has, at the time of writing, been no official disclosure of the terms of the September compromise, but the following account, again compiled from published sources, is probably not far off the mark. The overall ceiling on strategic delivery vehicles would be lowered from 2,400 (Vladivostok) to between 2,160 and 2,250. This would not pinch the United States, whose total strength stands a little short of 2,100, but would lop some 300 off the Soviet total permitted under SALT I. The Vladivostok ceiling on MIRVed missiles would stay unchanged at 1,320, but within it sub-ceilings would be introduced, namely 1,200-1,250 for ICBMs and SLBMs taken together, and 800-850 for ICBMs alone. And long-range bombers equipped with air-launched cruise missiles (ALCMs) would be counted, one for one, against the MIRVed missile ceiling. These provisions would be incorporated in a SALT II treaty to run until 1985. A protocol, to run for three years only, would embody substantial, if temporary, concessions by each side to the other. It would limit to 308 the number of heavy missiles permitted to each side (thus permitting the full deployment of the Soviet SS-18 force, numbering precisely 308, to be completed). It would impose a three-year limitation of 2,500 kilometres (1,550 miles) on the permitted range of ALCMs mounted on heavy bombers, and of 600 kilometres (372 miles) on that of sea- and ground-launched cruise missiles (SLCMs and GLCMs). And it would, with specific exceptions, forbid for three years the deployment of 'new' weapons. In addition, the Soviet Union would give a unilateral pledge not to expand production of Backfire beyond the current level of approximately two per month, and not to deploy it against intercontinental targets. No evidence emerged about the contents of the third 'tier' – the projected 'statement of principles'. Perhaps it had dropped from view. In any case, the problems of verification which the entry into service of the cruise missile would throw up would give future negotiators plenty to think about. For the difficulty of verifying the range of a cruise missile involved a high degree of reliance in future on mutual trust, as also did the virtually unenforceable pledges about the use of Backfire. And trust had so far been notably lacking.

These unsolved questions lent point to making a further attempt to constrain weapons development by the alternative route of a comprehensive ban on nuclear tests. This was one of the subjects on which a working group had been established at the time of Vance's ill-starred visit to Moscow in March, and the group's labours proceeded as the summer advanced. Addressing the UN General Assembly on 27

September, Gromyko surprised his audience by offering to join the US and Britain in a suspension of all underground nuclear weapons tests for an unspecified period. The offer was not, it appeared, conditional on Chinese and French compliance and there was no mention of PNEs. On 2 November Brezhnev, at a banquet in Moscow for the visiting Indian Prime Minister, lifted the curtain a little further by declaring the Soviet government's readiness to reach agreement on a 'moratorium' on PNEs, coupled with a 'ban' on all nuclear weapons tests for a definite period. The announcement was hailed in Washington as a 'major breakthrough', but talks between Soviet, US and British officials, which had begun in Geneva in October, soon established that the Soviet proposal was rather more *nuancé* than Brezhnev's prospectus suggested. It seemed that the Russians were seeking a treaty banning all nuclear weapons tests for a period of three years, together with a moratorium of the same duration on PNEs. If within the three-year period China and France did not accede to the treaty, it would lapse, leaving the signatories free to resume weapons-testing. They would meanwhile use the respite provided by the moratorium to devise abuse-proof procedures under which the Soviet Union would be able to conduct the 'peaceful' explosions it desired; if a satisfactory formula could not be found, the moratorium would lapse.

The Soviet proposals were open to criticism on two counts. If (perhaps a rather remote contingency) the treaty succeeded and became permanent, but the moratorium lapsed, the US and Britain would find themselves estopped from further weapons-testing, while the Russians would have the possibility, under the pretext of conducting PNEs, of carrying on nuclear research for warlike purposes. A more substantial objection was that the continued Soviet hankering after PNEs made nonsense of the opposition of the three powers to the conduct of allegedly 'peaceful' explosions by other countries and seriously undermined their efforts to contain nuclear proliferation. It seemed possible to hope that this latter consideration might in time overcome the Soviet government's addiction and enable a comprehensive test-ban to be concluded, if necessary with an escape clause permitting resumption should weapons-development in China or France come to pose a serious threat. A second-best solution might be to increase the duration of the treaty (perhaps to five or ten years) in the hope that with the passage of time the conflict of interests might become less acute.

Here we must perforce abandon the narrative unfinished and attempt to reach an interim verdict on the evidence so far available of Soviet intentions.

The main facts are not in serious doubt. The Russians have for more than ten years been systematically increasing the quantity and improving the quality of their nuclear armaments, and have continued to do so without pause even after they had achieved not merely broad equivalence but also invulnerability to an American first strike; and all this during a period when American strength was fairly static.

There are those in the West who contend that these preparations cannot be explained by preoccupation with defence and deterrence, and can only mean that the Russians are arming themselves to fight and win a nuclear war. Proponents of this view cite the writings of brass-hats and theorists in Soviet military journals (though the Russians might pardonably draw a similar inference from articles by some strategic analysts in the West). They adduce evidence that development is proceeding of yet another generation of Soviet offensive weapons even heavier and more deadly than the SS-18 and its contemporaries. And they cite Soviet preparations for civil defence as indicating the assumption that victory will turn on the relative ability of the civil population on each side to survive. While noting these points, we may fairly recall that received Soviet doctrine about the inevitability of war with the 'imperialists' had to be ignominiously discarded in Khrushchev's time, precisely in order to accommodate the troublesome recognition that there could be no winners in a nuclear conflict; and that recent US official estimates, while conceding that the United States would suffer more casualties than the USSR in a nuclear exchange, predict that losses even on the Soviet side would exceed 100 million dead. It seems inherently unlikely that the Russians have reached a fundamentally different conclusion and have, on the strength of it, reversed Khrushchev's judgment.

Others, while conceding that victory by force of nuclear arms is an unlikely Soviet objective, argue that the aim is to checkmate the Americans, without a shot being fired, by creating a 'disarming' nuclear capability, and that the entire Soviet negotiating strategy in SALT has been organized to this end. This view derives some plausibility from Soviet insistence on setting the missile ceilings in SALT I high enough to accommodate everything that they had under construction and in development; from their tenacity , then and later, in holding the road open for the modernization and qualitative improvement of their weapons; from their successful insistence on full deployment of their SS-18s as a condition of further progress towards SALT II; and from the evidence of Soviet testing of counter-satellite devices. A more imaginative dimension has been built on to this hypothesis by those who claim to detect evidence of Soviet research into wonder-weapons – a particle-charged beam (which would destroy any missile that entered its field) and a device to make the sea transparent to the satellite's eye (thus putting an end to the invulnerability of US missile-submarines). We cannot dismiss this evidence, both factual and fanciful, out of hand, nor lightly discard the hypothesis which it underpins.

But we are bound to note that, if the Russians are assumed to be playing for nothing less than unconditional surrender by the West, they have intermittently made moves on the SALT chessboard which are not too easily reconciled with such a purpose. They agreed, in 1972 and 1974, to arrangements which effectively closed the option of the ABM. They appear, in the September 1977 compromise, to be ready to concede (admittedly for value received) a reduction of the Vladivostok weapons ceiling which will cut their nuclear missile force while leaving the American force unscathed. And they seem, again for value received, to contemplate the introduction by the US of the strategic version of the ALCM, which will cause them much trouble and which they could not hope to match (if they decided they wanted to) for the better part of a decade. In conceding these substantial benefits (and banking the gains received in exchange) the Russians may indeed be pursuing a deceptive strategy of high sophistication: but it seems at least as likely that they are engaged, as the Americans are, in a process of give and take, in which (like their adversaries) they intend to take as much as they can get and give away nothing unless they have to.

But, if this premise were true, it would follow that the Russians are not after all aiming at victory or unconditional surrender, but a negotiated settlement of arms-control problems on terms of mutual advantage. Can the West place its faith in this much more comfortable hypothesis? And how, if it be true, are we to construe Soviet motives in carrying out the extraordinary build-up of nuclear strength which this chapter has examined? He would be a rash man who would give an unqualified answer to the first question. To the second we may reply, without prejudice to our caution on the first, that the build-up is in keeping with Russian and Soviet traditions – with the ideology which teaches that the USSR is surrounded by powerful and malevolent enemies, and with the much older assumption that military power in being is a good in itself, and that the more you have the safer you are. Add to this the doubling and re-doubling on American bets on the earlier laps of the arms race and the existence in the Soviet Union (as in the US) of a military-industrial bureaucracy which has acquired its own momentum, and you have what may be a sufficient, if not an exhaustive, explanation.

Despite initial errors of style, the Carter administration has shown great steadfastness in exploring the hypothesis that a serious arms-control bargain can be negotiated with the Russians. Defence Secretary Brown provided a glimpse of what they were after when, in June 1977, he professed his conviction that the Soviet leaders eventually would conclude that it was in their interest to make substantial reductions in strategic nuclear weapons. Having the option of matching or trumping every Soviet innovation (and thus evoking a further competitive response from the Soviet side) the administration have chosen not to exercise it, so long as the US second-strike capability, taken as a whole, remains unimpaired. For this restraint, caricatured as naivety or poltroonery, some of them have been most brutally and unworthily traduced by hawks and warhead-crunchers, who have accused them of playing ducks and drakes with national security. Mr Carter has faced criticism over the undoubtedly growing vulnerability of the Minuteman force to the new generation of Soviet missiles but, mindful of the cautionary tale of the MIRVing of the 1960s, has preferred not to raise the ante by deploying the Mark 12-A warhead or authorizing the production of the M-1 bomber. He has, of course, been able to show restraint in the knowledge that his SLBM force is at present fully capable of delivering a second strike should the United States be attacked, and in the reasonable certitude that superior technological capacity would enable the US, if things looked like going wrong, rapidly to recover lost ground. Both the relaxed tone, and the limits, of this policy came out clearly in a statement by Secretary Brown in June 1977 when the deadlock was still unbroken. There had been, he said, a 'rough equivalence' in the defence effort of the two countries in the preceding twenty years, but the US outlay had taken place mainly in the first ten years, and the Soviet in the second. 'We have', he added, 'probably lived off our earlier investment longer than we should. We have some catching up to do.'

At the time of writing, the enigma of Soviet intentions and behaviour still remained unsolved. Following the September compromise the auguries looked on the whole favourable to the conclusion of SALT II. This would narrow the field of dissension and uncertainty, and pave the way for SALT III which might at last bring some of those 'deep cuts' in armaments which had eluded Mr Vance in March 1977 and which were obviously necessary to the health of *détente*.

But it is well to remember the intractability of technical factors which, as the experience after Vladivostok has shown, can combine to frustrate even the political will of the leaders on both sides to reach agreement.

Problems of verification, which seemed in 1972 to have been tidily settled by satellite reconnaissance, have returned with the cruise missile. The fading of the distinction between strategic and non-strategic weapons threatens to drag on to the table of the SALT negotiators the future of the American forward-based systems and of Soviet weapons targeted on Western Europe and China. A situation might arise in which no conclusion could be reached in SALT which did not at the same time tackle and resolve the problems of force reductions in central Europe and take account of considerations lying outside the bilateral relationship of the super-powers. And, with technology meanwhile following its self-sustaining development, pressure on both sides could lead, in the absence of an early settlement, to another round of innovation and escalation. It would not necessarily, and with reasonable luck probably would not, lead to nuclear war, but it would set back for an indefinite period the hopes of a real relaxation of tension. For Secretary Vance was right when he told the NATO council in December 1977 that there was no prospect of stable US–Soviet relations without a SALT II; the conclusion of a treaty was in itself no guarantee of such stability, but there could be none without it.

7

Rights and Wrongs

One of President Carter's first acts, as was briefly noted in Chapter 1, was to nail the colours of the United States to the mast of human rights: the authenticity of *détente* with the Soviet Union would be measured by the Soviet government's performance in fulfilling engagements entered into at Helsinki to respect 'human rights and fundamental freedoms'. The present chapter attempts answers to three questions: what it is that the Soviet government has been doing to its citizens that has made its behaviour into a bone of contention; why it behaves in this way; and whether this behaviour is, as President Carter suggests, relevant to the health and viability of *détente*. The answers to the first two questions are closely intertwined and a good deal of ground will be covered in the process of unravelling them.

Every society strikes its own balance between freedom and organization. In the Soviet case the balance is tilted sharply in favour of organization, and this is no accident. For, as Chapter 3 showed, the Soviet Union was set up to 'build socialism', to establish, against domestic resistance, a new pattern of ownership of the means of production, to reorganize the life of Soviet man from top to toe and, in time, to transform him into a new creature, communist man. And, since the imperialist 'class enemy' was in control almost everywhere else in the world, the new society and its citizens had to be constantly on guard against foreign machinations. Small wonder then that the pattern of the Soviet state was one of dictatorship, nominally of the proletariat, but in practice of the Communist Party. Proletarian dictatorship received a decent burial at the hands of Khrushchev, and the USSR now styles itself a 'state of the whole people'. But under the new style, as under the old, the reality is the monopoly of power enjoyed by the Communist Party. Accordingly, such rights and freedoms as the individual may enjoy are exercised within the framework of the Soviet state and are qualified by correlative duties.

The environment in which the Soviet citizen exercises his rights and performs his duties to society is determined for him by the dictatorial and managerial role of the Communist Party. For a definition of this role we cannot do better than turn to Brezhnev's new constitution, introduced in June 1977. Article 6 reads as follows:

> The Communist Party of the Soviet Union is the leading guiding force of Soviet society and the nucleus of its political system. The CPSU exists for the people and serves the people. Armed with the Marxist-Leninist teaching the Communist Party determines the general prospects for society's development and the line of the domestic and foreign policy of the USSR, gives guidance to the great creative endeavour of the Soviet people and places their struggle for the triumph of communism on a planned scientific basis.

Here it is, without reticence or concealment. The party, as the custodian of Marxist-Leninist science, is the mainspring of the state and of society. It determines the goals of Soviet society, prescribes the path to be followed in reaching them and harnesses the strength and talents of Soviet citizens to the achievement of them. It claims to do these things for the people, but makes no claim to be of the people, nor that its rule is by the people. It is a machine with a job to do. Those who have ambitions to play a part in politics can do so only if they get themselves co-opted to membership of it. For the rest, life is a matter of fitting in with the party's plans, of conforming to the goals set by them. Human rights, as understood in societies built on different principles, that is to say a set of liberties held to be inherent in man's nature, inalienable and unconditional, lie outside the party's term of reference. It is concerned with applying Marxist-Leninist science to the problems of making the USSR strong and prosperous and leading its people into communism, with building the prototype and example of a new form of society. Absolute and abstract rights have nothing to do with this. Ask a party member what human rights are and he is likely to cite the right to work, the guarantee of a job and the assurance of having a roof over one's head: all of which Soviet society provides, after its fashion, but societies which are vocal on the human rights theme do not, or not always.

Despite the amplitude of its mandate, the party has not found the path of dictatorship smooth. It has, as an organization established for a purpose, and reckoning that it knows where it is going, been unfortunate, for about half of its sixty years in power, in its choice of leaders. In their different ways both Stalin and Khrushchev were disastrous for the party and each of them managed greatly to complicate its task of leading and guiding the Soviet people to communism. From about 1937 onwards Stalin usurped the power of the party, reducing dictatorship by a collective to dictatorship by one man, and government by the Marxist-Leninist rule book to government by caprice. Terror was his weapon and the state security police his instrument. Under Beria, the police became at once detective, prosecutor, judge, jury and executioner. An estimated 20 million people were killed, imprisoned or exiled to Siberia, many of them on groundless suspicion and many for no better reason than that Stalin, or the police, had taken an arbitrary dislike to them. Senior officers of the military high command and the state bureaucracy were liquidated. Worst of all, from the party's standpoint, Stalin unloosed the terror on to the party's own ranks, including his own close colleagues in the leadership, reducing this instrument forged to lead the country forward to a group of terrified yes-men.

The experience of Stalinism pulverized Soviet society. Stalin and his policemen had scared the living daylights out of everyone, 'conscious' and unconscious, party and non-party alike. If rule by the party was to become viable again, if the leadership were to give an effective lead, and the masses to emerge from apathy and respond, the terror had to go. Conformity was of course necessary, but Stalin had replaced it by paralysis activated only by his own daemonic and energizing will. With Stalin buried, a return had to be made to party rule and scientifically determined social goals. But if this was to happen, people, inside the party and out, needed to be told where they stood, what they might do without fear or exile, imprisonment or death, and what they might not do. Thus was born the principle of 'socialist legality' as the organizing principle of the Soviet state. It was compounded of several elements recognizable to Western jurisprudence – the interests of society, the rights (and duties) of the individual and the obligation of the state to comply with the law. Individual rights are part of it, but they are qualified by correlative duties, and the interests of society come first. Socialist legality was complemented by the reform of the police. Under Stalin they had been a law unto themselves, with direct access to the dictator and subject to oversight neither by state nor party, and had been used against both. Now, following Beria's execution, the police were cut down to size, becoming another, albeit still formidable, department of the state bureaucracy and, like other departments, subject in all things to the party's guidance and control. The party had learnt its lesson and would not be caught that way again. From the point of view of the common man, socialist legality was an unmitigated boon. Fear, as an abiding and pervasive feature of his life, had been removed. It might be a humdrum life, unexciting and deficient in creature comforts, but it was possible for those who conformed, and most did, to get on with their affairs with a peace of mind unknown in living memory. With the revolution almost forty years behind, party rule was not a sticking point for most and Khrushchev, as we saw earlier, set about revising the ideology, several of whose more objectionable and archaic features disappeared. And in due course most of Stalin's victims still living were repatriated from camps and prisons and many of the dead were posthumously rehabilitated.

But Khrushchev too, as he emerged from the ruck of the post-Stalin collective leadership, was to tax the equanimity of the party bureaucrats severely, though his aberration took a totally different form. His efforts to restore the body politic struck them as unscientific, spontaneous and potentially dangerous. He saw too much of Tito and had picked up from him notions which were bound to end in tears. The Hungarian counter-revolution of 1956 was an example of what happened if you started playing with ideas of 'liberalizing' the system. Yet Khrushchev, though no egg-head and a great philistine in most matters of art and aesthetics, seemed somehow to have a soft spot for the intelligentsia. His conviction that the ideology required revision and modernization made him accessible to all sorts of hare-brained notions. His revulsion from Stalinism moved him to sanction the publication of *One Day in the Life of Ivan Denisovich*, Solzhenitsyn's exposure of life in Stalin's prison camps. *Novy Mir*, under the editorship of Tvardovsky, became, with Khrushchev's blessing, the pace-setter for a new Soviet literature, quite different from the hack work of Stalin's days, telling the truth about the past, critical, often satirical about bits of the past that survived into the present. For a few, in the arts and in academic life, contacts with foreigners and travel abroad began to open up.

For those who took part in this flowering the Khrushchev years were a time of hope. The party bureaucrats in the professional unions – of writers, artists, actors, musicians and journalists – through which the party policed the cultural front, were on the defensive. It was no free-for-all, since the unions, a creation of Stalin's, remained in being and only their members in good standing could get their work before the public. And the censorship was still there, ably seconded by cautious editors and impresarios who did not wish to tempt fate too far. But it was now possible to make a living by literature, poetry or play-writing without selling one's soul, and hopes rose of further relaxation to come. In parts of the academic world too, notably among natural scientists, interests began to develop beyond the narrow confines of laboratory or institute. The Soviet Union had spent prodigally over the years on education, largely indeed of a vocational brand, but in the process had taught some of the more intelligent and independent to think for themselves. Unlike the majority of bureaucrats and ideologues, these people combined specialist knowledge with experience of how the world worked. They recognized shortcomings in the Soviet performance and were ready and anxious to suggest remedies.

How heavily Khrushchev's responsibility for the 'thaw' weighed in the eventual decision to throw him overboard is a moot point. His adventurism in foreign policy, his instant panaceas for Soviet agriculture and the liberties he took with party organization and appointments probably counted for more. But the party apparatus reckoned that safety margins on the intellectual front had been cut too fine for comfort. Unless a check were administered, unless party control were re-asserted, they foresaw that their entire defensive position might cave in. With revisionism rampant at home and Stalin's name a dirty word, it would take very little to get the Soviet intelligentsia right off the leash, hob-nobbing with the 'class enemy' abroad and corrupting Soviet youth with all sorts of ideas, religious, nationalistic, aesthetic and humanitarian, that promised, if they took root, to confuse Soviet society and disrupt the onward march to communism. Khrushchev's legacy might be no more than the thin end of the wedge, but it was a highly dangerous wedge and needed to be pulled out.

In Khrushchev's successors the party machine, after three decades of adversity, found men at the top who saw things in the same light as they did themselves. Khrushchev had fallen in October 1964. Within a year the check which the machine wanted was being administered. The exposure of Stalinism, which had been the source of, and the cover for, so much ferment in the public mind, was called off. Concurrently, a campaign was prepared to cut the intellectuals down to size. Seeing it coming, the intellectuals, for their part, discerned the thin end of another wedge, the wedge of resurgent Stalinism. The Stalin years had shown with terrible clarity what could happen in the Soviet Union if the levers of power got into arbitrary and irresponsible hands. From a cultural clamp-down to a renewed terror was, it seemed to them, but a short step, and the time to resist was before the point of no return had been reached. So it was that Brezhnev's redressment of the cultural line drew forth a response of activist dissidence. Both sides had over-rated the dangers. Neither wedge was as perilous as it was thought to be. The party certainly over-insured against risks which it greatly exaggerated. The activists certainly over-reacted if they conceived that Brezhnev was about to become a new Stalin. Be that as it might, Soviet dissent had been born, and from it was to grow the problem that the world calls human rights in the Soviet Union.

For a better understanding of what follows it will help to identify the categories of Soviet people who found themselves under pressure when the party under Brezhnev began to tighten the screws. Collectively, they are a mixed bag, not easy to classify and sort out. As a first shot at broad classification they may be divided into two main categories. They include, first of all, 'dissidents' in the proper sense of the word (the Russian word is *inakomyslyashchie*, meaning people who think differently). They include writers, creative artists, academics and scientists, of whom mention has already been made, but also others who dissent on religious or 'national' grounds. Second, there are those whose personal circumstances in one way or another bring them into conflict with the system. Typically, they include any who have connections, actual or potential, with the other world abroad and are therefore considered unreliable, unpatriotic and tainted with the contagion of the 'class enemy'. Among them are those with foreign wives, husbands or sweethearts; and Soviet citizens of Jewish blood. These two main categories are not exhaustive, but most Soviet dissidents or resisters whose names are known to Western newspaper readers fall into one or other of them. Or into both. For the categories are not mutually exclusive: they overlap in places. And like treatment (the party's package of repressive measures has a sameness about it) anyhow tends to draw them together, however different their points of departure, and in time to radicalize their attitudes. A copious literature exists chronicling the struggles of these people, whose plight has caught the imagination of journalists and scholars in the West. What follows here is necessarily superficial and selective, mentioning only a handful of names which seem representative of the various tendencies.

Dissidents proper have typically begun by criticizing Soviet reality, on grounds both practical and moral, from a position of acceptance of Marxism-Leninism. They set out from where Khrushchev left off, accepting the goals of Soviet society and the framework of party control, but advocating more 'liberal' socialism, embodying more of the underlying humanism of Marx and less of the manipulative social engineering of Lenin. Roy Medvedev, a philosopher-turned-historian, is the only prominent exponent of this position surviving today. (He should not be confused with his twin brother Zhores, a distinguished biologist and co-author with him of several books, who left the Soviet Union in 1973 and has travelled much further towards rejection of the system.) Any doubts about Roy Medvedev's orthodoxy or his assumptions are dissolved by a glance through his monumental five-hundred page denunciation of Stalinism *Let History Judge* in which, to cite one tiny point from many, he discusses Stalin's responsibility for muffing the great chance of bringing Western as well as Eastern Europe under communist rule in the aftermath of the Second World War. The flavour of his critique of latter-day Soviet performance comes out most readily in the memorial which, jointly with Andrei Sakharov and Valentin Turchin, he addressed in 1970 to the ruling triumvirate, Brezhnev, Kosygin and Podgorny. This is a well-documented plea for the 'democratization' of Soviet Society, which its authors see as a means to the better realization of accepted social goals and the overcoming of the basic malfunctions and lags of the system. These are attributed to the monopoly of decision enjoyed by ignorant and machine-minded bureaucrats. 'Democratization' as they use the term has nothing to do with pluralism: it means more open intra-party debate, bringing in those who have skills, knowledge and humanity to contribute, and a recognition of the fact that the Soviet people cannot be kept for ever in ignorance of the world around. Medvedev has held throughout the Brezhnev years to the essentials of this position, probably with tacit agreement of some in the apparatus who reckon that one day a source of new ideas might come in handy. His co-authors have moved on.

Andrei Sakharov, just mentioned, has graduated with time to be the godfather of Soviet dissent. A physicist of great distinction (in his thirties he played a leading part in developing Soviet thermo-nuclear weapons) and a member of the Soviet Academy of Sciences, he has, like Roy Medvedev, enjoyed by virtue of his position some immunity from the full rigours of the treatment reserved for lesser men. He has been harassed and publicly reviled but not yet put on trial, imprisoned or expelled. Under this treatment, however, he has travelled a long way from his initial position of advocating reform from within, concentrating his formidable intellectual powers and wide human sympathies on a campaign to prevent authority from bending the rules that it has itself laid down, to hold it to the 'socialist legality' which it proclaims, protesting, publicizing, and organizing the defence of those who are put on trial. Oppression has radicalized him and activized him, obliging him to burn his boats and turning him from hopes of future reform to agitation for a less crooked deal in the present. It is he and those who think like him that make it possible to speak of a Soviet movement for human rights. They are being thinned out by police action, but Sakharov is still there.

Those so far mentioned are at one in seeing the forward path as leading by way of economic development and progress to the overcoming of inherited backwardness and the emergence of a society which, depending whether they have retained or lost their Marxist beliefs, may or may not be qualitatively different from societies elsewhere, but which would in any case use the same tools, techniques and 'furniture' as developed non-Socialist societies. In this respect they are as different as chalk from cheese from Aleksandr Solzhenitsyn. Solzhenitsyn, veteran of Stalin's prison camps, champion of twenty-five years of struggle against tyranny, master of Russian prose-writing and Nobel Literature Prize-winner, rejects the system not merely because it is oppressive but also because it is un-Russian, godless, materialistic and has adopted the modern abominations of the West – industrialization and urbanization. Many Western admirers of his battle for freedom were taken aback, following his expulsion in 1974, to find Solzhenitsyn's lash falling with surprising impartiality on 'free' and 'socialist' societies alike, and to realize that their hero was, whatever his other merits, a latter-day Slavophil crank. (Slavophilism in Russian nineteenth-century history was a movement of protest against Westernization. Its adherents advocated the separate development of Russia in accordance with her ancient traditions of Orthodox Christianity and a peasant way of life.) For Solzhenitsyn's hatred of tyranny is inextricably bound up with his religion – he is an Orthodox believer – and with his Russian nationalism.

Nationalism, as the term is used here, denotes an individual's sense of identification with the culture and traditions of the national community from which he comes, rather than with the multi-national, proletarian culture which the Soviet system seeks to inculcate. The party regards nationalism as a grievous sin, since it errs against the Marxian ideal of proletarian international unity, which should embrace not merely the nationalities who make up the Soviet Union but also proletarians of all lands. It is also reckoned, on a less-elevated plane, to be dangerous, in that it promises, if left unchecked, to divide, weaken and potentially to split the monolithic power of the USSR, to weaken the grip of the party, which national unity re-inforces, even to divide the party itself. When we speak of the nationalities of the Soviet Union we are usually referring to the peoples of the main non-Russian Soviet Republics – the Ukrainians and Belorussians, who are Slavs and Europeans; the Moldavians, Estonians, Latvians and Lithuanians, who are Europeans but not Slavs; the central Asians – Kazakhs, Uzbeks, Tadjiks, Kirghiz and Turkmens, who are neither Slav nor European but Moslem in culture; the Caucasians – Armenians and Georgians – non-Slavs and belonging more closely to Asia Minor than to Europe, each with a Christian civilization older than Russia itself. Lenin condemned 'Great-Russian chauvinism' and his nationalities policy was liberal, offering the fullest degree of autonomy compatible with the overall interests of the Union. Today the nationalities continue to speak their own languages and retain, even in Brezhnev's 1977 constitution, a shadowy right on paper to secede from the Union. But the years of building socialism according to goals set from Moscow have, willy-nilly, meant a degree of russification, if not of the integument of national cultures at least of their social content. This inspires a degree of small-nation resentment and harking back to past glories which mingles with, and adds bite to, criticisms which other demerits of the system inspire, and intensifies the severity of the party's reaction to them. The correlative of it is the phenomenon of Russian nationalism. We saw one, rather special brand of it in Solzhenitsyn's case. In its commoner forms it is ugly and displeasing, not only to proletarian internationalists, representing as it does the equivalent in Soviet terms of the 'wogs begin at Calais' mentality. At times, notably in the Brezhnev era, the predominantly Great Russian leadership has shown a most un-Leninist degree of complaisance towards it. This is fuelled by the realization that some of the non-Russian nationalities breed like rabbits and that the absolute majority of the population will shortly be, if it has not already become, non-Russian.

Nationality becomes in its turn entangled with religion, and religion with dissent. The overwhelming majority of Soviet Christians are Orthodox, and the Orthodox church has produced many who dissent on grounds of conscience. But the minor denominations have had more than their proportionate share. A conspicuous case, exemplifying the link between religion and nationality, is that of Lithuania, where the Catholic church has given birth in the last decade to a movement of Christian dissent, the more vigorous because Catholicism is an important component of Lithuania's national consciousness, recalling her short-lived national independence at the beginning of the Soviet era. The party's attitude to religious belief, though periodically modified by concessions to expediency, is essentially hostile. 'Superstition' has no place in the new society: but the roots are deep and the tactics for pulling them up vary according to the conjuncture. Oddly, as it may seem, on the religious sector of the front the roles of Stalin and Khrushchev were reversed. In the 1941-5 war, with a patriotic resistance to be mobilized and Christian allies to be mollified, Stalin saw the utility of a measure of religious toleration and, then and until his death, the Christian churches enjoyed relative relaxation of pressure. Khrushchev, with characteristic over-reaction, reverted to the traditional party attitude with a vengeance, closing some churches and seminaries, and harassing priests, pastors and believers. Thus it came about that the beginning of religious dissent anteceded the growth of dissent on other fronts, which emerged only after Khrushchev's successors had re-drawn the frontiers of party control. When it came to power, the present leadership reckoned that, in a century of deepening secularism, religious belief was best left (subject always to safeguards against the preaching of sedition) to wither on the branch; persecution actually tended to consolidate religious opposition to the state. Khrushchev's zeal for activist atheism was discarded and today the state contents itself with installing more or less docile leaderships in the several Christian churches, and cultivates correct relationships with them. But the seeds sown by Khrushchev's persecutions have borne fruit, and activist clerics down the line, particularly in the Baptist and Evangelical churches, and among Catholic priests in Lithuania, bear witness to the contradictions between their beliefs and the demands of the system, with predictable results.

The case of Soviet Jewry is different. In old Russia, as elsewhere, Jews were maltreated, and latent anti-Semitic sentiment persists and periodically comes to the surface, particularly among Russians. Jews played important parts in the Bolshevik Party in the revolutionary years and today perhaps 3 million Jews, the residue of a much larger community reduced by pogroms and pre-1941 emigration to Western Europe and the new world, by early Zionism, and by Hitler, are scattered throughout most of the Union Republics. (Soviet statistics show $2^1/_4$ million as possessing Jewish 'nationality'. Many more of Jewish blood are undoubtedly buried in the figures of Russian and other nationalities.) Some, as in Georgia, are simple people and live in communities apart. More typically, Jews have been assimilated into the life of Soviet cities and have gravitated towards jobs in universities, institutes, the learned professions and the arts. Synagogues exist, subject to much the same constraints as other religious institutions, but for many if not most the faith of Judaism, and particularly the strict regime of orthodox Judaism, is something that their grandfathers practised but which does not seem very relevant today. Intermarriage between Soviet Jews and Soviet gentiles has been fairly common and, in urban Russia at least, the Jewish intellectual has in modern times achieved almost complete assimilation to, and identification with, Russian culture. But he has by the same token run up against the same barriers that his gentile counterpart has as a citizen of the Soviet socialist state, and the ranks of intellectual dissenters have included a substantial number of eminent Jews.

What distinguishes the Soviet Jew from other Soviet citizens is the fact that the existence of the state of Israel offers him the option of an alternative identity. It is not an easy option to take up, either psychologically, because the bonds of the acquired Russian culture are strong, or practically, since the Soviet state, regarding the desire to emigrate to the 'class enemy' as little short of treason, puts every sort of difficulty in the way. For many years the main takers of the option were old people who could not adjust and wished to die among relatives in the promised land. Two external factors galvanized this situation. At a moment when the lights lit by Khrushchev seemed to be going out all over the Soviet Union, Israel trounced the Soviet government's Arab protégés in the Six-Day War of 1967, staking a claim on the pride and loyalty of Jews everywhere. The option of emigration to Israel took on an attraction, and many Soviet Jews applied for exit visas. Applicants lost their jobs and their applications encountered all manner of bureaucratic resistance and vexatious delay. Some took the militant path, making demonstrations and running clandestine newspapers, even hijacking aircraft, to advertise their cause – and were dealt with by authority with predictable vigour. But by that time the quest for *détente* was already under way. An intensive campaign of publicity by Soviet Jewish militants mobilized the American Jewish lobby and alerted the US government and public to what was happening. The Soviet leadership, with its eye on American technology and credits, reckoned that this was an occasion where the use of the big stick would not serve its purpose. So the gates were opened to Jewish emigration, which rose steadily from 400 in 1969 to 33,500 in 1973. By 1974, 100,000 had left. Almost one-third of these were unassimilated Georgians, but the balance were for the most part intellectuals from the cities. A long waiting list remained to be processed. At that point American Jewry and its Congressional protectors overplayed their hand. The Jackson amendment to the Trade Bill made trade concessions to the USSR subject to the maintenance of a satisfactory rate of emigration (Senator Jackson let it be known that he would regard 60,000 visas a year as the minimum) and to a review at eighteen-month intervals of Soviet performance. The Soviet government, as we saw in the first chapter, declined these terms and the rate of Jewish emigration dropped to under

8,000 in 1975. The flow of exit visas tapered off and refusals multiplied. The Russians, with a straight face, insisted that nothing had changed. Jews were free to go if they followed established procedures. But fewer now wanted to do so. They saw that opportunities in Israel were limited by capacity (which was true). Some had found life there uncongenial and had returned (also true) and told their friends. As for refusals, they related to persons whose work gave them knowledge of Soviet military secrets. They would have to wait a while until their knowledge was sufficiently outdated to do no harm. And, of course, those who broke the law by causing disorders would be punished as the law required.

The package of repressive measures which the Soviet authorities employ against resisters and trouble-makers begins with loss of employment and livelihood. Once a dissident has been identified as such by authority (or, if he is a Jew, once he has made application for an exit visa) he is liable to be dismissed from the appointment he holds and subjected to obloquy and ostracism by his former colleagues. If he is self-employed and has made his way by writing, the arts or journalism, he will be expelled from the professional union to which he belongs, which effectually closes his access to his public. The prospect of these sanctions suffices to deter many, for in the Soviet Union there is no private sector, no non-governmental foundations and no alternative labour market. The dissident will be called in by the police, interrogated, bullied and pressed to reveal the identity of his friends. He may be harassed in a variety of ways, varying from broken windows and deflated tyres to being beaten up by plain-clothes hooligans. If he persists in his defiance, he may be brought to trial under the articles of the Criminal Code (nos 190 and 191) which punish 'fabrications discrediting the Soviet political and social system' and sentenced to three years in prison or five in Siberia. Or, if he has crossed the border that divides criticism from advocacy of change he may be tried (under articles 70 and 72) for anti-Soviet agitation and propaganda or anti-Soviet organization, with correspondingly heavier penalties; or even, if a charge of conspiracy with foreigners can be made to stick, for treason. As a nastier alternative he may be consigned, administratively or by judicial process, to a mental hospital, on the pretext that his dissenting activities can only be the work of an unbalanced mind, and there subjected to 'therapy' by drugs and other means. In recent years, in cases where the glare of international publicity has made it difficult to apply these various correctives, the alternative of expulsion from the Soviet Union, with deprivation of Soviet nationality, has frequently been applied, sometimes without the formality of trial, sometimes when a dissenter has served his sentence wholly or in part. Solzhenitsyn, for example, was arrested one day and bundled into an aeroplane the next, on the shrewd calculation that, once out of the Soviet Union, his nuisance value would fade. But even so it is a far cry from Stalin's terror. The law is oppressive and the judiciary amenable to party directions to convict, but the police have been bureaucratized and are forced increasingly to argue the case for the prosecution. The law is not equal for everyone who comes up against it. In remoter places it is no doubt applied to the full without anyone from outside hearing about it. In places like Moscow and Leningrad, where the world is watching, the police and its Party mentors have a range of flexible response which enables them to take political factors into account. But the punitive package has the effect of bringing together all those variegated elements who fall foul of the system into a single community of adversity. For they are all, whatever their initial motivation, in the same boat.

By 1965 the new leadership had settled what needed to be done and the repressive measures were ready. The first blow was a double one, struck in Kiev and Moscow. In Moscow, Andrei Sinyavsky and Yuli Daniel were arrested and put on trial for smuggling abroad and publishing there under pseudonyms satirical fiction critical of the accepted values of Soviet society. Their sentences – seven and five years respectively in prison – were immediately protested against, to no avail, in petitions signed by thousands of people ranging from eminent scientists and academics to writers, artists and professional people. In Kiev, twenty Ukrainian intellectuals were similarly sent away for long stretches because their writing on a variety of subjects was tainted with Ukrainian nationalist sentiment. Perhaps the best known of them, Valentin Moroz, was re-arrested after his release in 1969 and sentenced for a further term of prison and exile. By these means the Soviet literary world was put on notice that the relative licence of the Khrushchev era had been revoked. External events were the occasion for deterrent strikes on the other fronts. Soviet Jewry, as already noted, was dealt with in the wake of the Six-Day War of 1967. In 1968–9 it was the turn of any who harboured thoughts of 'socialism with a human face' in the USSR. The handful who, in August 1968, made their protest of conscience in Red Square against the invasion of Czechoslovakia were rounded up and imprisoned. But, apart from these, many Soviet liberals had been elated by the spectacle of the Prague spring, with its abolition of censorship and the general democratization of Czechoslovak society that followed it, seeing in Dubček's reforms an attractive model for social change at home. Once the Red Army had done its work in Prague, the police cracked down on the home front, arresting any who had declared their sympathies.

Inexorably, the pressures of the system were driving dissenters of whatever persuasion into collaboration. 1968 saw the appearance of the first numbers of the *Chronicle of Current Events*, a thick, well-documented bi-monthly periodical produced by the cottage-industry technique known as *samizdat* (literally, self-publication) employed by Soviet writers whose work no publisher would accept. *Samizdat* circulates from hand to hand among trusted readers, typed on thin paper and repeatedly re-typed as the chain of circulation lengthens. The *Chronicle* set out to provide an objective record of the activities of dissenters throughout the Soviet Union, and the steps taken against them by authority, reporting court proceedings and reviewing forbidden literature currently circulating in *samizdat* form. The devotion of its compilers and the loyalty of its readers are well attested to by the fact that it took the KGB almost four years to penetrate and silence it, and it resumed publication again after a fifteen-month gap, in May 1974. On a less conspiratorial level, Sakharov and two younger physicists, Valery Chalidze and Andrei Tverdokhlebov, in 1970 formed the Moscow 'Committee on Human Rights' to act as an independent centre of protest against the treatment of dissenters and to bring aid and comfort to those in trouble, organize their legal defence and advance proposals for law reform. Its importance was perhaps mainly symbolic, but its members in time developed the techniques and tactics of organized pressure groups in the West, making sophisticated use of the foreign press corps in Moscow and of the long-distance telephone as channels for the outlet of news to the outside world. After Helsinki, another committee came into being with the self-appointed task of monitoring the Soviet government's performance of its human rights obligations under the Final Act and bringing violations to the notice of humanitarian organizations abroad. Its work was bound to land its members in trouble and casualties among them multiplied as the new US administration's line on human rights unfolded. By the autumn of 1977 most of them had been imprisoned, exiled or expelled from the Soviet Union. This might, as the party no doubt hoped, presage the beginning of the end for Soviet dissent. But party pressure had welded disparate centres of resistance into a movement which had, over the years of the Brezhnev era, shown a striking capacity for self-renewal.

It is time to revert to the third question raised at the beginning of the chapter, namely the relationship between the campaign for human rights in the Soviet Union and international *détente*. Humanitarians in the West have frequently asserted that peace and universal respect for the rights of the individual are closely interlinked, indeed that the second is a condition of the first. In awarding the Peace Prize to Academician Sakharov, the Nobel Foundation went on record that 'for him it is a fundamental principle that world peace can have no lasting value unless it is founded on respect for the individual in human society'. The drafters of the Helsinki Final Act made the same point less generally and in a more persuasive context in no. VII of the 'Ten Principles', where they declare that respect for human rights 'is an essential factor for the peace, justice and well-being necessary to ensure the development of friendly relations and co-operation ... among all States'. This is indeed the hook on which the Russians, having subscribed to the Final Act, have found themselves impaled, and it is shrewdly barbed. But we are bound to ask ourselves whether the proposition is generally true. For relations between states are shaped by many factors, among which real interests generally have greater weight than ethical considerations.

A backward glance over the last twenty years shows that states which cherish human rights and respect for the individual in their own society have found no insuperable difficulty in maintaining correct and satisfactory relations, on the basis of real interests shared in common, with quite a number of others – with Franco and Salazar and the Greek Colonels, to name only those who have passed on – which have treated their own citizens, by Western standards, outrageously. And he would be a rash man who asserted that 'world peace' would have been the stronger had a different attitude been adopted. Moreover, the human rights paragraph of the Final Act comes next door to another (Principle no. VI) which binds all states to refrain from any intervention in one another's internal affairs, an obligation already explicit in the United Nations Charter and in countless other international documents. The Soviet Union's critics have no hesitation in claiming the protection of this principle, and telling the Russians to mind their own business, if they presume to interfere in other people's concerns – in Northern Ireland, in race relations or in residual colonial problems. Indeed it is arguable that 'world peace', so far from being strengthened by international busy-bodying, actually requires, for its health, a decent restraint on the part of all in not meddling in the affairs of others.

What then is it that makes the Soviet case an exception? Some may argue that a state which treats its own citizens in the way the Soviet Union does thereby demonstrates that it is capable of anything; and that the oppression of dissidents unmistakably betrays a disposition permeating the whole being of the Soviet state: it could not happen, the argument continues, except as part of a complex of evils which will make peaceful co-operation with the Soviet Union impossible (To transpose the argument to a different situation, this is as much as to say that, once it had seen how Hitler treated the Jews, the world ought to have realized that war with him was inevitable.) What we have so far learnt of Leninist ethics and of the motivation and organization of the Soviet state may indeed lend some colour to this thesis. But where does the argument lead us? War with Hitler was a rational option. War with the Soviet Union in the nuclear age is not. It surely follows that, whatever its intellectual and moral attraction, we cannot adopt the notion of an indissoluble link between peace and human freedom in the Soviet Union as a basis for policy.

So the discussion returns to the more familiar world of international politics with its awkward facts, moral preferences (not imperatives) and appropriate rhetoric. *Détente*, as was noted at the beginning of the book, is a modest objective, an easing of the sharpness of disagreements and a lessening of the accompanying risks, not yet a meeting of minds or a basis for long-term collaboration, though the path beyond *détente* might lead in that direction. *Détente* might reasonably be expected to include some alleviation of the miseries and iniquities inflicted on Soviet dissenters, if only because of the offence which they cause to the other side. But it is obviously beyond the scope of the operation (and in any case, given the balance of forces between the two sides, beyond the power of the West) to bring about comprehensive change in the nature and goals of Soviet society and the Soviet state. These are, as we have seen, the tap-root from which the requirement for conformity, the reaction of nonconformity, and the punitive counter-reaction of Soviet society spring. It is an illusion to look for much more from *détente*, in the human rights context, than a cautious cutting back by the Russians of their margin of over-insurance against disruption of their grand design. There is room for this and the West is right to press for it, though change may come rather through Soviet recognition of the inefficiencies and rigidities of their system than in response to external pressures.

If, as must be assumed, the search for *détente* is a shared interest of both sides, it follows that a policy which makes everything – arms limitations, trade and other forms of contact – conditional on the prior performance of Soviet obligations to respect human rights is something not to be attempted. 'Linkage' may be the essence of negotiation, but it needs to be used with discrimination. The case of Senator Jackson and the 60,000 exit visas should not be forgotten. The effects of this amendment on those it was meant to help were wholly counter-productive. This is not to say that the West should remain silent about Soviet inhumanities because the poor Russians, caught in the grip of their own preconceptions, are powerless to do anything about them. On the contrary, we are engaged, as the Russians never cease to tell us, in a 'struggle of ideas' which seems to entitle them to lecture us on the faults of our societies and to prophesy their inexorable collapse. Whatever these faults may be, Soviet practices offend *our* ideas and governments should not be deterred from saying so and from making sensible linkages in negotiation to secure improvement. For the Western countries have things which the Russians would like to have, and the case of Jewish emigration, before Senator Jackson and others got hold of it, shows what can be done if they retain a sense of proportion and a sense of occasion. Humanitarian groups in the West have their part to play too, but they need no prompting.

In September 1977, in an essay reproduced in the *Baltimore Sun*, President Carter conceded that 'human rights cannot be the only goal of our foreign policy, not in a world in which peace is literally a matter of survival'. The ability of the United States to influence other nations in the area of human rights was, he added, inhibited by the limits of American power. His readers might be forgiven for wishing that the penny had dropped in the President's mind nine months earlier.

8

One World after all

Autarky was Stalin's goal. Nature had endowed the Soviet Union with almost every mineral and raw material she could possibly need. The task of development was formidable but, provided the class enemy could be made to keep his distance, it was feasible. It would take several generations to complete and those whose lives were lived in the Soviet Union during those years would have a pretty thin time of it. But the country would emerge at the end immeasurably strong and, for all practical purposes, self-sufficient and dependent on no one.

The objective of self-sufficiency did not, of itself, imply the necessity of self-reliance in its achievement. Development could certainly be accelerated if foreign capital and foreign technology were to be harnessed to the task. But there were obstacles, both ideological and practical, to foreign investment. Foreign, in the 1920s, could only mean 'imperialist', and there was an inconsistency, which stuck in the throat of ideological purists, in resorting to the assistance of the class enemy and recreating in Soviet Russia a 'colonial' economic relationship which the revolution prided itself on having extirpated. On a more practical level the 'imperialists' could hardly be expected to lend capital to a state one of whose first acts had been to repudiate the foreign debts of its imperial predecessor, so external assistance, if forthcoming at all, would have to be paid for on the nail; and foreign exchange was, and was bound to remain, scarce. The combined force of these obstacles did not in the end suffice to prevent strictly limited and transitory recourse to the foreigner, and 'concessions', incongruously granted by Stalin to foreign firms, were the means of creating a number of plants deemed to be indispensable if the planned development of the economy was to be got off the ground. Thereafter the principle of self-reliance reasserted itself. Concessions were not repeated, but a policy of selective importation continued throughout Stalin's era. Essential imports were planned and goods set aside for export in sufficient quantities to pay for them; but the quantity was minimal, foreign trade claiming no more than one or two per cent of the national income. This pattern was substantially unaffected by the early consequences of the formation, in 1948, of Comecon (the council for mutual economic aid). The Soviet Union's trade with Comecon countries increased fourteen fold (from a rather low base line) in the first eighteen years of the council's existence but, consisting as it did of transfers of goods to which a value in inconvertible roubles was for accounting purposes attributed, it signified, initially at least, not so much a departure by the Soviet Union from self-sufficiency as an enlargement of the area in which self-sufficiency was the guiding principle.

Stalin's five-year plans made possible a concentration of resources, human and material, on the realization of economic goals on a scale never before attempted. The process was not an agreeable one for the common man. The plan set the level of accumulation necessary to cover expenditure on industrial development and social consumption (ranging from education and health to defence), the share of personal consumption being determined by what was left after these prior claims had been satisfied. Its success was due in large measure to the fact that the economic objectives set by the planners were relatively few and were pursued single-mindedly, without much regard for excellence. It was sharply biased in favour of industrialization. The task, as Stalin saw it, was to convert an agrarian into an industrial country; resources were not to be squandered on a sector that was already in being. Soviet agriculture, during Stalin's years in power, suffered purposive neglect, for which the economy was to pay dearly later on. Industrialization could not have been pursued at Stalin's pace without direction of labour, rationing and the widespread use of terror. Stalin's death and the necessary relaxation of pressures that followed it created a new environment in which the old methods would not work. Besides, size and ramification had brought complexity and directive planning, if it were to continue, called for a measure of sophistication that Stalin's techniques lacked.

Lenin had taught that socialism was immeasurably superior to all other forms of social organization, not merely when judged by human and ethical standards but also in its capacity to create material prosperity for those who lived under it. Khrushchev was realist enough to recognize that this claim was totally unsubstantiated by socialism's performance in the first thirty years of its stewardship, but optimist enough to tell the world that, now that the groundwork had been done, and the industrial base created, the Soviet Union would steadily catch up with the United States and the rest of the 'imperialists' and would, within a period of years which he was rash enough to define, overtake them. His specific targets were, by and large, realized. The Soviet Union became, in due course, the world's largest producer of steel and crude oil. But meanwhile the capitalist countries had escaped his notice in carrying out a second industrial revolution, applying to production the fruits of scientific research. The Soviet Union had spent hugely on science. But though very important results had been achieved in some, mainly defence-related, fields, the spin-off from scientific research, that is the development of its manufacturing applications by the civil economy, was negligible. The secrecy in which scientific research was shrouded had a good deal to do with this, but so also had the rigidity of the planned economy, noted in Chapter 3, and its built-in resistance to innovation. In the West, by contrast, new products, new processes and new techniques of management had been developed which left the Soviet Union, despite its successes, trailing far behind the capitalist economies; and the gap between the two, so far from narrowing, was widening from year to year. This was happening at a time when, as Khrushchev saw, the consumer needed to be brought in from the cold, and agriculture, whose contribution to consumption was indispensable, needed to be rescued from the neglect of the Stalin years.

Krushchev had picked up several bright ideas from his travels in capitalist countries, which led to a spate of imports in the early 1960s. Synthetic fibres struck him as a quick way of doing something for the consumer, and artificial fertilizers as a means of boosting food production. The Soviet Union could provide the feedstock for both and a sheaf of contracts were placed with Western engineering firms for turnkey projects. The contract with Fiat for erecting the Togliatti plant for mass production of passenger cars was signed after Khrushchev's fall. His main attention was, however, focused on agriculture (where instant remedies – the development of virgin lands, and the mandatory production of maize for fodder – were applied) and on economic reform. The economy had been equipped by Stalin to do some very big things, but it did not do them as well as it could and would not do so unless, somehow, the energies of the manager and the skilled worker could be released. Stalin had tried the expedient of paying them more, but they had generally been content to do no more than what they were told, and pocket their bonuses. The bureaucratic structure that directive planning had created had become an obstacle. But how to change it?

Ideology and politics both stood in the way. Tito had done the trick by scrapping directive planning, falling back on an increasingly insubstantial indicative plan and leaving demand and the forces of the market to determine, within very broad limits, product, quantity and price. Khrushchev could hardly follow him. To do so would mean discarding the power to determine what was good for the Soviet people and the means of ensuring that it was produced. It would mean replacing the labour theory of value, one of the pillars on which the whole system rested, by a subjective standard, random in its effects and neutral in terms of social values. No less seriously, if more concretely, it would crack, if it did not actually break, one of the party's most important levers of control over the course taken by Soviet society. The market option was not a starter and Khrushchev fell back on tinkering with the machine as he had inherited it. Over-centralization was an obvious vice. Too many jacks-in-office were sitting and polishing their trouserseats in Moscow while they devised more and more constraints on the initiative of the industrial manager.

Khrushchev, never one for half measures, abolished at one month's notice, in 1957, the central industrial ministries in Moscow (defence production and a handful of key heavy industries excepted) and concentrated the oversight of industrial production in the hands of economic councils (*sovnarkhozy*) created at provincial (*oblast'*) level. The move was intended to bring industrial production under the eye of the party's provincial committee (*obkom*) secretaries, each a small tsar in his own domain, who were reckoned to be able, if anyone could, to put some ginger into industry. In the event the reform succeeded merely in making confusion worse confounded. The province was too narrow a geographical base, for many large combines had sub-units spreading into several provinces and the *sovnarkhozy* were incapable of maintaining the essential flow of supplies and components between them. To keep production moving, makeshift organs of re-centralized control had to be rigged up and the bureaucratic apparatus re-expanded, reaching a size even greater than before. The *sovnarkhozy* were abolished, to the relief of all concerned, as soon as Krushchev fell from power. but the problem of stimulating the economy without rocking the ideological boat remained to confront his successors.

In 1965 Kosygin began a further round of tinkering, this time with the enterprise manager's terms of reference. If the planning framework was immutable and the superstructure had to stay, the argument ran, the manager could at least be nudged into improved performance by linking his remuneration and that of his staff to required levels of profit and sales, by making enterprises pay a charge on the capital which the state made available and by providing him with modest funds, freely disposable, for incentive payments. The requirements were generally met, but the fire still refused to light. It could probably have been got to burn merrily if the reform had gone a bit further in freeing the manager to follow his commercial judgment – for instance, in procuring the plant and materials that he reckoned he could use profitably, and in adopting a rational pricing policy. But such freedom was unthinkable. So attention shifted once more, this time to the methodology of planning.

Groups were despatched to inspect Western management training institutions; the techniques used by the capitalists for maximizing profit could surely be mastered and adapted to socialism's more edifying goals. The tardy advent of the computer opened up new vistas of scientific regulation of the economy, permitting the compilation of input–output matrices on a gigantic scale and the rapid construction of, and comparison of, alternative models. Hitherto, with the growing complexity of the economy, planning had seemed to be a losing battle. Some had no doubt cherished the hope that the attempt would sooner or later be abandoned in favour of a reversion, at whatever ideological cost, in market socialism. For any such rational defeatists, computerization spelt hope deferred. Science had come to the rescue of the party and mathematical economists were everywhere in demand. Their methods offered at least the theoretical possibility of an escape from stagnation without sacrifice of social objectives.

But it might take years to establish whether the possible was also practicable, and meanwhile the economy would have to muddle along as it was, overweight, overmanned, wasteful of resources and increasingly lagging behind its imperialist competitors. Besides, population growth had flattened out in the European parts of the country presaging labour shortage to come; rates of economic growth, though respectable by the standards of more developed countries, were beginning to flag, and the productivity of labour and the return on capital had turned downward. It was an unsatisfactory state of affairs when viewed against the claims of Soviet spokesmen about the shift of the 'correlation of forces', economic and other, in socialism's favour. And it augured ill for the safe resolution of the socio-political problems that the party would have, before long, to face at home – the problems of consumer expectation and the emergence of a new generation that had known neither Stalin nor the war.

A new expedient was badly needed. The party, after due deliberation, decided to go for long-term economic and technological co-operation with the 'class enemy'. The decision was announced, amid general acclamation, at the twenty-fourth congress in 1971, becoming an important component in Brezhnev's 'programme of peace'. By so deciding, the party turned aside from the course of autarky and self-reliance by which it had steered, with minor and temporary aberrations, for forty years. It was an admission of defeat, far-reaching in its implications, but an infinitely lesser evil than the sacrifice of the planned economy, with all that that would entail for the goals of socialism and the supremacy of the party.

Considerations of technology played a large part both in prompting this change of course and in its implementation. Preoccupation with the Soviet Union's technological lag and with the scientific-technical revolution in the West dated back at least to Khrushchev's day, and two precautionary steps had then been taken. In 1962 a Soviet agency (*Litsensintorg*) had been established to buy foreign know-how and industrial licences and, hopefully, to license a reverse flow of Soviet technology to foreign firms. In 1965 the Soviet government, having till then unashamedly pirated any foreign process that aroused its interest, acceded to the International Convention on the Protection of Industrial Property. Thus equipped, the Soviet Union was ready, when the moment came, to negotiate transfers of foreign technology.

Transfer of technology means making use of other people's

experience, as an alternative to finding things out the hard way, making one's own mistakes. It is concerned with innovation, that is with making new products and with better − cheaper, quicker and more efficient − ways of making products already known. It saves the beginner the delay, uncertainty and expense involved in undertaking his own research, development, design and testing, providing him, ready made, with the results of the old hand's experience. A crude and chancy form of technology transfer consists simply in getting hold of someone else's innovation, discovering by inspection how it works and attempting to copy it. But the more normal and surer course is to proceed by negotiating an agreement with the innovator who, in exchange for a fee (for he will want to recover some of what he has spent in developing the innovation), may be prepared to assist the newcomer in a variety of ways. Forms of technology transfer vary greatly, including the mere handing over of know-how, the licensing of manufacture and marketing of a product, and the delivery by the innovator of a complete plant or plants. Depending on the nature of the arrangement, the innovator may additionally undertake to provide training in the use of the equipment or assistance in its erection and maintenance. Most technology worth having is, in the West at least, in private hands, and its transfer presupposes that the innovator is a willing seller. But, not being also a philanthropist, he will not necessarily transfer his very latest innovations, and will be keen to satisfy himself, by restrictive covenants, that the recipient does not rapidly emerge as a competitor in other markets.

The Russians, when they decided to go for foreign technology, were reasonably well acquainted with these procedures. They had indeed long been on the look-out for foreign know-how and possessed, in the State Committee for Science and Technology, a talent-scout whose job it was to nose out and evaluate foreign innovations, gutting the foreign scientific and technical press, using industrial espionage where practicable, and buying odd copies of a product for dissection and replication when all else failed. The State Committee's covert operations were in part a normal Leninist use of available methods to reach the goal, but in part also a response to the embargo placed by the West in the early cold-war years, on the export to communist countries of goods, including technology, reckoned on a rather broad definition to be of strategic importance.

Once the Soviet Union had set its new course the conjuncture of the early 1970s was highly favourable to a rapid follow-up. *Détente* was in the air. Political obstacles looked increasingly surmountable. Western economies, after twenty years' uninterrupted prosperity, showed signs of faltering and the prospect of Soviet orders was attractive. The Soviet government, besieged by suitors, set out methodically to examine what each had to offer. By the end of 1974 it had negotiated a sheaf of co-operation agreements with each of its principal potential partner-governments, defining the possibilities of scientific, technological, economic and commercial dealings with them. The agreements, in themselves, were little more than symbolic, merely conferring official blessing on, and providing a framework for, such bargains as Western firms might strike with Soviet trading corporations; for governments had neither goods nor know-how to sell. But agreements were reckoned to facilitate access through the maze of Soviet bureaucracy, and the mixed commissions established under them were used to good purpose by several countries.

Western industry had far more to offer than the Soviet Union could afford to buy. Not surprisingly a great deal more business was proposed and discussed than was ever actually concluded. The problem for the Russians was one of priorities. Purchases were made on a strict calculation of utility in the modernization of Soviet industry and of the need to open up bottlenecks. Many, perhaps most, transactions have involved a combination of know-how and hardware, but there is no separate record, either in Soviet statistics or in those of partner countries, of the value of the know-how element. Soviet figures of imports from developed capitalist countries show a sharp rise (in billions of roubles – one rouble = 1.30 US dollars) from 2.5 in 1970 to 3.4 in 1972, 6.1 in 1974 and 10.8 in 1976. The fields covered are extremely diverse, including chemicals and petro-chemicals, ships, transport, mining, food processing, computers, photo-copying, aerospace and steel-making, to name only a few examples. In most fields there is a wide spread, running from components to complete plants, with or without licences for local manufacture. A characteristic of many transactions is their long-term character, the Soviet Union having often entered into commitments running for a decade or more and occasionally running into the twenty-first century. Frequently, agreements have provided for technical help in erection and operation of the plant supplied, and today small groups of Frenchmen, Americans, British and Germans are to be found living on construction sites or in industrial complexes in unexpected corners of the Soviet Union. Many Western exporters and banks now maintain offices in Moscow, and the Soviet trading apparatus is learning, after a slow start, to cope with these hitherto rare visitors. The size of the individual transactions varies greatly. In the first years, multi-billion dollar figures were frequently bandied about, as in the case of Dr Hammer's proposals, since much reduced in scope, for a massive deal in gas and fertilizer plant. However, a contract of comparable size with Ruhr interests, for technology and equipment for direct reduction of iron ore from the Kursk basin, was successfully concluded, involving commitments covering thirty years ahead. The general run of contracts have been of less spectacular size and, in the case of the huge Kama River truck plant, the high-technology business was split into blocks and divided between several Western suppliers.

Imports on this scale could not be paid for out of the receipts from Soviet trade with developed capitalist countries, still running at no more than about 3 per cent of total national product and still, despite the growth of Soviet manufacturing industry, consisting mainly of primary products. Payment was not just a short-term problem, since high-technology imports were likely to continue over a period of years, perhaps of decades. The long-term solution – a substantial increase in exports to the convertible-currency area – would take time. The modernization of the Soviet economy at which the new policy aimed should help in the longer run, as also would the removal of continuing discrimination against Soviet goods. In the meantime, despite sales of gold, of which the Soviet Union is a major producer (they amounted to an estimated total of four-and-a-half billion dollars in 1971–6), the Soviet deficit on current account has continued to increase. Deferred payment helps by spreading the repayment burden over a term of years and the Soviet government has been skilful in promoting competition between its partners in providing government-guaranteed commercial credit on concessional terms. With notable exceptions – the FRG (which has refused to go below normal commercial interest rates) and the United States (which was caught by the Jackson amendment) – the Soviet Union's main suppliers have been ready to comply. The Russians have been less successful in concluding so-called 'compensation' deals, intended to eliminate any transfer whatever of foreign exchange, payment for the supply of industrial plant being made by deliveries of its product. This technique lends itself well enough to resource-development projects where the payment comes in raw materials which the exporting country would have to import anyhow. But it has no attraction – indeed it is tantamount to importing unemployment – if the exporter is expected to take payment in a manufactured product of which it already has all that it needs.

Continuing deficits have therefore had to be financed by external borrowing. There has been no shortage of lenders. The Soviet Union's credit rating is excellent, and Western banking representatives are increasingly thick on the ground in Moscow, seeking opportunities to lend convertible currencies, chiefly eurodollars, to the Soviet Foreign Trade Bank and the two Comecon banks. In the latter case this is mainly for onward lending to Eastern European countries, where the policy of modernization through technology imports has gone as far as, and in some cases further than, in the Soviet Union itself. Recent estimates put the Soviet Union's cumulative deficit, covering the years 1972–6, in convertible currencies at over eleven billion dollars, and that of the Comecon countries as a whole (including the Soviet Union) at over forty billion. On present trends both figures might be expected to double by 1980. Western bankers have shown no sign of disquiet at the growth of Soviet indebtedness. The Soviet Union's past record is one of absolute punctuality in meeting its obligations. If any crisis should now arise, the USSR, as a planned economy accustomed to supplying its own needs, should have no technical difficulty in shifting into hard-currency-earning exports resources which had been destined for domestic use. True, banking convention, fortified in some countries by legislative provisions, places limits on how large a part of the lender's assets may be lent to a single borrower, and normally discourages further lending when his accumulated indebtedness exceeds a given percentage of his annual export earnings. As and when these amber lights begin to flash, the Soviet Union's creditors and their govern-ments will have to consider where they go from there, and on what conditions.

It must, however, be added that, in the Soviet case at least, the accumulated deficit was not solely the result of increased imports of high-technology industrial equipment. The other factor was the harvest failures of 1972 and 1975. Soviet agriculture, as noted earlier in this chapter, suffered total neglect for thirty years, but since Khrushchev's time heavy investment had gone into irrigation, mechanization, fertilizers and improved seeds. Materially, agriculture was much better provided for but its organizational weaknesses – Stalin's pattern of state and collective farms remained substantially unchanged – and its vulnerability to weather, persisted. Losses from drought in 1963 had forced the Soviet Union to buy abroad and put one of the final nails into Khrushchev's coffin. In 1972 the weather struck again, reducing grain production to a level eighteen million tons below the 1970 crop. To make good this shortfall Soviet buyers without warning entered the world market and in no time the price of wheat and maize had rocketed. Eventually the US government rescued the Russians and the market by supplying cheap grain from its stored surplus. In 1975 drought, rain and early frost, in different areas, produced disaster on a scale without precedent. The harvest fell sixty-five million tons short of the planned target and eighty million tons short of the bumper crop of the preceding year. The prospect of a further Soviet foray on the world market, this time in search of even larger quantities, was too much. The United States prohibited American sellers from dealing and informed the Soviet government that it could not be permitted to use the market as a convenience, neglecting it most of the time, resorting to it only in disaster conditions and causing great disruption and price instability in the process. The negotiations that followed led to an agreement binding the Soviet Union to buy, on commercial terms, a basic quantity of six million tons of wheat and maize in each of the succeeding six years. When American supplies were plentiful the Russians were free to buy an additional two million tons as a matter of course, and more still by special arrangement. In a year when the US government was itself short of grain it retained the right to sell less than the basic six million tons. The agreement established the practice of recurrent consultation between the two signatories, thus bringing a relationship which had become an international nuisance into an orderly way of going.

If this chapter seems to have strayed from one subject to another – from autarky and the plan mentality to economic reform, and from that to technology transfer, Soviet external indebtedness and the vicissitudes of Soviet agriculture – its meandering course has not been accidental. The thread that connects the highly variegated elements in the story is the slow and reluctant recognition that the objectives which Soviet society had set itself were not being achieved, and that they could not be achieved by the old recipes of self-sufficiency and self-reliance. Going it alone would not deliver the goods. The co-operation of others had become indispensable, and the price of co-operation was a measure of interdependence. The Soviet Union did not seek interdependence, indeed the preconceptions with which its founders set out forcibly discouraged them from having any truck with the 'class enemy'. Nor was it sought by the United States or other Western countries who lacked both the inclination to promote it and the power to force it upon the Russians. The beginnings of interdependence which have made their appearance in the last decade are the product of circumstances, willed by neither side, which have brought the two together in practical ways. Is interdependence the right word? Would it be more exact to say that the manifest irrationality of the Soviet system has obliged those who run it to acquiesce in a degree of dependence on the capitalist West? That is a fair enough description of one side of the relationship, but it is not exhaustive. If the Soviet Union has discovered that it needs the West, so also have Western countries discovered that a world run without regard for the Soviet Union's needs and interests carries disadvantages for themselves. By trading know-how and advanced machinery with the Russians, or lending them money, the West is not performing an unrequited act of grace. Western bankers lend money to Soviet banks (instead of putting all their funds elsewhere) because it can earn comparable interest in the Soviet Union and the risks of default are minimal. If Western manufacturers, who are free to choose between alternative projects, opt to enter the Soviet market, they do so basing their judgment on criteria of opportunity and profitability – because, in a given case, the Soviet market offers them a better return, enabling them to recover past outlays on research and development and to finance further such outlays in the future. Western governments who, unlike the Soviet leadership, periodically need to get themselves re-elected, have a solid interest in maintaining the level of domestic employment, and Soviet orders come in very handy, particularly in times of recession. By the same token, the US–Soviet grain agreement did not have the primary aim of relieving Soviet need, though it certainly had that effect as well. It was undertaken because the orderly functioning of the world market in grain could not be left at the mercy of recurrent but unpredictable Soviet plunges into the pool. So let us admit that the dependence is not one-way.

Interdependence is not a particularly novel thought, reflecting, as it does, the truism that we all live in one shared world. The novelty is that the Soviet leadership, having ploughed its own furrow for over fifty years, has begun to accept its implications. The concluding passage of Chapter 5 floated an hypothesis which needed to be tested against external evidence. The hypothesis was that, appearances to the contrary notwithstanding, Brezhnev's 'programme of peace' might have been adopted not as offering an alternative and less perilous route to the victory of socialism, but actually as an objective necessity dictated by the real (as opposed to ideological) interests of the Soviet Union. That hypothesis was to stand or fall by whether such real interests were found to exist. The present chapter has identified one such interest: the fact, desired or undesired, of interdependence with the West.

But the mere fact that the Soviet leadership has opted for a degree of interdependence with the West does not, of itself, imply that interdependence with the Soviet Union is something that the West should wish to encourage. There are, in fact, at least two schools of thought which regard it as a thoroughly bad thing. There are, first, those who criticize interdependence on what are basically protectionist grounds. They object that Western bankers, by putting capital at the disposal of the Soviet economy, are diverting abroad resources that could better be used to strengthen the economies of the West; that Western manufacturers, by exporting know-how and machinery, are raising up Soviet industries to compete against themselves, both in the Soviet domestic market and in third-world markets, thereby promoting recession and unemployment at home; and that Western governments, by allowing these things to happen, and indeed encouraging such exports by providing credit facilities, are acting against the interests of their own economies. These are arguments which, if they were true, would apply not merely to the case of the Soviet Union but to exports of capital, know-how and machinery regardless of destination. It need merely be noted that they run counter to the basic assumptions on which the multilateral system of international trade works, namely that the exporter, applying his own criteria, makes his own choice as between domestic and foreign projects; and that the state should be chary of intervening. If the exporter concludes, as he often does, that profitability, lower costs, maintenance of employment and the funding of research and development will be better served by involving the foreigner in co-operative arrangements – instead of insisting on his buying the finished product or doing without – the state, in the absence of some factor of extraordinary national importance, should let him get on with it.

The second line of criticism fastens on this last point – national, and particularly strategic, interest. Since 1947 the West, originally in compliance with conditions attached to Marshall Aid and later by common consent, has operated a multilateral system of controls on 'strategic' exports to the Soviet Union and Eastern Europe. A body known as COCOM (the co-ordinating committee of a consultative group of Western governments) has placed an embargo, monitored by the mutual vigilance of its members, on the export to the East of goods reckoned to be of strategic importance. COCOM's criteria have narrowed with time. In the early cold-war years it regarded as 'strategic' almost any goods that might contribute to the growth and modernization of the Soviet economy. Nowadays, COCOM is still in business but its embargo list has shrunk to include only items with a more or less direct bearing on the expansion of Soviet military power. Nevertheless, in the changed circumstances of today the old assumptions of COCOM continue to crop up in various forms. Credit sales of machinery to the Soviet Union are assailed on the ground that they free Soviet resources which may be channelled into military production. They could indeed have this effect, though who can say for sure that the resources liberated might not find their way into food processing or hospitals? In any case the containment of military expansion is better dealt with directly by negotiating reciprocal reductions in armaments.

A more substantial critique invokes the concept of 'market power', a notion which will be familiar to the reader from experience (quite unrelated to the Soviet Union) of successive Arab embargoes on oil shipments and OPEC's fourfold increase in the price of crude oil after 1973. 'Market power' derives from the existence of relatively few sellers (or buyers) for a given commodity and raises the question of critical dependence upon a single market or source of supply. Applied to the interdependence of the economies of Western countries and of the Soviet Union, it prompts Western governments to consider whether, already or at some future date, growing involvement may not make them vulnerable to Soviet arm-twisting, whether by withholding supplies, cessation of purchases, dumping, price-extortion or otherwise. At various times in their history the Russians have shown themselves ready to use any of these tactics, as Yugoslavs, Finns, Chinese and Albanians can testify. Who can be sure they would not try to do so again?

The existence of Comecon, and the Soviet Union's continuing ability to make its allies dance to its tune, provides another dimension of pressure. On a less ambitious scale, the existence of competing Western suppliers enables the Russians to favour one partner and to penalize another for reasons which have little or nothing to do with economic co-operation. Western governments would be foolish to lose sight of these possibilities, but they need not take counsel of their fears. Large as the Soviet economy is, its share of international trade, even today, is tiny, as also is its share of the world market in the main products that it exports. A contest in 'market power', if the Soviet Union were to seek it, would mean confrontation with the United States and the European Economic Community, each formidable individually and infinitely more so in co-operation with one another.

Western economies have prospered over the years by the freest possible access to raw materials and the freest possible exchange in manufactured products. By these means stable economic relationships have grown up which have benefited all participants in international trade. If the Soviet Union now seeks to share these advantages those taking part will be wise, without forsaking prudence, to give it a fair wind.

Prudence imposes limits of the speed and scope of advance. International commerce is not a form of philanthropy. Soviet readiness for economic co-operation is the product of a Western lead in technology which needs to be maintained. Acceptable co-operative arrangements need to bring advantages to the Western partner going beyond the proceeds of sale. One such advantage is the stability that flows from long-term commitments; and stability in economic relations can contribute in very concrete ways to a wider relaxation of tension. But until *détente* has progressed a good deal further, close attention will have to be paid to the size of transactions and the risks of critical dependence.

Those who have followed the ideological background set out in earlier chapers may take additional comfort from Soviet moves towards a policy of economic interdependence. For it is not rational to make long-term arrangements to interdepend with partners whose early extinction is a foregone conclusion. Without breathing a word about it, the Soviet leadership has revised the myth of the impending crash of capitalism.

9

Guns or Butter

The socialist transformation of Russia was carried out on the promise, still unfulfilled, of abundance to come. Things are of course much better than they were and continue gradually to improve. But not fast enough. There are still people in the Soviet Union who are poor, and those who are better off increasingly take what is for granted and ask for more. The failure of abundance to materialize after sixty years of socialist construction has begun to pose a socio-political problem for the Party and its leadership. Its symptoms do not yet affect more than the vitality of the system; but, if left untreated, it could in time undermine the system's apparent stability. The party has seen the trouble coming and reckons that *détente* could help internally in freeing resources which will be required for dealing with it. This chapter examines the nature of the problem and its relevance to the main theme of the book.

At the time of the Bolshevik take-over there were about 160 million people in Russia, of whom 85 per cent lived on the land. Today, the population of the Soviet Union exceeds 255 million and nearly two-thirds (61 per cent in 1976) live in towns. The flow from the villages into the towns has been continuous and steady. Town-dwellers first became the majority element of the population around 1960. The shift was the planned consequence of industrialization, and would, no doubt, have been still greater but for strict controls over change of residence. The natural increase (births less deaths) slumped during the terror and the war and rose sharply in the post-war years, but has tapered off since

1965 and now stands at 0.9 per cent for the country as a whole. But rates vary sharply as between developed and less-developed regions – in the three Slav republics (RSFSR, Ukraine and Belorussia) with 0.64, 0.57 and 0.79 per cent respectively, the rate is less than a quarter of that in central Asia, where Tadjikistan leads the field with 2.95 per cent. In the developed regions the one-child family is normal and more than two children a rarity. This is the consequence not of state planning – in principle the state would like more babies – but of family planning, itself a response to the urban environment of small flats, working mothers and rising material aspirations. Nevertheless, for the present, the Soviet Union is a country of young people: 51 per cent of the population is under thirty, 36 per cent under twenty and 16 per cent under ten. The under-thirties missed two of the great formative experiences of their grandparents and parents, the revolution and the great patriotic (or, as we would say, Second World) War. The oldest of them were infants when Stalin died and teenagers under Khrushchev. None of them has any recollection of Stalin's terror. Their consciousness of the world around them took shape in conditions of relative relaxation, free both of acute privation and of the fear of sudden death.

Inheriting a largely illiterate country, the party has been tireless in educating the young. It believes in education, because its ideology teaches that man is perfectible and because education was necessary for development. It is a massive undertaking. In the academic year 1974–5 $4^3/_4$ million undergraduates and graduate students were attending 842 universities and other institutions of higher learning. Those finishing university courses at the end of the preceding academic year numbered nearly one million. A further $4^1/_4$ million were, in the same year, receiving 'specialized secondary' (i.e. vocational) education and 49 million pupils were attending ordinary ten-year schools (bracketing primary and secondary education as defined in Britain) graduating a class of nearly $5^1/_2$ million school-leavers in 1974. The emphasis of higher education is heavily on applied science, engineering and technology, which account for more than half the output from universities and institutes, and on teacher-training and economics. Law and the humanities bring up the rear. The first task of the educator is to produce specialists to man the economy and staff the bureaucracy, and intake and output are planned accordingly. But the impact of learning

on enquiring minds is imponderable; in decanting annually into society
so many young people who have been taught, with whatever safeguards,
to think, the party has also complicated its own task of ruling.

The Soviet Union prides itself on having banished unemployemnt.
Stalin's constitution (only superseded in 1977) laid down that 'he who
does not work shall not eat', and those without jobs are liable to
prosecution for 'parasitism'. In fact, the need to eat has generally
sufficed to prevent idleness, and the insensitivity of the growing
economy to cost factors has normally ensured that all comers were fitted
in somewhere. As late as 1952 the minimum monthly wage stood at a
beggarly 22 roubles, since when it was raised in successive steps to 70
roubles in 1972. Soviet statistics show the average monthly rates of
wages and salaries in the entire economy as having risen by 50 per cent
(from 96 to 146 roubles) between 1966 and 1975. In addition to wages
the worker also receives social benefits in kind and in cash (education,
medical service, pensions, student grants) which the state quantified in
1975 at an average of a further 52 roubles per worker. No figures of
actual distribution of income are published, but the average rate just
quoted includes salaries as well as wages and masks differentials as
between branches of industry and (though the higher minimum wage
has narrowed these) within branches. The collective farmer, who had to
exist on a bare pittance in Stalin's time, supplemented by what he could
grow privately, has about doubled his money income since 1955. The
proportion of the population living in actual poverty (that is on *per
capita* incomes falling below the minimum subsistence budget) has been
reduced since the late 1950s but even today may include one family in
every four or five, particularly where there are many children (as in
central Asia) or old relatives to be kept. Means-tested social benefits are
now being used to raise minimum standards, with the aim of eventually
eliminating acute need. But, the really poor apart, the Soviet worker is
now substantially better off and, at the upper end of the ladder, has
begun, in money terms, to enjoy modest affluence. The working wife is
a common feature of Soviet life and where she and her husband are
earning well, and there are no, or few, children, there is money to
spare.

Housing has contributed greatly to the improvement of urban
conditions since the Second World War. In Stalin's time, those who
were brought in from the villages to work in the towns were piled into

existing housing stock, as many as six or seven families sharing a 'communal' flat, and there was no money, manpower or materials for repairs and maintenance. Rents were of course minimal, being like other basic necessities subsidized, but the congestion, squalor and lack of privacy were appalling. War devastation made things worse, but the inflow to the cities continued. The tide began to turn with the fifth (1951–6) five-year plan, and since 1956 the Soviet Union has built upwards of $2^1/_4$ million flats each year, an impressive achievement by any standards. Many of the old dwellings have been demolished and others, perhaps for the first time since the revolution, have undergone major repairs and modernization. The 'communal flat' is not yet extinct, but its days are numbered. Soviet newly-weds, when they get accommodation (shortage still obliges many to live for a time with parents or in-laws), are likely to find themselves housed in new communities of high-rise blocks some way from the centre of the city but connected to it by underground and surface transport. Space in the new blocks is, by Western standards, tight – the childless couple will get one room, plus diminutive kitchen and bathroom, and a flat with two or occasionally three rooms is as much as a larger family could hope for. The finish is often poor, as workmanship suffers in the rush to get one block finished and move on to the next. Khrushchev, who set the pace for the great housing drive, prudently kept blocks down to five storeys, being the maximum height to which tenants could reasonably be expected to climb on foot. His successors, keen to make the best use of land and pre-fabrication techniques, have built up to twelve storeys, and recently higher still, necessitating the installation of lifts, whose temperamental performance often brings much trouble and frustration to the users. Tenants cannot complain that they are not getting value for money, for rents continue to be subsidized, rarely claiming more than 10 to 15 per cent of the monthly pay-packet, with heating and light thrown in. But many would be prepared to pay quite a lot more for a little more space. A small minority from among the better off manage to do so by joining with colleagues from their place of work in co-operative construction projects and building flats, on mortgage, which eventually become their own property.

    The construction industry will take many years longer to complete the task of re-housing the Soviet population (and by that time the flat-dweller will no doubt be demanding more space and better quality), but it has tried, and goes on trying, to solve the problem on a mass scale.

The record of Soviet consumer goods industries, including the food industry and the sectors of agriculture on which it relies, is a good deal less satisfactory. The reasons are structural and historical: the consumer-goods sector suffers from the ailments that afflict all manufacturing under Soviet directive planning, but also from others that are specific to itself. All, to quote Brezhnev's report to the twenty-fifth congress, suffer in greater or lesser degree from 'loss of working time, idling, variable rhythm of work and poor labour discipline and technological discipline'; which means, translated into ordinary language, short-time working while waiting for supplies to turn up, feverish spurts to meet the end-of-month plan deadline, absenteeism, corner-cutting and evasion of quality control. Despite all efforts to refine plan targets, the old traditional yardstick of gross ouptut retains much of its strength, because of the difficulty of enforcing other indicators. Having learnt by bitter experience that outside suppliers will let it down, the manufacturing enterprise often sacrifices the benefits of specialization to the convenience of getting as much as possible under its own hand. It accumulates and hoards reserves of material and labour. It resists innovation, preferring a steady return from making the obsolete product to the uncertain gains that change might bring. These are all aspects of the plan mentality, distortions which flow directly from the mode of operation of Soviet planning.

Group B, broadly speaking that part of the economy – including the food industry – which caters for the consumer, has its own additional troubles. Traditionally, it has always been at the end of the queue for resources, taking its place behind the priority claimants – defence production and the development of the heavy industrial base – and having to content itself with what was left over when their demands had been satisfied. Although the leadership now takes a different view of priorities, the attitudes of the past live on. To quote Brezhnev again, Group B industries are treated as 'something secondary and ancillary'. Being held of little account, they have consistently come off worst. Enterprises engaged on big contracts for powerful clients – the armed forces or important state agencies – have their own means of getting out of the muddles and hold-ups that are endemic in the system. When they run out of supplies or need extra labour they invoke the influence and protection of the customer, and old-boy contacts on the local party network ensure that their needs are met, by robbing someone else. The victim of the robbery is all too often the nearest 'group B' enterprise, which wakes up one morning to find that the resources allocated to it by the planners, and on which it had counted to fulfil its own production plan, have been diverted to purposes of supposedly higher priority. Group B, though its customers are numbered in millions, has suffered from having no lobby, no important protectors and no political clout.

Today the most basic foodstuffs, bread and flour, potatoes, some vegetables, and oil, sugar and milk, are generally available at prices which, like those of all necessities, are kept low and stable. Quite a wide range of less homely (and dearer) food is produced, but in insufficient quantity, and distribution varies enormously from one place to another and from time to time in the same place. Big cities do better than small towns and Moscow and Leningrad better than any. On a good day the Muscovite shopper, if he has a full purse, may find quite a wide choice, running from hams and poultry to canned goods and instant coffee. But supplies come and go. There is a chronic overall shortage of meat which, outside the main cities, may disappear from the shops for weeks on end. Peasant markets (which sell the produce of small plots which most collective farm workers cultivate privately) are an important subsidiary source of food but prices, fixed by supply and demand, are high. Shopping is generally slow and laborious, especially on a cold night after a day's work.

The faults are the same, but more obvious, when it comes to clothing and household goods, furnishing materials and textiles. Articles of mass consumption, from pots and pans to shirts and underclothes, are manufactured in ample quantity, but distribution is variable, quality uncertain and design and styling often poor. The product that was acceptable in the days of greater austerity is now all too often recognized by the shopper as ugly or obsolete and left unbought. Meanwhile, personal incomes have gone up, under the last two five-year plans; Russians are prepared to pay quite heavily for occasional luxuries, but in order to find something a little out of the ordinary to eat, to wear or to make the home attractive the (usually working) housewife will have to shop around, spending much time in queues. The longest queues are often for East German, Polish or Czechoslovak products, which are better made and better looking. The shopper has become increasingly choosy and is prepared to pay for quality. His basic expenses – rent, light and heat, telephone, public transport and basic foodstuffs – are very low, his home is small (so he is more interested in the quality than in quantity) and so a relatively high proportion of his income is available for food, clothes and consumer goods.

Industry has been turning out consumer durables for twenty years or more. Some products – watches and television sets (black and white – colour sets exist but are still scarce and dear), and transistor radios – are within reach of most people and are not hard to find. The labour-saving household appliances – washing machines, vacuum cleaners, refrigerators – would find a ready market if reliable models could be mass-produced cheaply. At present, only the better-off can afford them, but limited availability (and doubts about performance) are probably stronger constraints than price. The Soviet citizen is a considerable saver and generally has some cash put by; deposits in the state savings bank have doubled since 1970 reaching a level not far short of 100 billion roubles. They earn a modest 2.5 per cent interest, but the return is acceptable given the relative absence of inflation (prices of most consumer goods have not changed for years, though rising import costs are beginning to be felt and 'new' models, or variants of old products, tend to cost more). Savings would certainly be smaller if there were more on sale that the citizen wanted to buy.

Very few can afford to buy a car, and until recently car-ownership was not a serious option for the ordinary mortal. Soviet-made passenger cars went to chauffeur-driven bosses and senior bureaucrats, civil and military, or were used as taxis. But from the early 1970s onward the Zhiguli (the Soviet-made version of the Fiat 1100) began to come off the production lines, opening up entirely new, if still distant, horizons for the consumer. It can be bought by any who have both the cash to pay for it (the equivalent of about £5,000) and the patience to wait their turn or the contacts to enable them to jump the queue. Such people can be only a very small proportion of the population, but there are more of them than there are new cars for sale. Meanwhile a second-hand market is beginning to flourish. The Soviet Union built 1.2 million passenger cars in 1976 (a tenfold increase over 1966), of which perhaps half were Zhigulis, but the number available for sale on the open market, after the claims of export, state agencies and those with foreign currency to spend had been met, must have been much smaller. In deciding to manufacture cars for private ownership the leadership has reversed its long-standing policy of exclusive reliance on good and cheap public transport, which had much to commend it on social and environmental grounds, and have incidentally let themselves in for a big future bill for roads. By doing so they have opened up new and alluring prospects for the citizen, even though it may take him twenty years to reach the goal. They would hardly have done so had they not convinced themselves of the importance of car-ownership, as an incentive initially to the enterprising few but, in the longer run, to the working masses.

The part played by incentives in the Soviet economy has increased greatly in importance and merits closer examination. The ideological premises on which the Soviet system is based assign to the manager and to the worker roles which are in important ways a good deal more passive than those of their counterparts under capitalism. Under capitalism, the entrepreneur makes his own forecast of demand and organizes production so as to maximize profit in meeting it; and the worker bargains with him for wages, overtime and productivity bonuses. Under Soviet socialism the plan (not demand) is sovereign. The plan sets out to produce goods not because it is profitable to do so but to achieve social goals. The manager's function is not entrepreneurial but administrative. And the worker receives a wage determined not by bargaining but by the plan. (The plan also prescribes what goods shall be available for him to spend his wages on; he is not obliged to buy these goods, but the alternative is to do without them.)

Initially, it was hoped that the passive attitudes inculcated by this system could be offset by 'moral' incentives – by appeals to patriotism and ideology, organization of 'socialist competition', mass campaigns and 'actions' and the like – but these were found to appeal mainly to the committed, leaving the inert and agnostic mass fairly unmoved. Stalin, who was in a hurry to get the economy moving and growing, applied the stick (including the direction of labour) supplemented by the carrot of material incentives. There was ideological sanction for the latter in Marx's principle that, under socialism (i.e. until communism and abundance had been achieved, permitting distribution according to need), remuneration should go 'to each man according to his work'. Stalin introduced first, a wide range of wage differentials (to attract manpower into the jobs held to be of special importance) and second, a system of production bonuses to be paid both to the manager and to the workers if they fulfilled (or over-fulfilled) the plan.

In modern times Stalin's stick has fallen into disuse, though managers and workers can still be brought to justice for economic 'crimes'. Direction of labour has gone. The spread of wage differentials has been narrowed, and the carrot of bonus remains as the primary instrument of economic stimulation. Constant efforts have been made to build into the plan targets requirements more sophisticated than mere volume of production – requirements as to quality, unit cost, labour productivity, etc. – thus restoring in ideologically acceptable form some of the motivations that got excluded from the system when the entrepreneur (who minded about these things but for socially objectionable reasons) was banished. But these indicators have proved easier to formulate than to enforce. What is more serious is that, with the basic needs of the Soviet worker already satisfied, the stimulative effect of the bonus system has begun to flag and seems unlikely to pick up again until there are more things on sale that the worker would like to buy.

Around 1970, the party woke up to the fact that consumer goods production, so far from being a secondary and ancillary matter, was actually an indispensable propellant of the system of incentives on which the growth and modernization of the economy had come to depend. This thought was in Brezhnev's mind when he addressed the twenty-fourth party congress in 1971:

> Improvement in the well-being of the working people is becoming a more and more urgent requirement for our economic development itself, one of the most important pre-requisites of the rapid growth of production.

The ninth five-year plan introduced at that congress was intended to bring about just this improvement. It projected a substantial rise in personal incomes (which was realized), a record level of investment in agriculture to increase food production (the benefits of this investment, which exceeded the total funds invested in agriculture in the first fifty years after the revolution, were unfortunately swamped by the harvest failure of 1975) and a higher growth of output from group B industries than from the heavy and defence industries of group A (also not realized, perhaps owing to the continuance of old bad habits of 'robbing' group B by unofficial diversion of materials). Brezhnev was back on the same platform at the twenty-fifth congress in 1976, repeating the same message but in sharper language. The party must understand, he said, that an increase in both quantity and particularly in quality of consumer goods, including consumer durables, and the provision of services, had become a matter of immense importance, not merely economically but politically. Those who had frustrated the intentions of the ninth plan in this regard bore a heavy responsibility. Personal incomes had been increased, but the goods on which the money was to be spent had not come forward as they should. Heavy industry had not done what was asked of it in providing the machinery which was essential for the expansion of consumer goods capacity. All concerned must get it into their heads that the overall growth of the economy was being held up by the failure of group B to deliver the goods, and responsibility for this failure rested partly on the consumer industries themselves, partly on the heavy industry sector, and partly on the planners. Unless the Soviet worker found in the shops the things he wanted to buy, he would not give of his best. A comprehensive increase in the availability of food was crucial. As Brezhnev put it, 'nothing must be missing from Soviet man's dinner table'. It was no good asking him to make do with potatoes when he wanted onions or to use tomato juice for cooking oil. He should have the lot. The secretary-general's peroration merits quoting at length:

> To the 40 million people who work in the branches of industry making consumer goods, in shops, in catering establishments and in the services sector – and they include one and a half million party members and three million members of the Komsomol [the party youth organization] – I should like to say this: it is on you and the work you do that the wellbeing, and also the mood and temper of the Soviet people substantially depend. Remember this. Work better. Show more initiative. Bring your industries up to the level of the best we have. This is the charge the party lays on you. This is what the party expects of you.

Soviet man's desire for a better life had, as a matter of fact, been inspired not only by the absolute level of the satisfactions which the Soviet state offers him – indeed, as already noted, most people's standard of living had improved notably since the bad old days – but also by the comparisons he had begun to make between the quality of his life and that of others, both at home and abroad.

At home, Soviet man had become familiar with the spectacle of Soviet super-man. Privilege in the Soviet Union dates back to the early post-revolutionary decrees which gave special rations and special feeding facilities to party workers and to the armed forces. In the conditions of the time it may have seemed reasonable that those on whom so much depended should not be distracted from their work by anxieties about where the next meal was coming from. But, once established, the principle of privilege for the party – and for the military – had come to stay. The least attractive aspect of it was the preoccupation, in an environment of continuing shortages for the common man, with ensuring that the favoured few had plenty of good things to eat and drink, and at concessionary prices. Most benefits came in kind, or against token payment, but at times in earlier days party members received supplementary (and unacknowledged) cash payments. Today, privilege has been expanded and systematized into what amounts to a separate way of life for its beneficiaries. Food and drink remain the backbone of the system. They come from special shops – a separate nation-wide distribution network, closed to the ordinary citizen, and offering cheap and plentiful supplies of things either more expensive or rarely available outside. But much more has been added, clothes, housing, recreation, special medical treatment, holidays, transport, even real estate. Of course not all super-men have access to all these facilities, for the system is highly diversified. Those at the very top, that is to say the Politburo, the party secretaries and the bosses of the constituent republics, live like lords at minimal personal expense, drawing without limit on the special distribution network, migrating from spacious flats in the town to weekend *dachas* in the country, transported everywhere in chauffeur-driven limousines (for which many cities provide special traffic lanes). Below them, privileges spread downwards on a descending scale, carefully stratified, to members of the central committee and the republican central committees, of the councils of ministers at the centre and in the republics, of the party and state bureaucracies, and so on down the line. In the lower-middle levels the privilege package will normally include limited access to the closed shopping network, a place at the head of the queue for private car purchase, cheap holidays at special resorts, easy access to tickets for the opera and theatre and especially good canteen facilities.

These privileges strike a jarring note in a society whose professed principles are so explicitly humanitarian and which came into being to eradicate man's exploitation of his fellow man. There is something slightly furtive about the way in which the beneficiaries go about enjoying their good fortune. The special shops are externally indistinguishable from ordinary office premises and display no shop-sign. But the comings and goings of the fortunate few cannot be concealed and the common man knows well enough what is going on. Moreover, the recipients of privilege of one kind or another form, in the aggregate, quite a large body. Party membership (which is by co-option, so this is a matter for decision at the top) has grown from almost 7 million in 1952 to over 14 million in 1973, that is at a rate just faster than the increase in the population, but the rate has slowed down in recent years. Brezhnev claimed in 1971 that one in every eleven adults was a party member. So Soviet super-man has become rather too numerous a species to escape notice.

And privilege, in the sense of better access to better things, is not confined to the party and the state. In a secondary ramification it spreads, in part at least, to those who in the post-revolutionary generation have come to the top in the various walks of life in which they are active. These are scientists, academics, engineers, doctors, sports stars, theatre and film directors, actors and ballerinas and a lot more, including, not least, managers of big enterprises. All these people are well paid, and a minority of them – members of the Academy of Sciences for instance – very well paid indeed. Some are members of the party, but many are not. They are on terms of familiarity with the ruling class, and their sponsoring body – be it institute, enterprise, university or professional association – takes care of them. They are better housed, better dressed, better equipped than the generality of Soviet citizens. What is more, since they have achieved a degree of excellence in their own line of activity, it sometimes falls to them to go abroad to represent their country – to international conferences and professional gatherings, to give performances and recitals, to play games, to buy and sell. Foreign travel, so long a forbidden fruit, has now become the most sought-after of privileges. The Soviet Union's growing bilateral links with the outside world have created new opportunities for trips abroad, inspiring intense competition among those who consider themselves candidates. Foreign travel is no bed of roses, for security screening of all who go abroad is severe and the possibilities of putting a foot wrong are considerable. But, all else apart, the shopping is an irresistible draw and travellers come back with empty wallets and full suitcases, having spent the last kopeck that their foreign exchange allotment will allow on clothes and consumer goods.

A third and quite separate category of privileged persons consists of those whose job it is to staff, often in quite menial capacities, the apparatus of Soviet links with the world outside. The most numerous of them are seamen of the fast-growing Soviet merchant navy, whose calling keeps them in contact with foreign places and foreign goods. Others are air-crews of Soviet international air services and, at home, the employees of the tourist industry – interpreters, guides, hotel staff, travel agents and couriers. Others still are the numerous ancillary staff of Soviet missions overseas, clerks, technicians, drivers and domestic servants. The common characteristic of these people is that, because of their employment rather than any particular merit, they live to a greater or lesser extent by Western, not Soviet, standards. They too, of course, are carefully screened, indeed as a group their links with the security authorities are probably closer than most. They are not in any way Western-oriented in sentiment, and are usually intensely proud of their country. But they have a vested interest in the continuance of Soviet contacts with the West, on which their continuing enjoyment of the good things depends; and they have wives, husbands, sweethearts and cousins and friends at home, who are reminded when they see them of the deficiencies of Soviet living standards.

Reminders of these deficiencies come in much more direct ways, and not only from the West. Illustrated papers from the countries of the Warsaw Pact circulate freely in the Soviet Union. It only takes a glance at an East German fashion magazine, or at the 'homes and gardens' section of a Czechoslovak or Hungarian weekly, to realize that here are people, and from socialist countries, who are living at a totally different level of material wellbeing. Besides, travel to other socialist countries is not difficult or unduly expensive, and many Russians have seen for themselves in the course of package-trip holidays. The same message, but louder and clearer, is picked up by the television viewers in the Baltic Republics and in the north-west corner of the RSFSR, who compare the life around them with that portrayed by Finnish television; and the Finns may be safely acquitted of ideological axe-grinding. Western sound broadcasts naturally make the most of the West's claims to offer a superior quality of life, but it is doubtful whether this adds much to their appeal. People listen for two main reasons. One is that they provide news of events in the world – and indeed in the Soviet Union, for despatches from Western correspondents in Moscow are relayed back in press summaries – which never finds its way into print in the USSR. The main radio services in the West, the BBC, the Voice of America and Deutsche Welle, have done this with some success and with greatly increased impact since the Soviet authorities ceased jamming them in September 1973. Radio Free Europe and Radio Liberty are still jammed, being regarded, with a certain plausibility, as hostile and subversive.

The other reason has little or nothing to do with the political calculations and contrivings of Western governments. It is quite simply that Western broadcasts hold up a mirror to the pop culture which has captured the imagination of youth in the West and now bids fair to do the same thing in the Soviet Union. The cultural diet which the party offers to the Soviet people caters amply for their appreciation of classical music, literature, drama and painting (though much that is both new and good is excluded as decadent and pessimistic) but it leaves largely unsatisfied their not inconsiderable talent for casting aside inhibitions and enjoying themselves. So Western entertainment finds ready listeners. Original Western records are highly prized and are taped and re-taped, as also are the sound-tracks of Western broadcasts. The words and music, in time, percolate into the repertoire of the dance bands whose electronic blare deafens the diners in Soviet restaurants. Russians enjoy dancing on a night out and until recently foxtrotted decorously around in the manner of the 1950s. Adults, in the cities at least, have now begun to shed their inhibitions and, as happened in the West, to follow, a little sedately and a few years behind, in the steps of their teenage children. Along with the music have come changes in style. Teenage hair is longer, the mini-skirt has come and nearly gone, jeans, T-shirts, platform shoes and smart boots are the acme of fashion. They are hard to get, though easier for the children of the super-men or those with foreign-travelling friends. Ideological purists no doubt deplore this trend as a slavish aping of foreign ways, but it is a fair bet that before very long the gear and accoutrements of the new culture will have been added to the list which group B is required to produce. 'Soviet man' evidently wants them and, if we are to believe Brezhnev, the higher interests of socialist construction will make it advisable that his wishes should be fulfilled.

The evidence so far cited suggests that a variety of factors – urbanization, education and relative relaxation at home are the chief – have combined to expand the expectations of Soviet man. What the Soviet state has been able to do for him has aroused his appetite for more and the spectacle of plenty in other countries has further whetted that appetite. His rulers, for their part, have concluded that the best, and perhaps the only, way to move upward from the plateau to which past exertions have carried the economy is to offer what he has come to expect, in return for the effort without which the ascent cannot be resumed. Experience suggests that he will not bestir himself unless satisfied that the offer is genuine. So how are the rulers to deliver the goods? To do so, they will have to find from somewhere the resources, real and human, with which to expand consumer goods production. Theoretically, they could do so in one of two ways, or by a combination of both: they could squeeze out of the economy as at present deployed a net addition to national product – by more efficient use of plant, better management of production and less wasteful use of materials and labour; or, they could cut back some other sector of the economy and shift to consumer goods production some of the resources currently employed in it. The first alternative is plainly the more attractive, requiring as it would no sacrifice of present objectives. If Soviet criticisms of the system are any guide, there must certainly be a good deal of under-utilized capacity, under-employed labour and hoarded reserves of materials knocking around somewhere in it. If these could be unearthed and put to productive use, the problem could be solved with a minimum of pain and dislocation. But this is what Soviet planners have been trying for years, and for various purposes, to do, and their efforts have always failed. Had it been open to them to discard some of the paraphernalia of administrative allocation of materials, centrally directed production plans, managed prices and the rest, and to allow freer play to the forces of demand and the market, they might have succeeded (though success might have brought other problems): and they might succeed in the present case too. But this path is closed to them on ideological grounds. Besides, the scope offered to individual (not private) initiative would entail a politically unacceptable dilution of the principle of democratic centralism. So they are obliged to persevere with the old game of tinkering with plan indicators, improving forecasting techniques and pursuing, with the help of bigger and better computers, the will-o'-the-wisp of omniscience. The only new factor is the import of foreign know-how and equipment described in the last chapter. Great hopes are entertained that technology imports will work the miracle of modernization and increased efficiency that has so many times eluded them. Brezhnev was betting heavily on these hopes at the twenty-fifth congress when he declared:

> Like other countries we use the advantages offered by foreign
> economic arrangements in order to have additional possibilities of
> carrying out our economic plans, to gain time, to increase the
> efficiency of production and to accelerate scientific and technological
> progress.

But modernization by implantation of foreign technology will be a long haul. Its contribution to improved living standards will take time to mature. And it seems unlikely by itself to do the trick.

The alternative course – the diversion of resources currently otherwise employed to production for the consumer – involves choosing a victim; and the choice is not easy. Of the big spenders, agriculture must be ruled out. Its contribution to the standard of living is every bit as important, perhaps even more so, than that of the consumer goods industries themselves. Nor, for similar reasons, would it make sense to touch the social services. The finger seems to point to heavy industry: but here too prudence intervenes. The great projects for the development of Siberia – the Baikal-Amur railway, the hydrological projects, the extraction of non-ferrous metals, the exploitation of vast reserves of oil, gas and coal – can go forward only if the heavy engineering sector continues to produce the necessary capital goods. To defer these plans would be to mortgage industrial growth in the 1990s and after. But what of the industries catering for the armed forces, and indeed what of the armed forces themselves, one of the largest consumers of Soviet manpower? In the context of *détente* the idea has very obvious attractions.

How great is the burden of defence on the Soviet economy? The truth is shrouded in obscurity which published Soviet statistics do nothing to dispel. The Soviet state budget, published annually, has shown defence expenditure as running throughout the 1970s at a steady rate of between 17 and 18 billion roubles, representing a steady 7 to 8 per cent of government spending. It taxes credulity too far to suppose that the share of defence in total expenditure, however denominated in money terms, is as low or as constant as these figures assert. The observed volume of Soviet military effort over the period has been too large and has expanded too fast for that. Western analysts have suggested that much or all of the outlay on weapon procurement and on research and development of new weapons is not included in the defence budget but buried under other heads, the engineering industry and the science budget being the most likely candidates. But even when adjusted to take account of this factor, the budget figures are of little use, either as a guide to the actual size of the defence burden or for comparative purposes.

One difficulty is the arbitrary nature of the prices attached to all the products of the Soviet economy. The declared budgetary cost of a given Soviet defence package is simply the sum of whatever costs the managers of the economy choose to impute to each of its components. Another is that, when it comes to making comparisons, there is no reliable exchange rate to use. The rouble is inconvertible and the official rate does not, and does not claim to, reflect its purchasing power in relation to other currencies. Much effort and ingenuity has been employed in estimating the true burden by constructing, on certain assumptions, 'real' costings and 'real' rates of exchange, but for many years the results were too divergent and too subject to radical alteration to inspire any great confidence.

Of late, however, the conclusions of the two main schools of analysis, one official and the other academic, and each working by different methods, have begun to converge on an estimated defence burden of between 11 and 14 per cent of the Soviet Union's gross national product. Such estimates naturally invite caution and it is a fair comment that generals, arms manufacturers and legislators representing industrial constituencies in the West have an interest in ensuring that the Soviet danger should not be underrated. All the same, give or take a percentage point, the analysts' results accord pretty well with the evidence of direct observation. The Soviet Union today mounts a military effort, in material terms as large as, if not larger than, that of the United States; and it does so out of a gross national product of approximately half the size. In the American case the burden of defence has run in recent years at around 6 per cent of GNP. The effects on the rest of the Soviet economy of a pre-emption of resources on this scale can only be punitive, and the relief that would follow from a reduction of the defence burden correspondingly beneficent.

A cut in defence spending would no doubt be hotly resisted by the Soviet armed forces and by those sections of Soviet industry that owe their prosperity to defence orders. Hitherto they have been able to see off anyone who was rash enough to suggest such a thing by invoking the imperialist threat and pointing to the risks that the motherland, and the socialist commonwealth, would run if they were so imprudent as to lower their guard. The national leadership, having these interests every bit as much at heart as the soldiers, have had no alternative but to let things go on as before, with the results for the vitality of the economy, and for the common man's living standard, with which we are familiar. But if there were now to be a relaxation of international tensions, the arguments for maintaining the defence effort on its current scale, regardless of the attendant penalties, would be seriously weakened. And if *détente* were to become, as Soviet propagandists have never ceased to insist, 'irreversible', the case for rationalizing the allocation of public expenditure, and diverting to consumption the resources needed to cope with the Soviet Union's socio-political problem, would be very hard to answer.

Old ways die hard and, as noted, Russian habits of thought attach great importance to the maintenance in being of substantial military force. But, sooner or later, the Soviet leadership will have to face the consequences – and they are no longer merely economic; they are becoming social and political as well – of over-commitment. It may be that, for the present, the prospect of a reduced defence bill represents no more than a gleam on the distant horizon of the sorely tried managers of the Soviet economy. But, of all the reliefs that *détente* could bring, surely the most potent and far-reaching would be a decrease in the claims which defence makes on national resources; and the leadership cannot afford indefinitely to ignore the fact. For, if we are to take Brezhnev at his word, we must conclude that the future health and prosperity of the Soviet Union will depend every bit as much on butter as on guns.

Not for Export

10

In his much quoted rejection of the notion that revolution can be 'exported', Lenin was merely endorsing the theoretical proposition that revolutionary situations develop by a dynamic of their own and cannot be anticipated or imposed. A far better guide to his intentions is his other dictum that it is the 'internationalist duty' of a socialist state to give aid to revolutionary movements in capitalist countries. Whether such aid counts as 'export' or not, and whether it is given out of duty or interest, or a combination of the two, the fact is that, from Lenin's time onwards, the Soviet Union established itself in the business of promoting revolutions in foreign countries. In doing so it has greatly undermined confidence between East and West, leaving a legacy of suspicion which today seriously obstructs the search for *détente*. What is less obvious, though no less important, is that successive failures to organize and control the international revolutionary movement have over the years so discredited Soviet revolutionary efforts that the path of internationalist duty has run into the sand. The present chapter examines how this result has come about.

Before Lenin's time, all efforts to organize an international revolutionary working-class movement had ended in disappointment. The First International (the International Workingmen's Association founded by Marx in 1864) had disintegrated in doctrinal disputes. From the 1890s onward the socialist and social-democratic parties who made up its successor, the Second International, had been torn by conflicts between 'revisionists' and orthodox Marxists. The revisionists, who believed that Marx's prophecies had been largely invalidated by subsequent social developments, thereafter sought progress by way of evolutionary change within the capitalist system. In the First World War socialists had, for the most part, thrown proletarian solidarity to the winds and rallied to the cause of patriotism; and when the war was over and a measure of international co-operation between parties was resumed, it was the revisionist proponents of evolutionary socialism who controlled the re-established Second International. The relatively few who had remained true to Marxist revolutionary orthodoxy, and had been defeatists during the war, were the nucleus in each country around which there grew up communist parties dedicated to the revolutionary overthrow of capitalism and the establishment by force of proletarian dictatorship, following the course charted by Lenin and the Bolsheviks in Russia. One of the first steps taken by the Russian revolutionaries in pursuance of their 'internationalist duty' was to bring these unfledged communist parties together in the (third) Communist International, or Comintern.

The relationship was from the outset one of master and pupil. The Soviet Communist Party was the patentee of Lenin's development of revolutionary technology. It had the experience of a successful revolution behind it, and its authority within the movement was unquestioned. Alone among the member parties it had the material means of funding and equipping the revolutionary struggle in other countries. For the time being, the interests of the international movement were synonymous with that of the Soviet Communist Party, and these were, of course, also those of the Soviet state. The master set about his task with proper seriousness and in the years between the wars the future leaders of communist parties in the capitalist world were brought to Moscow and subjected to rigorous training in their duties. Many whose names became household words in Europe after the Second World War – Georgi Dimitrov in Bulgaria, Matyas Rakosy in Hungary, Maurice Thorez in France, Palmiro Togliatti in Italy, Wilhelm Pieck in East Germany, Josip Broz in Yugoslavia, to name but a few – were graduates of the Comintern's revolutionary school in Moscow. The discipline in which they were instructed was in part theoretical – the scientific socialism of Marx as modernized and interpreted by Lenin and applied by him in Russia – but in part practical – the revolutionary professionalism which had enabled Lenin to take and hold power. National loyalties had no place in the curriculum, which taught absolute fidelity to the overriding interests of the movement as a whole of which the Soviet Union, the first socialist country, was the standard bearer.

The master–pupil relationship was already second nature to communist parties in Europe and the New World by the time that, following the Second World War, world revolution resumed its forward march. The Comintern, it is true, had been formally dissolved in 1943, but its disappearance made no difference for it had throughout been wholly controlled and operated by the CPSU which continued, as before, to direct the movement after the Comintern's demise. When, after the war, coalition governments of the left were installed by the Red Army in newly liberated countries, the Moscow-trained communist leaders proceeded like clockwork to eliminate their bourgeois partners, as they had been taught to do, and to establish proletarian dictatorships. A socialist camp whose nucleus consisted of Poland, Hungary, Bulgaria and Romania began to take shape. It included also two atypical recruits, Yugoslavia and Albania, who had fought and won their own wars of liberation. And to it were added Czechoslovakia in 1948 and eventually East Germany in 1951. The Chinese People's Republic, owing hardly anything to Moscow's influence and efforts, was established in 1949 and formally welcomed into the community of socialist states, as were the communist secessionists in North Korea when they declared independence in 1951. But the socialist camp proper was an East European affair, consisting of a group of states where Soviet geographical and strategic interests were paramount, all of them ruled by parties and governments consciously modelled on the Soviet pattern. The Communist Information Bureau (Cominform), to which the more substantial of the communist parties of Western Europe were also admitted, was the CPSU's instrument for directing the camp's policies.

'Proletarian internationalism' was the guiding principle of the socialist camp. In theory this required nationalist sentiments, a regrettably durable by-product of the defunct bourgeois state, to be laid aside in favour of the wider loyalty to, and solidarity with, the world-wide interests of the proletariat. But since the latter were now firmly identified with the interests of the first country of socialism, proletarian internationalism approximated in practice to acceptance of the CPSU's writ in all matters of Marxist-Leninist faith and morals, and strict adherence to the dictates of the Soviet state in international affairs. Yugoslav communists, who were the first to kick over the traces, dubbed the first of these aspects 'ideological monopoly' and the second 'hegemonism'. Both were exceedingly irksome to proud East European nations several of whom had suffered bitterly in past centuries from subjection to alien despots, Ottoman, Hapsburg and Romanov, and had achieved independence and national identity as states only after the First World War. The ideological monopoly of the CPSU was perhaps the more pervasive and objectionable of the two, since it gave the Soviet party a *droit de regard* not only over the correctness of the line of the fraternal parties of the camp and thus over the whole conduct of their internal affairs, but also, by extension of Soviet practice, over appointments to leading party and state positions in each country. Soviet advisers, specialists and policemen were deployed in the ministries and the armed services of the fraternal countries, reporting regularly to Moscow on any signs of deviation from the prescribed path and securing the dismissal of any functionaries considered to be unreliable or incompetent. Soviet diplomatic missions ensured that Soviet hegemony in foreign relations was effective. They kept a sharp lookout for signs of unwholesome friendships developing between the member states of the camp or of ties of economic interest developing between any of these and the outside world.

Yugoslavia was the first to break out of this strait-jacket. Though he had graduated with honours from the Cominform school for revolutionaries and turned the Yugoslav party into the most promising, zealous and active of Moscow's pupils, Tito had in four years of war, won without substantial assistance from the Red Army, become the leader of an intensely patriotic national movement. Though wholly loyal to the cause of proletarian revolution, he contrived by his style of leadership to convince Stalin that he had got too big for his boots and an unsuccessful *putsch* was mounted to depose him and his closest colleagues and instal new leaders acceptable to the CPSU. Expulsion from the Cominform, an economic blockade, military threats and border provocations followed, but the Yugoslav party stood its ground. The United States and Britain, later joined by France, paid Yugoslavia's import bills, and Tito kept afloat. In time Yugoslavia responded to the pressures of the camp by propounding its own 'road to socialism', rejecting the bureaucratic centralism of the Soviet model in favour of new forms of industrial democracy, and by adopting an increasingly pronounced non-aligned stance in relation to both East and West. Stalin, resolved to prevent any spread of infection, proceeded to depose, and imprison or execute, the leaders of the other fraternal parties on spurious charges of 'Titoism' and nationalist deviation.

Inheriting this state of affairs on Stalin's death, Khrushchev set out to restore unity and amity in the camp and by the summer of 1956 had normalized state relations with Yugoslavia and re-established intercommunion between the Soviet and Yugoslav parties. To achieve this he was obliged at Belgrade in 1955 to endorse the equal status, territorial integrity and independence of all socialist states and to abjure intervention in their internal affairs; and at Moscow in 1956 to recognize the right of every communist party to choose its own road to socialism. With the rejection of Stalin's worse excesses following the twentieth CPSU congress in 1956 it seemed that the lessons of the Yugoslav secession had been learnt and that the socialist camp might evolve into an association less uncomfortable and dangerous for its non-Soviet members. But the new deal left intact two institutions – the Comecon and the Warsaw Pact – whose establishment in the intervening years had immensely strengthened the Soviet Union's position of pre-eminence; and, as soon became clear, the Soviet Union never accepted the full implications of national independence and 'separate roads' to which it had ostensibly subscribed. When in the autumn of 1956 the new liberal leadership of the Hungarian communist party declared their country's neutrality, withdrew from the Warsaw Pact and were on the point of introducing parliamentary pluralism, Soviet military forces intervened to preserve the gains of the socialist revolution. The point was abundantly clear. Separate roads and formal equality were acceptable within limits, but when they led to radical departure from the Soviet model of socialist society, or to severance of the bonds of alliance, they posed a challenge to the overriding interests of socialism and of the Soviet state and would be brutally suppressed.

Meanwhile tensions had begun to develop between the CPSU and the only other communist party that was of comparable size and weight in the world. The Chinese communists since their accession to power in 1949 had stood apart from the narrower association between the CPSU and its East European clients, but they counted themselves as members of the broader international socialist movement and acknowledged the primacy of the CPSU in it. The CPC's institutions and techniques were copied from Soviet models, the Chinese state relied heavily on Soviet assistance in economic development and a treaty of friendship was signed between the two countries in 1953. But the two parties, so different in revolutionary experience and called upon to operate in such widely divergent environments, were in serious disagreement on the practical application of the Marxist-Leninist doctrines which were their common inheritance. They disagreed about the nature of the socialism they were supposed to be building in their respective countries, and about revolutionary strategy towards both developed and underdeveloped countries.

In particular the Chinese rejected the 'modern revisionism' which the CPSU had embraced at the twentieth congress, which they stigmatized as 'taking the capitalist road' at home and as a betrayal of proletarian revolution abroad. And ideological dissensions were compounded by national characteristics, clashes of economic interest and old hostilities inherited from the past. Unlike the East Europeans the Chinese were too big to be bullied, and in a series of stormy international meetings after 1956 they moved over to the offensive. Not content with rejecting the CPSU's claim to dictate to them in ideological matters, they impugned the Soviet practice of socialism at home and abroad as mistaken and heretical and claimed for Peking the role of sole authoritative interpreter of doctrine. By the middle of 1963 the international movement was definitively split. Several parties in Asia and Africa followed the anti-Pope in Peking, reckoning that Mao Tse-tung's gospel was better adapted to their condition of undevelopment, and they were joined by Albania, economically the most retarded of the countries of the camp in Eastern Europe. The rest (Yugoslavia, of course, excepted) remained tied by vested interest to the Moscow papacy, as did the more influential of the communist parties of the West, though the Chinese scored minor successes in procuring splits in some of them.

The most unsatisfactory outcome of these events for the CPSU was not so much the multiplication of different 'roads' to socialism: a measure of diversity was recognized, following the Yugoslav experience, as inevitable and, provided always that the revolutionary gains of socialism were not endangered (as had happened in Hungary), could be lived with. The really serious casualty was the authority of the Soviet Union as the hitherto unquestioned leader of the movement. The CPSU accordingly set out to prepare a synod in Moscow of the world communist parties, at which the Chinese party, if it persisted in its heresies, would be put on trial and formally excommunicated from the movement, and unity under Soviet leadership re-established. But preliminary inter-party discussions, intended to fix this outcome in advance, revealed that the sentiment among the fraternal parties had hardened. With the exception of a few Maoist splinter groups, no parties in the West, and none among the East European parties in power, felt any affinity for the barefoot socialism of the Chinese. But the schism in the movement represented for them a godsent mitigation of the CPSU's position of ideological monopoly which the synod was designed to re-establish, and they set their faces against Soviet schemes to convoke it. For Yugoslavia, walking the tightrope of non-alignment between East and West, the schism in the movement had become a vital interest. The party in neighbouring Romania began, despite Romania's membership of Comecon and the Warsaw Pact, to move in a similar direction. It was not for the Romanians a question of separate roads, for their road to socialism was closer to Stalin's than any other in Eastern Europe. Their interest was in emancipating themselves from Soviet hegemonism in foreign affairs; and to this end they set about distancing themselves from the common positions of the camp, cultivating bilateral relations with China, Yugoslavia and, in due course, with Israel. Less daring, the other East Europeans were content to go slow, supporting Soviet polemics against China but dragging their feet when action to put China in the corner was proposed. In the West the communist party of Italy (CPI), as the Moscow-trained generation thinned out, began to propound the notion of 'polycentrism', which contemplated the concurrent existence of several 'centres' of communist doctrine and inspiration. The Italian communists threw themselves enthusiastically into exchanges with the Yugoslav party and a close relationship unfolded from 1961 onwards, directed less to the replication in Italy of the singular institutions devised by the Yugoslavs than to the development in the longer term of a separate centre of socialist thought and practice appropriate to conditions in Western Europe.

Baulked of its purpose of re-establishing world-wide unity of the movement, the CPSU found its attention claimed in the later 1960s by events nearer home. The camp, properly speaking, now consisted of Poland, Hungary, Romania, Bulgaria, Czechoslovakia and the GDR, united to one another and to the Soviet Union by a network of bilateral treaties, by the integration of their defence forces under Soviet command in the Warsaw Pact and of their production and trade plans in the Comecon, and by common acknowledgment of Moscow as the fountain of doctrine and the arbiter of socialist practice. Mongolia, wedged between Siberia and China, was admitted to Comecon in 1962 but, though militarily linked with the USSR, was not a member of the Warsaw Pact. Nor was Cuba, whose bourgeois revolution had broken new ground by embracing Marxism-Leninism, but which was separated by the Atlantic from the main nucleus of the camp.

Into this orderly and well-regulated environment the change of generations which in 1968 replaced the party leadership in Czechoslovakia introduced new elements of instability. In the name of 'socialism with a human face', the new leaders abolished the censorship and were well on the way to abolishing the Communist Party's monopoly of political power. Once more, as seen from Moscow, the question was posed not of a separate road to socialism but of a basic change of direction involving the adoption of different goals, and one with serious implications for Warsaw Pact defence. Once more, as in Hungary eight years earlier, the Soviet Union, assisted this time by contingents from its allies in the Warsaw Pact (less Romania), moved in troops, and Czechoslovakia was brought back by force on to the straight and narrow party path.

The disciplining of Hungary in 1956 had been undertaken *ad hoc* because of a perceived need to salvage the 'gains' of the revolution. In the wake of its intervention in Czechoslovakia the CPSU moved forward to erect this need into a principle. The so-called 'Brezhnev doctrine' propounded by *Pravda* when the 'events' in Prague were in full course, and formalized later by its eponymous inventor, postulated that the sovereign equality conceded by Khrushchev to Tito in 1955, and subsequently extended to the relations between socialist states generally, was after all subject to limitations. These flowed from the fact that the socialist character of socialist states, gained by revolutionary struggle, constituted the common patrimony of all of them, which all had a right and duty to safeguard. Each of the fraternal countries was, in this respect, his brother's keeper, and to that extent each enjoyed only limited sovereignty. Naturally the CPSU, creator of the original socialist homeland and first country of socialism, was the keenest, and reckoned itself to be the most experienced, judge of the circumstances in which developments in fraternal countries threatened socialism's gains. And since the countries of the socialist camp occupied territory vital to the national security of the Soviet state, and all of them were shackled to the Soviet Union by ties of defence and economic integration, the considerations of true ideology were strongly reinforced in the Soviet mind by others of material interest. Czechoslovakia, once the surgery was completed and a reliable and conservative leadership installed in the room of the reformers, was called upon to sign a new treaty of friendship with the Soviet Union, enshrining the doctrine of limited sovereignty. The new Czechoslovak rulers thereby recognized the Soviet right of intervention should internal developments again imperil the achievements of the revolution. Further treaties on the same model were proposed by the Russians to the other fraternal countries of the camp and in due course Bulgaria and the GDR obliged by subscribing to them. Others took evasive action. These new-style friendship treaties contractualized the Soviet right of intervention and left the Soviet government free to determine when the *casus foederis* justifying its exercise might have arisen.

The repercussions abroad of the invasion of Czechoslovakia were uniformly destructive of the remaining cohesion of the international movement. The spectacle of Soviet tanks rolling into Prague had shown that nothing – not even the most basic requirements of international law – would stand in the way of the Soviet Union if it thought that its real interests were endangered. Even within the camp, Romania had declined to take part in the Warsaw Pact's military operation and had sided with Yugoslavia in condemning it. Both countries passed an uncomfortable three months under the implied, but in the event unrealized, threat of punitive military action. But the more damaging consequences were felt in the communist parties of the Western world. Many Western communists had applauded Dubček's experiments in democratization, believing them to be good in themselves and good also for socialism's image and appeal to the masses in developed societies. The use of naked force to suppress the Czechoslovak liberals left the rank-and-file aghast and many tore up their party cards in instinctive revulsion. But more serious from Moscow's point of view was the realization, born of the Czechoslovak events and spreading thereafter among the party leaderships in Europe, that continuing identification with the Soviet Union was a liability which communist parties in the West would need to shed if they were ever to acquire mass support.

'Eurocommunism' is the name given to the stock of ideas developed by parties in Western Europe in response to the challenge of 1968. Its standard bearer has been the communist party of Italy and its roots go back to the CPI's advocacy of polycentrism in the early 1960s. Having participated briefly in post-war coalition governments, the CPI, though enjoying substantial trade-union and mass support, spent twenty-five years in the wilderness, and it was only when the longstanding Christian Democrat ascendancy began to run out of steam that prospects of a return to shared power revived. Setting as its target coalition with the Demochristians as the basis of an 'historic compromise', the party began to refurbish its image with a view to mustering the necessary electoral support. The obstacles were daunting and all of them arose from the Soviet connection. Perhaps the hardest to surmount was the pervasive belief of democratic societies everywhere that communist parties and their members were agents of a foreign power. Abundant evidence for this belief was provided by the anti-national, if not treasonable, activities of communist participants in the popular fronts of the past in Western as well as in Eastern Europe; and the outrageous about-turns executed by communists when the Ribbentrop–Molotov pact was signed, and when Hitler attacked the Soviet Union, were not forgotten. Besides, as Moscow never ceased to tell the world, communist parties in capitalist countries were there to promote revolution; and the last thing that increasingly affluent Western electorates wanted was the violent overthrow of state institutions and their replacement by proletarian dictatorship. And, finally, there was the ideology which taught that, once socialism was established, the historical process was irreversible: there was no going back. So communists, once elected to power, would never allow themselves to be dislodged from it. The democratic process would be turned into a mockery. The CPI accordingly set out to efface the labels of disloyalty and devotion to proletarian dictatorship and to persuade the electorate that it would abide by the rules of the parliamentary game.

The platform which the CPI built itself to meet these specifications offered socialism as the remedy for Italy's manifest social and economic ills, but the theoretical basis of socialism was shaded out and it was to be a socialism reshaped by Western humane and democratic traditions. Revolutionary aims were disavowed; the socialist transformation of society was to be achieved peacefully by democratic means. To this end the party would seek election on the same terms as other parties, would work in loyal co-operation with them and would withdraw with a good grace into opposition if it lost the confidence of the electorate. It would be a staunch defender of the country's interests and, in foreign affairs, would maintain Italy's membership of the North Atlantic Treaty Organization and of the European Economic Community. It looked in the longer run to a Europe independent of both the Soviet Union and the United States, deplored the division of the world into hostile blocs and would work for relaxation of the tensions which this division set up.

The French Communist Party (CPF), with an established tradition of fidelity to Moscow, was slower to move, but its conversion to a Eurocommunist line, when it came, was to all appearances more explicit and demonstrative. The party had seemed to weather the storms of 1968 more successfully than most, but its own crisis of conscience came later over human rights. The tightening of the screws on Soviet dissent which accompanied Moscow's moves towards *détente* abroad was the straw that broke the camel's back. In 1975 a newly elected leadership swung the party into a position close to that of the CPI, and a new line was formalized at the twenty-second party congress in the following year. Proletarian dictatorship was ostensibly discarded, signifying the end of the party's commitment to revolutionary violence and political monopoly and, in disclaiming allegiance to any philosophy or official doctrine, it seemed to have cut itself loose from its Marxist-Leninist origins. It was to work by peaceful means for the democratic transformation of French society and the economy, maintaining and extending the freedoms that Frenchmen traditionally enjoyed, accepting the rules of party pluralism and engaging itself to respect the verdict of the electorate in all circumstances. In foreign affairs, if its pronouncements were any guide, it might be expected to be every bit as assertive of French national interests as General de Gaulle himself had been. Some, both in France and abroad, found the CPF's conversion to democracy too complete to be wholly credible, given the continued presence in its ranks of life-long supporters of the Moscow line, and wondered how durable it would prove to be. Of course with the CPF, as earlier with the CPI, electoral considerations had played their part in shaping the new line. At the elections due in 1978 the CPF was to campaign on a common programme (on which it has since reneged) with the socialists and its share of the spoils, if victory came, would depend on its performance at the polls. Prospects looked hopeful if only the damaging label of past Soviet and revolutionary associations could be effaced.

Of several others (including the communist party of Great Britain) who took the Eurocommunist course, the most notable was the Spanish communist party. Its members had been driven underground and its leaders into exile after the Spanish civil war, but the end of the Franco regime was in sight and preparations for a return to active politics were well advanced. Its secretary-general, Santiago Carrillo, had for some years been distancing himself from Moscow. The party's headquarters had been transferred to Paris and from there Carrillo established increasingly intimate links with the CPI, leading in 1974 to a broad understanding with the Italians on common aims which attracted adverse notice in Moscow. The platform on which his party campaigned in the Spanish elections of 1977 – the first for forty-five years, and held shortly after his return to Spain – was scarcely distinguishable in essentials from that of the CPI, but considerably more explicit in its disavowal of the Soviet model of socialism. His book, *Eurocommunism and the State,* published in Madrid in 1977, roundly denounced the 'monstrous aberration' of Stalinism and declared that the electoral victory of socialist forces in Western Europe must not, and must be seen not to, mean any increase in Soviet state power or any expansion of Soviet single-party socialism.

The emergence of Eurocommunism poses problems of varying seriousness for East and West. For the governments of Western countries which are the neighbours of France and Italy, and linked to them by the North Atlantic Treaty and the Treaty of Rome (to either or both of which post-Franco Spain might quite possibly accede) questions arise about how the Eurocommunist parties of those countries would behave if they should find themselves in office. Would assurances before the event of loyalty to NATO and to the EEC prove reliable on the day? Would communist ministers prove secure custodians of their allies' defence secrets, or of public order and security in their own countries? Could they really be relied upon to depart into loyal opposition if the next election should turn them out of office?

The conventional wisdom replies that a communist is always a communist and is bound by his ideology, whatever he may say to the contrary, to hold firm to his revolutionary aim. Such was broadly the position of Dr Kissinger and it is still widely held, though it begs the question what the man will do if he has actually escaped from the ideological bond. Western attitudes have been a good deal influenced by the unhappy, but fortunately short-lived, experience of communists in government in Portugal in 1974–5. But it is fair to note that the Portuguese communist ministers were very far from being Eurocommunists; indeed they were unabashed revolutionaries bent on producing in Lisbon a carbon copy of Lenin's takeover of the Russian revolution of 1917. To turn the question round, is it suggested that the Eurocommunist platforms have been rigged up simply and solely to bamboozle the electors, and are destined to be cast aside as soon as power is won? If so, surely their proponents have done far too thorough a job of deception, for neither they nor their parties can easily survive the return to revolutionary business as usual. It would of course be naive to suppose that no backsliding is possible or to assume that the democratic turn of recent years could not be reversed by shifts of sentiment and changes in the composition of the leadership. But given the obvious trepidation with which the CPSU contemplates the prospect of Eurocommunists in office, it is reasonable to infer that the contingency might not, after all, prove to be an unmitigated disaster for the West.

In fact, for the CPSU and the Soviet government, though they were a little slow to recognize the full implications, Eurocommunism raised questions of a far more serious and fundamental character. With the tide of *détente* flowing strongly, they believed that new opportunities were opening up for communist parties everywhere. Their first idea – the convening of a new world-wide inter-party synod – was briefly considered, but as soon, for familiar reasons, dropped. Instead it was decided to call a meeting confined to the parties from European countries, Western and Eastern. The intention was to concert strategy for a new offensive in Western countries, to be launched following the successful conclusion of the CSCE, and directed to the widest possible participation of Western communist parties in united front governments of the left. The preparatory stage of the conference ran into trouble from the outset because of fundamental disagreements about revolutionary tactics, separate roads to socialism and the nature and purpose of co-operation with non-communist parties. For the Russians it went without saying that alliances concluded with bourgeois parties could be no more than tactical, undertaken with the sole purpose of preparing a subsequent seizure of power and establishing proletarian dictatorship. But, as they discovered, a number of the Western parties not merely rejected these tactics as impracticable but actually rejected the revolutionary principle and denied the right of the CPSU to hold them to it. The running was made by the Yugoslavs and the Italians, with some tactical assistance from the Romanians.

The conference preparations lasted, with intermissions, for more than two years, despite the periodical interventions of high-level trouble-shooters from Moscow and, with the French and others joining the opposition, it became clear that the CPSU would not get its way. Having successfully frustrated the imposition on the meeting of an unacceptable basic document of Soviet manufacture, and replaced it with a draft of their own, the Yugoslav–Italian team retained the initiative and secured the issue of a final communiqué by the summit conference in East Berlin on 30 June 1976. In signing this final document, the party leaders endorsed the unqualified sovereign independence of all participant parties, the voluntary character of the co-operation between them and the important role of Christian and other democratic forces in defending working-class interests in Western countries.

What most preoccupied the CPSU during these exchanges was the deplorable example which Eurocommunism set to the parties and peoples of Eastern Europe. If Italian and French communists could live with a pluralist system which allowed them to be turned out of office for failure to please their electors, how long would it be before Poles, Czechs and Hungarians claimed the same facility of changing their rulers? Worse still, if ideology, the class struggle and the dictatorship of the proletariat could be jettisoned with impunity by West European parties, for how long could the fraternal parties of the camp be restrained from seeking similar licence? Parties and peoples alike could of course have this sort of nonsense knocked out of them by use of the big stick: but that would mean repetitions of 1968 all over again, which the USSR, in the wider context of *détente,* could ill afford.

Accordingly, as memories of the Berlin meeting receded, the Soviet theoreticians moved in to regain lost ground and to queer the pitch for the Eurocommunists. The campaign was addressed, though they did not say so, to those party members in the West whose orthodoxy and militancy had been submerged by the anti-Soviet waves of 1968 and after. Carried on through the party journals with occasional assistance from *Pravda,* it recapitulated the arguments about revolutionary tactics that had failed to carry the day in 1975 and 1976, and the overt anti-Sovietism of Carrillo's book, when it appeared, enabled them to add charges of disloyalty to those of ideological heresy. Their message was that exclusive reliance on the parliamentary road could only end in failure. It was a prime example of what Lenin had called 'parliamentary cretinism' to suppose that power could be won, and control of a state seized, by relying on a mere arithmetical majority of votes and without the use of revolutionary violence at the decisive moment. Deluded Eurocommunists might actually believe what they said, but they were flying in the face of the laws of history whose objective validity had been confirmed by Soviet revolutionary experience. The party leaders in Paris and Rome had nothing to say in reply, doubtless reckoning that a public debate with the Russians on so sensitive a theme could do nothing but harm to their electoral prospects. But it was less to the leaderships, already publicly committed to heretical positions, that the Russians were speaking, than to the doubters who might one day unseat them. It seemed, as 1977 advanced, increasingly probable that the CPSU, unable any longer to control the Eurocommunist parties, had resolved on the desperate course of splitting and destroying them. If they did so, it would be in obedience to the same bitter logic that makes the soldier spike his own guns before the position falls into enemy hands. But it would be a sad end to a long journey begun in hope.

For Western governments seeking *détente* with the Soviet Union the history of the international movement over the past thirty years offers grounds for comfort and reassurance. In 1947 the Soviet Union exercised unchallenged authority over a world-wide movement of like-minded parties, owing allegiance to Moscow and dedicated to procuring the downfall of capitalist institutions everywhere in accordance with the laws of history as propounded by Marx and Lenin. Proletarian revolution was the Soviet Union's secret weapon, which exercised a mesmeric influence on its intended victims, imparting to the reality of Soviet power a supranatural aura of inevitability. Since then Soviet authority has shrunk in response to repeated challenges, so that today Moscow's ideological writ runs with certainty only in the narrow strip of territory on Russia's Western frontier, and even there more by virtue of military muscle than by doctrinal conviction. In Africa and Asia the lead has been lost to China, though chances of opportunist intervention periodically occur. In the West the apostles of revolution have resigned their mission and told their Soviet mentors that converts can be won only by jettisoning doctrine and abjuring the name Moscow. Today the old game of the Communist International is up. Shorn of the revolutionary magic, the Soviet Union is revealed as another large power on the make, playing politics against other large powers, keeping tight control of its Western *glacis* and making predatory, but not uniformly successful, sorties into the third world when targets of opportunity present themselves. The Russians remain formidable people, but they no longer look ten feet high. If *détente* with them seems attainable on otherwise tolerable conditions, suspicions of their revolutionary intent need not trouble us unduly. For Lenin spoke truer than he knew. Revolution is not for export.

11

Prospects for Change

The problem of co-existing with the Russians would be enormously simplified if only the Soviet Union would change its ways. This thought prompts us to consider whether any factors are discernible in Soviet life today which could give rise to change, and thus give grounds for hoping that the course of East–West relations may prove plainer sailing in future. Several candidates for consideration emerge from what has been said in previous chapters, and these must now be examined. The short list (shorthand titles only) consists of: education, loss of faith, the change of generation, urbanization, technology, Western example and nationality.

Soviet education has a heavily technical bias, but if you teach a man to think about the problems of pre-stressed concrete, or oil-drilling or micro-wave circuits you are awakening a rational faculty in him which cannot with certainty be kept confined to his specialist field. And if you turn out engineers and technicians in hundreds of thousands annually the odds are that at least some of them, and perhaps a majority of those who go on to become doctors of science, will develop analytical and critical abilities which will in time affect their attitudes as citizens. It is noteworthy that several of the ideological free-thinkers who achieved prominence in the movement of Soviet dissent have been people whose academic formation was scientific. The example of these people has been important; it has focused the world's attention on the shortcomings and injustices of the Soviet system and thrown the Soviet leadership onto the defensive. But in going into opposition they have burnt their boats and forfeited any prospect of influencing the evolution of the system from within.

If education is to prove a factor for change it will operate not through the heroic defiance of a few choice spirits whose convictions have impelled them to self-immolation or exile, but through its pervasive effects on the social consciousness, assumptions and attitudes of a much wider section of the Soviet educated class, whose members are scattered through industry, the academic world, government, the learned professions and even the party apparatus and police. These are people who do not stick their necks out, but their critical faculty and their experience of the world must tell them that the reality with which they are dealing bears less and less resemblance to the stereotypes of official Soviet historiography. They are private revisionists, if they have retained their belief in the underlying framework of Marxism, or private agnostics, if they have lost it. What can be expected of them? In the very long term it is conceivable that their frame of mind will spread to a point where it captures the inner strongholds of the party. In a less distant perspective, if change were to be forced on the party for reasons not of their making, they would no doubt emerge as enthusiastic supporters and executants of new policies. But there are, as will appear below, powerful countervailing pressures which tend to keep them tied to the system.

The widening gap between theory and practice, between the promise and the performance of Soviet socialism, has led, over sixty years, to a decline of ideological conviction which spreads far beyond the confines of the highly educated. Lenin, for all his worldly wisdom and hard-headedness, committed his party to dogmas so absolute and a programme so all-embracing that any result short of total success could hardly fail to damage its credibility. Experience has taught Soviet economists and administrators that economic planning and the state ownership of the means of production do not, of themselves, ensure rational allocation of resources and efficiency in production. Nor, as the man in the street knows, does proletarian dictatorship produce a classless society. The proletarian vanguard – the party – and their allies have formed a new class every bit as self-seeking as its bourgeois predecessor; while at the other end of the social scale their fellows live on bare necessities. The capitalist states beyond the border who were supposed to crash in ruin have, at least until very recently, flourished, and created material prosperity on a scale which socialism has not remotely matched. What is more, the party has not scrupled, when reality has diverged from the dogmatic blueprint, to mislead the public by falsifying events.

Khrushchev let a number of cats out of the bag at the twentieth congress, particularly about the revolution and the Stalin years. The Soviet people do not know the whole truth but they know there is a lot to learn. Viewed against this background, the myths that started it all have an increasingly hollow ring. Marx's nineteenth-century abstractions — the forces of production, the historical process and the laws by which it was meant to unfold, the class struggle and the inevitable triumphant proletarian revolution — have little visible relevance to the world in which the Soviet people live, and the age of plenty and the brotherhood of man, to which the revolution was to lead, are still immeasurably far off. It is by any standard a serious thing for a society if its members, including those in positions of authority, come to regard the beliefs of the founding fathers as so much abracadabra to be gabbled or assented to on prescribed occasions.

But any who expect that the whole edifice will collapse now that the foundations of belief are crumbling are likely to be disappointed. It is too securely buttressed for that, and too firmly underpinned by institutions. The party dictatorship cannot admit that the myth is dead, for that would mean abdicating its claim to govern. But it has equipped itself to get on well enough without the support that belief formerly supplied. Being self-sustaining and self-perpetuating it can maintain itself in power so long as it retains its will to rule. And the vested interest of its members, and those of the state apparatus that it has created, in holding on to their jobs, status and privileges, can be counted on to ensure that the will to rule will not flag.

A factor for change more potent, because more general, more pervasive and in the long run inevitable is the replacement of the present generation of rulers, and ruled, by younger men and women whose historical experience has been quite different. The process of replacement, which in theory should be continuous, works more jerkily in the Soviet Union than elsewhere because of the static and conservative character of society, which tends to lengthen the active life of those in positions of responsibility. But with old men at the top getting older and the under-thirties now forming a majority of the population, the next jerk can hardly fail to bring forward a crop of men and women of whom little can be said with certainty except that they will be very different from their predecessors.

What do we know of the under-thirties? Generalization is hazardous since for Western observers the field of vision is confined mainly to the larger cities and even there more is known about that part of the population that goes on to complete higher education. But, with these caveats, a few pointers can be noted. Families in the more developed Soviet republics are small. Parents, remembering their own privations and anxious to do everything for the best, tend to spoil their children who grow to adolescence taking for granted what they find and in time become impatient for more and better. The young are bored with their parents' tales of hardship; and the war, which they do not remember, leaves them cold. For them life is the present day, but it is a life which many of them find lacking in excitement and disappointing in terms of material amenity. Marxism-Leninism, an obligatory school subject, inspires about as much enthusiasm in most of them as did Old Testament history when religious instruction was obligatory in the West. Military service knocks some of the nonsense out of them, but many who go on to higher education obtain deferment, which with good luck and good management can become permanent. A number drop out after the first two or three semesters at the university where it is possible for a while to play the fool in ways unheard of in days gone by. But those who survive the early hurdles almost invariably graduate, for even universities have their production plan to fulfil. The minority who join the Komsomol and go on (normally around the age of twenty-five) to obtain party membership may do so less from a sense of vocation than on the calculation that this is the path to career and privilege, as indeed it is. Fewer are now admitted to the party's ranks than was the case ten years ago, for recruitment has been brought back into step with the decelerating growth of the population.

The party itself suffers more acutely than other sections of society from the tenacity with which the elderly hold onto their jobs. The leadership itself has become a gerontocracy. At seventy-one Brezhnev heads a Politburo and party Secretariat whose average age is in the high sixties and whose members include half a dozen as old or older than himself. The old men prop one another up, their collective survival effectively blocking the kind of *putsch* that unseated Khrushchev. It is noteworthy that of the few dismissals from the top in the last few years Shelest, Shelepin and Polyanski were all men with some mileage left in them, Podgorny, seventy-three, the only one of the old-timers to be sacked, was replaced by a man three years older than himself. On the level below the top the provincial party committee secretaries, who form the backbone of the party in the country, are now mostly men in their sixties. It cannot be very long now before death breaks up the old men's cartel at the party summit and in ten years, perhaps less, the last of Stalin's collaborators will have been gathered in, and new men will take over control of a nation which will itself have undergone renewal. It will be a society with a different tone, more critical and discontented but not necessarily freer or more tractable internationally.

Some of the signs of social unease already perceptible can be attributed to the tensions which industrialized societies create for themselves by urban concentration. The Russians, in their zeal to outstrip the capitalists in industrial expansion and material progress, have managed to repeat a number of the errors made by Western societies thirty years ago, and with results which are beginning to look very similar. The high-rise building has become the Soviet construction industry's standard answer to slum conditions and inner-city congestion. Literally hundreds of thousands of such buildings have mushroomed around Soviet cities, and the tower blocks are getting higher as technology advances. Life in them is cleaner, healthier and tidier than in the old congested tenements, and they give a degree of privacy formerly unknown, but the isolation from the surrounding world has disturbing effects, particularly on adolescents.

The traffic arteries of Soviet cities are already becoming clogged, bringing frustration, traffic blocks and exhaust fumes, and the advent of the private car makes things worse. In recent years authority has become conscious that all-out industrialization has brought pollution to the environment on a scale which the West would regard as intolerable, but has realized that cleaner air adds hugely to industrial costs. Factory noise deafens the industrial worker. In some plants he is even encouraged to break off at intervals and spend ten minutes in rest-rooms with soft lights, soothing music and pictures of rural scenes. Though the yen for country outings is strong, spectator sport, especially football, and television, claim more and more of leisure time. Soviet cities are still much more orderly after dark than New York, Chicago or London, but teenage delinquency – vandalism, mugging and occasional cases of drug addiction – is increasing, and the party is in two minds about how to cope with it. Drunkenness, the Russian's traditional escape from a hard world and the rigours of his climate, is nothing new, but boredom and increased wages encourage recourse to the bottle. Westerners are ill-placed to feel pharisaical about these phenomena, which are the common lot of 'advanced' societies and will no doubt get worse as the Soviet Union develops further. But they may reflect that, though Marx hit the nail on the head in identifying alienation as the curse of industrialized society, he was wildly wrong in supposing that it could be exorcized by a change in ownership of the means of production. Soviet man is today considerably alienated from his natural environment and from his own nature; and this makes life more difficult for his rulers. But this could as easily lead to greater rigidity as to increased relaxation of the system.

Another relevant aspect of industrialization has been the emergence of a managerial class – the Soviet enterprise director is no longer the poor fish that he used to be. He quite often finds himself running a very large organization and his training and experience have taught him a great deal about how to do it. He could not have survived and, in Soviet terms, prospered, unless he had become adept at beating the system. His talents could be used to much better purpose if he and the system were pulling in the same direction, but he is obliged to work with one hand tied behind his back. He is no counter-revolutionary, reckoning that public ownership and some degree of economic planning have come to stay. But he knows that he could make a much better job of it if the strait-jacket of detailed directive planning were relaxed and the weight of the economic bureaucracy reduced; and he would dearly like to have a shot. Nor is he wholly without bargaining power, for he is, from the point of view of his bureaucratic superiors, a goose that lays golden eggs. They may get cross with him and replace him with another, but in the long run they are dependent on him or his successor for the production of the goods they need. Production is no longer a job that can be taken on by any know-nothing party hack. Specialization and the division of labour have gone too far for that.

Plainly, some quite far-reaching consequences for the system would follow if ever the leadership were forced – by falling growth rates or mounting pressures for more and better goods – to give the industrial manager his head. A more pragmatic, technocratic Soviet Union would certainly be more efficient, probably more stable and possibly, though not necessarily, an easier bedfellow for other countries. But such a development would involve something approximating to a take-over by the managerial class of the powers at present held by the bureaucrats. The lesson of successive attempts at economic reform – by Khrushchev in the 1950s, by Kosygin in 1965 and by Brezhnev in 1973 – has been that the men in the ministries will not easily be got to relinquish control and, if deprived of it, have ways of clawing it back over time. And bureaucratic resistance to change would, in the circumstances we are discussing, be likely to attract support, for reasons examined below, from the party apparatus.

Earlier chapters have identified various ways in which Western influence and example have impinged on Soviet practice. Brezhnev, like Peter the Great before him, has recognized the need to borrow from the West, but reckons, with Peter, that he can turn his back on the West once the need is satisfied. The Soviet Union borrows technology, as he told the party at the twenty-fifth congress, in order to gain time and to cash in on the benefits of research in the West. A degree of intermingling and involvement with the West has resulted from which disengagement, if attempted, would not be easy to achieve. The impact of these Western involvements on the man-in-the-street is limited by the party's continuing efforts to insulate him from all avoidable contact with foreigners.

What is possibly of greater importance as an agent of change is Soviet man's growing acquaintance through radio and television, and to a lesser extent from books and pictures, and the beginnings of foreign travel, with Western life-style. He may find a good deal to shock and disturb him and he can shudder, in company with the most straitlaced of his ideological mentors, at its more flagrant degradations, from pornography to soccer vandalism. But he has been taught to count progress in terms of material satisfaction and he sees that life in the West, though it be naughty, is nice. The minority of Soviet people who have actually sampled any of the sweets of Western materialism is small though growing, and the persistence with which Western visitors are importuned to sell spare clothing and foreign exchange attests the strength of the addiction. So also, perhaps, does the vehemence with which Soviet ideologues continue to attack the notion, popular in the West some years ago, of a 'converging' trend of capitalist and socialist societies. Few things are more repugnant to the Soviet theoretician (as also incidentally to the Western cold-warrior) than the idea that, confronted with similar concrete problems, capitalist societies are becoming less capitalist and socialist societies less socialist. The absurdity of such a thought is easy enough to demonstrate in ideological terms but the demonstration would suffer seriously in credibility if it were found that, regardless of the arguments, a convergence of the life-styles of the two sides was taking place.

For completeness' sake it is right to mention the last item on the list, namely nationality. The Soviet Union is a multi-national state in which ethnic Russians will shortly be, if they have not already become, a minority of the population. The constituent republics retain, even under the new constitution, a formal right of secession and in most of them the sense of national identity is strong. But, though history suggests that empires are not eternal, the decline and fall of the USSR is not a serious possibility in the present century. The Soviet Communist Party effectively controls each of the constituent republics. Their economies are integrated by the plan into a single Soviet economy. The less advanced of them are heavily dependent on the Union for investment. And most of them lie in strategically important border regions which the Soviet military would not readily surrender. More may be heard of Russian nationalism, though it is unlikely to promote change. Its ancestor, nineteenth-century Slavophilism, relied heavily on Orthodox Christian belief, now swamped by twentieth-century secularism, and on nostalgia for the peasant communal way of life, which urbanization and rural collectivization have effectively obliterated. All that remains of its stock-in-trade is a latent racialist contempt for non-Slav peoples at home and abroad and an abiding grudge against the Westernizing influences which have denatured Russia's indigenous culture. It is hard to see how Russian nationalism could, as some have suggested, provide a viable alternative philosophy for Soviet conservatives who dislike *détente* and external entanglements, but the attitudes of mind to which it panders will no doubt be around for some time to come.

If some of the factors just examined are conducive to change – notably, the accession of a new generation, the spread of education and the emergence of a managerial class – their effects seem likely to be spread out over a considerable period of time, and meanwhile the factors operating against change are potent and active. The obstacles to change are deeply rooted in the claim of the Soviet Communist Party to a monopoly of political power and in the integral character of the system that it has built up to accommodate its monopoly. The party rules not by virtue of any popular mandate – no one has elected it: it is self-appointed, self-renewing and immovable – but because it holds the copyright of, and has made itself the sole authorized exponent of, Marxist-Leninist social science, which contains the answers to all problems. Possession of this copyright is the sole foundation of the party's claim to be the legitimate ruler of the country. For this reason, if for no other, the party must cling, through thick and thin, to the mythology, however obsolete or exploded parts of it may today seem. The system that it has set up is purpose-built for the achievement of its self-chosen goals. Its features, good and bad, are all of a piece, differing essentially in this respect from Western systems which are the product of random factors, many of them historical and irrational, and constantly patched, modified and renewed. Because the party's power is monopolistic and its goals all-embracing, the system had to be all-embracing too. Where other systems content themselves with ensuring that the citizen shall not do certain things that are held to be anti-social, the Soviet system, which aims to create a new man, sets out to sublimate his unruly passions and canalize them into edifying channels, and accordingly must decide what it is good for him to know and do and read. Because it aspires to extirpate exploitation and to create abundance, it must control the economy, prescribing in detail what should be invested, produced and sold, and at what price. Because the security of the system depends on keeping the class enemy at arm's length, it finds it necessary to control the good behaviour of its immediate neighbours, imposing on them replicas of its own institutions. All of these fields of activity are interlocked and constitute a single nexus of policies and measures, none of which can be disentangled and straightened out, in whole or in part, without partly or wholly undoing the others. The centre of the knot is the dictatorship of the party. Almost any conceivable change risks undermining the dictatorship in one way or another. Relax the reins on culture, or recognize the rights of individuals, and you are cutting at the roots of your own power at home and putting ideas into the heads of your vassals over the border. Start playing with market socialism, or let the technocrats have their head, and you will lose your grip on the economy and deprive yourself of your primary means of control.

To these built-in and principled impediments to change must be added others of a more political and pragmatic character. For one thing, the party has built up, in discharging its monopoly functions, a great apparatus of control, both within its own ranks and in the organs of state power. They include the officials of the state planning commission and the industrial ministries and of the party itself, both at the centre and in the localities, cultural bureaucrats, accountants and policemen. All of these have a vested interest in maintaining the system as they know it because it is the source of their status and livelihood. They are well dug-in and, on the odd occasions when efforts have been made to dislodge some of them, they have generally managed to hold their ground.

For another thing the party has succeeded in concluding an unwritten social compact with its citizens which has been very effective in restraining any impulse to break out of the system or advocate change. In essence, the citizen is offered a steady but often undemanding job, a slowly rising standard of living, social services and a pension, on the understanding that he minds his own business and does not make trouble. The implications of the compact are that much stronger where the citizen is a person of some consequence. The party has devised quite sophisticated means of tying status and privilege to conformity. So long as the scientist, engineer or academic continues to conform, he will enjoy the respect of his fellows, he will be better housed, he may have the use of an official car, his wife will be able to dress herself nicely and his children can be got into better schools. But if he gets odd ideas and attempts to buck the system, he will lose all this and much more, because he may find himself out of a job and deprived of the means of practising his calling. For writers and artists of all sorts the incentive to conformity is even more explicit, owing to the control which the professional unions exercise over their members by their control of access to the public. It is by means such as these that the critical faculties of the educated class are kept under restraint and the potentially disruptive effects of education, examined earlier in this chapter, neutralized. If the attitude of the Soviet intelligentsia towards the system seems unheroic, it is well to remember that the enjoyment of even moderate affluence and of modest status is a new experience for most, that there is no alternative employer for any who put a foot wrong and that emigration (save with obloquy and impoverishment) is not an option.

We must concede that major change is unlikely so long as the *status quo* continues to suit the party as well as it does. The present leadership did not come to power in order to preside over the dissolution of the CPSU's dictatorship. Its room for manoeuvre is pretty limited. It no doubt believes that it is right to stand pat. But, right or wrong, if it should do otherwise, it would soon put the party's sovereignty at risk, and the personal positions of its own members as well. Some Western sovietologists canvas the idea that, as in Washington, so also in Moscow, there are hawks and doves, conservatives and liberals, contending with one another when policy decisions are taken. Brezhnev, because of his personal identification with the policy of peace, is sometimes identified as the dove-in-chief and presented as carrying on a running battle in the Politburo and the Secretariat against the military-industrial complex and the ideologues. This schematization owes more to the preconceptions of the 'interest group' theorists in the West than to any observed pattern of Soviet behaviour.

That there is a military-industrial complex is not in serious doubt. Ustinov, the civilian minister of defence, an arms procurement man by trade, is eminently well qualified to represent it at the summit. There are ideologues too in Suslov and Ponomarev. Each of these men, no doubt, speaks up in debate for the interests of the portfolio which he holds. But all of them are collectively responsible for what is decided, whether the subject is defence, foreign affairs, public order, culture or the economy. Policy is a mix of different constituency interests and democratic centralism provides the means for resolving any continuing disagreements. To portray Brezhnev, an arch-conservative if ever there was one, as the champion of peace and sweet reason against the schemings of bellicose marshals and hide-bound fundamentalists, is absurd. More absurd still is the notion which Soviet spokesmen sometimes propagate *sotto voce,* that Western governments should 'help' Brezhnev by doing what he asks, lest he lose his job and they their best friend.

The present leaders are coming to the end of their natural span and, whether their replacements come piecemeal or all at once, a new team will, before very long, be running the CPSU. Their style and their perceptions of the world are bound to be different. But their interests will be the same and their monopoly of power as essential to them as it is to their predecessors. It is hard to conceive that they would do anything that might impair their monopoly, save only in dire necessity, and if they were convinced that only by taking great risks did they have a hope of saving the system. The only obvious contingency of sufficient magnitude to fit this specification would be if economic stagnation worsened to the point at which its effects began tangibly to impair the stability of society. If that happened, they might conclude that the least disastrous course open to them was to unleash some of the spontaneous forces in the economy which have for so long been kept under severe restraint. And once the conservative line had been breached at one point some of the other long-pent-up factors for change might begin to operate. The time-scale in which such a *dénouement* could occur is unpredictable, but we may reasonably guess that it would be just as long as the Soviet Communist Party could make it. It follows that unless *détente* is to be postponed until the Greek Kalends, we must count on negotiating it with the Russians as we have known them.

Further Outlook

12

The prospects for *détente*, like stock-market values, are continually obscured by the volatility of men's perceptions of them. The first chapter of this book traced the rise of *détente*'s stock to the high point of spring 1972, and then watched it plummet to the nadir of spring 1977. By the autumn of the same year sentiment was again on the upswing, with SALT (despite Gromyko's 'never') back on the rails, comprehensive test-ban negotiations moving forward and hints of a US–Soviet summit. Those in the West who had dismissed Helsinki as a sell-out and the Belgrade follow-up meeting as a non-event were discovering that the CSCE had its uses after all, and chuckling at the discomfiture of the Russians impaled on their own hook. Our task, in summing up the conclusions of this enquiry, is to look beyond the conjuncture of the moment, with its constant oscillations between euphoria and despair, and attempt a more objective valuation of the prospects.

What we have called the bones of contention – the terms of peaceful coexistence, the arms race and the controversy about human rights – are the outward expression and embodiment of a much deeper underlying antagonism. The antagonism has been shaped, on the one hand, by the clash of global interests between Russia and the West, whose origins long antedate the revolution of 1917, but which has been intensified by the subsequent growth of the principal contestants to super-power status; and, on the other, by the clash between the ideologies to which each side is dedicated. The fusion in the external policies of the Soviet Union, and to a lesser extent of the United States, of global interests and ideology is what has propelled the two contestants towards confrontation. Each of them has convinced himself that right is on his side and neither is deficient in the will to win.

For at least twenty years it has been plain to both sides that unlimited competition will have disastrous consequences for both of them and for the world; and for the second half of this period they have, with variable success, sought to bring about a relaxation of tension, which we call *détente*.

Where the strengths of the parties are pretty evenly matched, as is the case here, such a relaxation can come about only if it is freely assented to by both sides. Neither is in a position – though both Russians and Americans on occasion may have imagined that they were – to coerce the other into *détente*. What brought them together in the first place was a recognition, once each had equipped itself with nuclear weapons, that war, the logical outcome of unlimited competition, promised the impartial extinction of both. A shared interest in survival is a solid enough foundation for accommodation, as far as it reaches; but it does not reach far enough, particularly so long as the attitudes born of sixty years of hostility, including thirty years of cold war, continue. Far less is it, if experience is any guide, a sufficient basis for a comprehensive settlement between East and West. No such settlement would be complete if it did not tackle and resolve the deep-seated ideological antagonism between them.

The Russians are, on a proper construction of the words, perfectly correct when they insist that there is a continuing ideological struggle between the two systems, socialism and capitalism. Just as the Marxist-Leninists look for the revolutionary transformation of capitalist societies in accordance with their view of the historical process, so also the free societies of the West reject a system calling itself socialist which contemptuously dismisses liberties regarded by themselves as axiomatic and inalienable. A resolution of the clash of ideologies is obviously not possible save in the very, very long term, since it logically calls for a complete reassessment by both sides of their social goals and, on the Soviet side at least, could hardly come about without dismantling the structure of the dictatorship. The defeat of the US administration's efforts in 1977 to make *détente* conditional on respect for human rights sufficiently illustrates this point.

So *détente*, if it is to have any practical meaning, will be not a comprehensive settlement of all differences, but an accommodation between two groups of nations whose aims differ widely and whose conflicting interests threaten, unless restraint is shown by both sides, to lead to the destruction of both. The generalized prescription for such an accommodation is no mystery. All the necessary ingredients are to be found in the 'basic principles' proclaimed by the Soviet and United States leaders in Moscow in 1972. They pledged themselves to recognize one another's security interests as equal, to renounce the threat or use of force, to settle differences peacefully by negotiation and constantly to exercise restraint.

What an accommodation must tackle and, if it is to succeed, restrain, is not the ideological conflict itself, which is likely to be with us for a long time, but the policies and actions which have been undertaken in its name, though they are often pursued as much for reasons of global interest and ambition as on strictly doctrinal grounds. Neither side has a wholly unblemished record but the root of the mischief is not in doubt. The Russians have not been content to proclaim, as their beliefs entitled them to, that capitalism was doomed, and to leave the laws of history to take their appointed course. They have regarded it as their bounden duty to couple belief with action to accelerate the onset of doom, and have thereby justified to themselves comprehensive policies of hostility towards capitalist interests everywhere. If, as the Russians like to remind us, capitalist governments have periodically shown bitter hostility to the Soviet Union (memories of the intervention of 1918–21 and of the Dulles era of Western policy are not allowed to wither), they need not look far for the reason. Hostility begets hostility. It is an essential component of any enduring accommodation that means should be found of containing the 'struggle of ideas' on the level of ideas, of severing the link between it and the hostile actions taken in its name, which are incompatible with *détente*.

This may seem to make extraordinary demands on the Soviet leadership, but *détente* is a demanding concept. And the demands may strike them as less exorbitant in the situation of today than they would have done sixty, or forty or even thirty years ago. For, formidable and wilful though the Soviet leadership remains, it knows that its plans have been blown off course.

The Bolsheviks embarked in 1917 on a project of extraordinary scope and grandeur. Their aims were to transform the world by proletarian revolution and to make Russia a model socialist state as an example for revolutionaries everywhere to follow. Sixty years later they have had to admit substantial failure on both counts. The vision of an expanding socialist commonwealth has shrunk to include only their immediate neighbours, who are kept within the fold more by Soviet power than by ideology, with outliers, under uncertain control, in Cuba and Vietnam and a changing handful of cupboard-loving clients in Africa. The 'oppressed peoples' of the backward countries look in the main to China for inspiration (though they periodically look to Moscow for arms) and the communist parties of the developed world are falling over themselves to abjure revolutionary tactics and the Soviet connection. The grand design for a revolutionary world controlled from Moscow lies in ruins. What survives is a strong Soviet state with a few strategically placed clients, now for the most part integrated militarily and economically with their protector. It is, of course something worth having, but it is a pale shadow of what was originally intended. The outcome for the Russians could have been much worse, for they dreadfully mismanaged the affairs of the camp in better days and might, but for their military strength, and their willingness to use it, have lost the lot. Today their diminished empire offers valuable elements of security, but it needs constant policing, and integration has saddled them with responsibilities for keeping their clients solvent and maintaining their peoples at the standard to which they, though not yet the Soviet people, have become accustomed.

Likewise, the Soviet Union has not developed into a model for the world to copy. The Soviet design worked effectively enough, though at a high cost in blood and misery, so long as it was a matter of dragging the country out of backwardness and into the twentieth century. The planned economy mobilized resources in a way, and at a speed, that probably no other system could have done. But once the foundations had been laid the shortcomings of the system became increasingly apparent. In opting to run the economy by command rather than by harnessing market forces, the leaders of Soviet Russia had set themselves problems which they could not solve. The system turned out to be highly resistant to innovation, though it spent lavishly on science.

From the 1960s onwards it began to show increasing signs of torpor and stagnation. Though a vast labour-force was continually expanded, productivity was low; increased wages and stimulative payments failed to boost it because the economy was not making the things on which they could be spent. What had started as an economic problem was on the way to becoming a social and political one. Food production, a central element in the people's living standards, demanded prodigious inputs of capital into agriculture to make good earlier neglect, but the bizarre system by which Soviet farming was organized periodically broke down in face of bad weather, bringing crop failures, slaughtering of live-stock and the need for large imports of grain. Overall, Soviet resources were stretched unbearably by the competing priority demands of industrial modernization, agricultural investment, defence, social security, education and consumer living standards. By about 1970 it was plain that relief must come from somewhere. To scrap the planned economy in its existing form was not a serious option: it would have meant jettisoning too much of the ideological ballast of the system and relinquishing the dictatorship's main lever of control over society. Brezhnev and his colleagues chose what was for them the lesser evil of accepting a measure of dependence on the capitalist countries. The pill was not swallowed whole. The first bite was the acquisition of foreign technology, represented as a device to gain time, to restore momentum and push the USSR forward once more towards its proclaimed goals. But when it was followed by the emergence of an increasingly complex pattern of long-term economic co-operation, by a rapid growth of Soviet indebtedness to the West, and then by arrangements for substantial annual imports of American grain, the goals themselves began to lose some of their definition and cogency. Put at its lowest, the demise of the capitalist system was no longer a desirable end, at least until the benefits in prospect had been harvested and the vigour of the Soviet economy restored.

So it was that the imperative of survival in the nuclear age was reinforced by considerations, economic, social and political, arising from the shortcomings and necessities, internal and external, of the Soviet system. For reasons of their own, independent of the concurrent appearance on the scene of Dr Kissinger and Chancellor Brandt, and of the international conjuncture of the early 1970s, the Soviet leaders found themselves involved in negotiating an accommodation with the West. It was not by choice that they had come to contemplate a relationship with capitalist countries which, whatever precautions were taken to limit the damage, represented a quite distinct departure from what had gone before. They did so reluctantly, obliquely and under the compulsion of circumstances.

We may accordingly, without abandoning due caution, discard one widely canvassed construction of the Soviet government's conversion to the line which made its appearance in 1971 in Brezhnev's 'programme of peace'. For if, as appears, the move towards accommodation was the product, in greater or lesser degree, of failures of the Soviet system to cope with its tasks, it cannot also be true, as some have contended, that the 'programme of peace' is nothing more or less than a tactical gambit to bamboozle Western governments, to induce in them a false sense of security, and soften them up in preparation for a new offensive of hostility and pressure. The hypothesis of simple deception derives some plausibility from the way in which the Russians, their need for accommodation notwithstanding, continue to behave. But the evidence suggests that it is itself deceptive and misleading.

All the same, the probability that we are dealing with something more substantial and less disreputable than a simple case of fraud does not in itself afford any very far-reaching reassurance. In opting to go for a relaxation of international tensions, the Russians have, as yet, made only the minimum adjustments that overriding necessity made inevitable. There has been a pragmatic adaptation but no systematic reformulation of objectives. The accepted need for accommodation has not brought about the abandonment of the old goals: the two subsist side by side. The result is contradictory and highly confusing for the Western mind. Marxist-Leninists no doubt find it easier to live with since they can justify in dialectical terms the concurrent pursuit of logically incompatible ends. The doctrine of peaceful coexistence epitomizes the incompatibility. The Soviet Communist Party cannot, of course, afford to let on that it has been forced seriously to breach the line dictated by its ideology, and must therefore present its deviation in language which suggests that *détente* is simply an alternative, more sophisticated and less dangerous route to the victory of socialism, thereby greatly impairing its credibility as an interlocutor. But that is only half the story. For, questions of presentation apart, they would like to regard their breach with the past as no more than partial and pragmatic.

They realize that, in order to make *détente* a reality, in order to bring about a relaxation of tension sufficiently durable and credible to yield the benefits they seek, they will have to pay a price in terms of improved international behaviour. But they see no point in changing their ways more radically than they have to; and their instinct for hard bargaining tells them that, with persistence and a bit of luck, the price can be beaten down; for they rightly calculate that the West needs *détente* too. Thus, notwithstanding the comprehensive assurances of restraint and respect for the interests of others given at the Moscow summit of 1972, and at similar bilateral meetings with their other Western partners, the Russians have, while picking up anything that attracted them in the way of technological and economic co-operation, loans, commerce and grain, cheerfully continued to conduct business as usual — that is on the old assumptions of struggle and hostility — wherever they reckoned that they could do so with impunity.

It may seem too severe a judgment, given the literally vital nature of the interests involved, to cite under this heading Soviet handling of the problem of strategic arms limitation; but the dogged evasion, continuing at least until mid-1977, of the palpable need for qualitative restriction of armaments suggests that, in this regard at least, the recognized requirements of *détente* had not subdued the old, instinctive urge to make assurance doubly sure. And we cannot be sure, even today, that the conclusion has been drawn. A clearer case is the Soviet stone-walling operation, now in its fifth year, in the negotiations on the reduction of forces and armaments in central Europe (MBFR). Another is the continuing itch to disrupt Western societies from within, and the correlation between communist leaderships and union militancy is no accident. Political subversion in its broader sense, the traditional weapon of the Comintern, has lost much of its effectiveness in recent years, as Eurocommunist ideas have spread and groups of the further left have outflanked the traditional communist parties. But espionage, though the supply of ideological traitors recruited in the depression years has about run out, continues to be widely employed, both in Western capitals and against Western officials serving in the Soviet Union, to the continuing detriment of mutual confidence and good relations.

But the most striking instance of the vitality of old bad habits is the Soviet proclivity for overseas adventures whenever targets of opportunity present themselves, in odd corners of the world, offering the chance of altering the global balance of strength against the West. *Détente* or no *détente*, the Russians have not abandoned their old objective of procuring a shift in the 'correlation of forces'. A number of the adventures have ended badly, for third-world politics are notoriously unpredictable. The Russians have been flung out of Egypt and Somalia, losing in each country base facilities – in the Mediterranean and in the Indian Ocean – which they had paid dearly in money and arms to obtain. Their attempt in 1973 to exploit India's hour of need has not yet yielded benefits, in terms of either influence or facilities, commensurate with the effort and expense involved. But they continue undeterred by failure, apparently convinced that they will one day pick a winner. The intervention by proxy in Angola, carried out in 1975 by Cuban troops armed and equipped by the Soviet Union and ferried in Soviet aircraft, was undertaken on the shrewd calculation that the Congress, in its post-Vietnam mood, would successfully block any counter-action by the United States administration. The Soviet-backed faction in due course won the Angolan civil war but the operation was mounted in wilful disregard for Soviet undertakings at the Moscow summit, and its impact on American opinion, already deeply disillusioned about the prospects of accommodation with the Soviet Union, was disastrous. Yet in the autumn of 1977, when hopes of *détente* had somewhat recovered, Cuban troops were at it again in Africa, this time to intervene on the Soviet Union's behalf in the Ethiopian-Somali war.

These instances point to an entirely unsatisfactory state of affairs which provides no basis for a lasting relaxation of tension. The first task facing Western governments is to make clear to the Soviet Union that the advantages which it seeks from *détente* can be had for nothing less than a cessation of hostile action across the whole front of East–West relations. There can be no exclusions. An armistice on a few sectors of the Soviet government's choosing will not do.

How can this essential point be brought home to the Russians? Western governments have a hand to play which, if it is less strong than it was four years ago, is not without bargaining power. Circumstances have placed the Soviet Union in the position of *demandeur*. It badly needs know-how, equipment and finance which will not be forthcoming unless it is prepared to adopt and loyally carry out a policy of no exclusion. This may be easier said than done for Western governments who, in current conditions of recession, would otherwise welcome the employment which Soviet orders would provide. But if they are seriously interested in getting East–West relations on to a satisfactory permanent basis, they will need to summon the strength of mind to say no. More generally, they will need, if they are not to come off second-best in a process of negotiation about *détente* which may take years to complete, to hold fast to the principle of no concessions unrequited by full counter-value. *Détente* is about mutual benefit, and no agreement for the time being may be better than a bad agreement.

A balance of mutual benefit will not be achieved without linkage between the desiderata of both sides. There is nothing wrong with linkage as such, but, as experience over human rights and Jewish emigration shows, it requires some finesse and it cannot accomplish the impossible. It is a misapplication of effort to demand, as the price of advantages sought, that the Soviet leaders should knock away the props on which their system, iniquitous as we find it, rests. Nor is it essential to the purpose of *détente* as we have defined it. The more promising course is to pursue Dr Kissinger's concept of a web of shared interests between the two sides. For reasons of their own, the Russians have become susceptible to the attractions of interdependence. Western governments would be silly to run away from interdependence simply because the Russians would stand to gain something from it. If they hold tight to the rule of mutual benefit and no unrequited concessions they have nothing to fear.

In the light of all that has happened since the search for *détente* began we must admit that the euphoria which periodically captures men's minds is misplaced. All the evidence suggests that the going will continue to be rough and there is no absolute guarantee of arrival at the destination. But there are equally no grounds for despair. We have identified some of the conditions which must be created if *détente* is to become a reality. The Russians have already travelled some of the way towards creating them and the logic of their situation may reasonably be expected to carry them further still, provided that Western governments keep a clear view of their own interests. They may not always find this easy, for the Soviet Union is not the only country whose system is today functioning less than perfectly. Unemployment, inflation and strikes divert the attention and weaken the hand of the West in negotiations with the Russians. But these problems no more portend the terminal illness of capitalism than the patent insolvency of Marxist-Leninist ideology portends the early disappearance of the Soviet Union as a world power. If either hypothesis were true, the necessity for *détente* would not arise.

Short Bibliography

Amalryk, A., *Can the Soviet Union Survive until 1984?* (Harper & Row, New York, 1970).

Arbatov, G. A., *Ideologicheskaya bor'ba v sovremennykh mezhdunarodnykh otnosheniyakh* (The war of ideas in contemporary international relations) (Progress, Moscow, 1973).

Barghoorn, F. C., *Politics in the USSR* (Little, Brown, Boston, 1972).

Barghoorn, F. C., *Détente and the Democratic Movement in the USSR* (Free Press, New York, 1976).

Brezhnev, L. I., *Report of the CPSU Central Committee and the immediate tasks of the party in home and foreign policy* (Novosti, Moscow, 1976).

Brown, A. and Gray, J., *Political Culture and Political Change in Communist States* (Macmillan, London, 1977).

Brown, A. and Kaser, M., *The Soviet Union Since the Fall of Khrushchev* (Macmillan, London, 1975).

Burt, R., 'The cruise missile and arms control', in *Survival* (Jan/Feb 1976).

Carr, E. H., *The Bolshevik Revolution* (Pelican, London, 1976).

CPSU, 'Programma KPSS', in *Kommunist*, Moscow, No. 16 (November 1961).

CPSU, *Materialy XXIV s"ezda KPSS, 1971* (Politizdat, Moscow, 1971).

CPSU, *Materialy XXV s"ezda KPSS, 1976* (Politizdat, Moscow, 1976).

Deutscher, I., *Stalin* (OUP, Oxford, 1949).

Edmonds, R., *Soviet Foreign Policy, 1962–73* (OUP, Oxford, 1975).

FCO, London, *Select Documents Relating to the Problems of Security and Cooperation in Europe, 1954–77* (HMSO, London, 1977, Cmnd 6932).

Griffith, W. E., *The Soviet Empire, Expansion and Détente* (Lexington, Mass., 1976).

IISS, London, *The Military Balance* (International Institute for Strategic Studies, annually).

Kaiser, R. G., *Russia* (Secker & Warburg, London, 1976).

Kaser, M., *Soviet Economics* (Weidenfeld & Nicolson, London, 1970).

Kissinger, H. J., Statement to the Foreign Relations Committee of the Senate (State Department, Washington, D.C., 19 September 1974).

194 Short Bibliography

Kohler, F. (ed.), *Soviet Strategy for the '70s* (Center for Advanced International Studies, Miami, 1973).

Korbel, J., *Détente in Europe* (Princeton University Press, 1972).

Khrushchev, N. S., *The 'Secret' Speech* (Spokesman Books, Nottingham, 1976).

Khrushchev, N. S., *Khrushchev Remembers: The Last Testament* (Little Brown, Boston, 1974).

Labedz, L. (ed.), 'The future of East–West relations', *Survey*, double anniversary issue (1976).

Lenin, V. I., *Collected Works* (Lawrence & Wishart, London, 1960).

Marx, K. and Engels, F., *Selected Works* (Foreign Languages Publishing House, Moscow, 1958).

Medvedev, R. A., *Let History Judge* (Spokesman Books, Nottingham, 1974).

Medvedev, R. A. and Z. A., *Khrushchev, The Years in Power* (OUP, Oxford, 1977).

Medvedev, Z. A., *Ten Years after Ivan Denisovich* (Penguin, London, 1975).

Meyer, A. G., *Marxism: The Unity of Theory and Practice* (Harvard U.P., 1954).

Meyer, A. G., *Leninism* (Praeger, New York, 1956).

Morton, R., *The U.S. Role in East–West Trade* (Department of Commerce, Washington, D.C., August 1975).

Nalin, Y. and Nikolayev, A., *Sovetskii Soyuz i Evropeyskaya bezopasnost'* (The Soviet Union and European Security) (Progress, Moscow, 1973).

Nove, A., *The Soviet Economy* (Allen & Unwin, London, 1968).

Pipes, R. (ed.), *Russia Under the Old Regime* (Scribners, New York, 1975).

Pipes, R., *Soviet Strategy in Europe* (Macdonald and Jane's, London, 1976).

Ponomarev, B. N., *Some Problems of the Revolutionary Movement* (Peace and Socialism, Prague, 1975).

Remington, R. A., *The Warsaw Pact* (MIT Press, Cambridge, Mass., 1971).

Sakharov, A. and others, 'Appeal of Soviet scientists to the party and government leaders of the USSR, 19 March 1971', from *Survey* (summer, 1971).

Seton-Watson, H., *The Russian Empire, 1801–1917* (OUP, Oxford, 1967).

Shub, D., *Lenin* (Doubleday, New York, 1948).

Smith, H., *The Russians* (Sphere Books, London, 1976).

Solzhenitsyn, A., *The Gulag Archipelago* (Collins, London, 1974).

Tökes, R. I., *Dissent in the USSR* (Johns Hopkins Press, Baltimore, 1975).

Urban, G. R., *Détente* (Temple Smith, London, 1977).

USSR, *Narodnoe Khozyaistvo SSSR* (Statistika, Moscow, annually).

USSR, *The USSR in Figures* (Statistika, Moscow, annually) (In English).

USSR, *Vneshnaia Torgovlya, statisticheskii sbornik* (Ministry of Foreign Trade, Moscow, periodically).

USSR, *Konstitutsiya SSSR 1936* (Moscow, 1975).

USSR, 'New draft constitution of the Soviet Union,' *Soviet News*, London, No. 5885 (14 June 1977).

Vance, C. R., *Second Semi-Annual Report to the Commission on Security and Cooperation in Europe, December 1976–June 1977* (Department of State, Washington, D.C., 1977).

Wolfe, T. W., *Soviet Power in Europe, 1945–70* (Johns Hopkins Press, Baltimore, 1970).

Yanov, A., *Détente after Brezhnev* (Institute of International Studies, University of California, Berkeley, 1977).

Glossary

ABM	Anti-Ballistic Missile
ALCM	Air-Launched Cruise Missile
BBC	British Broadcasting Corporation
Comecon	Council for Mutual Economic Assistance (CMEA)
COCOM	Co-ordinating Committee (of Consultative Group on strategic exports)
CP	Communist Party
CPC	Communist Party of China
CPF	Communist Party of France
CPI	Communist Party of Italy
CPSU	Communist Party of the Soviet Union
CSCE	Conference on Security and Co-operation in Europe
EEC	European Economic Community
FBS	Forward-Based Systems
FRG	Federal Republic of Germany
GDR	German Democratic Republic
GPU	*Gosudarstvennoe Politicheskoe Upravlenie* (State Political Directorate)
ICBM	Inter-continental Ballistic Missile
IRBM	Intermediate-range Ballistic Missile
KGB	*Komitet Gosudarstvennoy Bezopasnosti* (Committee for State Security)
KT	Kiloton (1,000 tons of conventional explosive)

MAD	Mutually Assured Destruction
MBFR	Mutual and Balanced Force Reductions
mfn	most favoured nation
MGB	*Ministerstvo Gosudarstvennoy Bezopasnosti* (Ministry of State Security)
MT	Megaton (one million tons of conventional explosive)
NATO	North Atlantic Treaty Organization
NEP	New Economic Policy (in 1920s)
NKVD	*Narodniy Kommissariat Vnutrennikh Del* (People's Commissariat for Internal Affairs)
OPEC	Organization of Petroleum Exporting Countries
PNE	Peaceful Nuclear Explosions
RSFSR	Russian Soviet Federal Socialist Republic (incorporating Russia proper and Siberia)
SALT	Strategic Arms Limitation Talks
SLBM	Submarine-Launched Ballistic Missile
SLCM	Sea-Launched Cruise Missile
UN	United Nations
USA	United States of America
USSR	Union of Soviet Socialist Republics

Index